JOIN US

DENVER
POWDERHOUNDS

DENVERPOWDERHOUNDS.COM

SCARPA

NO PLACE TOO FAR™

BIG
DAY
EVERY
DAY

F1 | ANDREW MCCLEAN, ANDY DORAIS | SILVERTON, CO | PHOTO: LOUIS AREVALO

VOLUME 2 NORTH OF INTERSTATE 70
MAKING TURNS
IN COLORADO'S FRONT RANGE

INCLUDING INDIAN PEAKS

A Backcountry Ski & Snowboard Guidebook
By Fritz Sperry

A Giterdun
GUIDE

MakingTurns in Colorado's Front Range
Volume 2: North of Interstate 70
Including Indian Peaks

A Backcountry Ski & Snowboard Guidebook
Written By Fritz Sperry

© 2016 Fritz Sperry

Edited by Jill Redding
Design by Allison Seymour/gravitygirlgraphics.com

All photos by Fritz Sperry except where credited
Front cover painting by Fritz Sperry
Back cover photo: Fritz Sperry, athlete: Gary Fondl

Photo contributions by Allison Seymour, Joe Brannan, Jeremy Dobish, Miriam Green, Gary Fondl, Doug Evans, Cory Reppenhagen, Dave Reed, Andrew Steger, Erik Stevens, Jon Bloomfield, Becca Orig, Jason Kilgore, Natalie Moran, Rob Dickinson

Published by Giterdun Publishing Ltd.
www.giterdunpublishing.com
Edgewater, Colorado

ISBN: 978-0-9884012-4-2

*This book is dedicated to the memory of those the mountains have taken.
If you play in the hills long enough you will eventually lose someone. It's especially
painful when they are your friend or family. But the effects of any loss in
the backcountry touch all of us, in our tight knit community. Mistakes happen;
it's the nature of the game. The mountains can be a very unforgiving place.
May the fallen continue to make turns with us, in our memories, ever after.*

I'd like to thank the following people and sponsors that helped make this book happen. I couldn't do it without you. You put up with my obsession for the hills. Thank you for the love and support.

Allison Seymour, Calvin and Wilson Sperry, Mom and Fred, Dad and Suzanne, Gary Fondl, Dave Bourassa, Miriam Green, Frank Bowman, Aaron Carlson, Cory Reppenhagen, Mike Records, Doug Evans, Mark Morris, Eben Mond, Dan Moroz, Jason McGowin, Gary Apostolou, Mark Kelly, Kevin Riley, Jerome Consoli, Scott Wescott, Don Bushey, Ian Borgeson, Skylar Memsic, Jeremy Dobish, Andrew Solod, Kim Ross, Scott Edlin, Kihm Beyer, Frank and Brittany Konsella, Michael Waesche, Darrell Haggard, Tom Armento, Larry Hall, Homi Kapadia, Doug and Emilie Mock, Scott Sutton, Jon Ridnell, Dalton Kieta, Joe Brannan, Lou Dawson, Danny Medved, Eddie Schuster, Dustin Schaefer, Louise Lintilhac, Jon Bloomfield, Joel Bettner, Mark Fusco, Rob Dickinson, Ryan Halverson, Mark Cavaliero, Billy Hebert, Stephanie Ring, Otina Fox, Henry Wood, Anthony Orig, Scott Yorko, Casey Riva, Bruce Edgerly, Phil Lindeman, Ryan Banker, Travis Hightower, Justin Ibarra, Mike Stem, John Popper, Spin Doctors, Pretty Lights, Yonder Mountain String Band, Rapidgrass, Mosquito Pass Experience, Climb Talk Radio, Big Agnes, Julbo, Goal Zero, G3, Pepe Osaka, Backcountry Pizza, Tin Shed Sports, Trident Cafe and Bookstore, The Alpine Restaurant, Lionhead Coffee, Icebox Mountain Sports, Deno's, Honey Stinger, Scarpa, Dynafit, Bent Gate Mountaineering, BCA, Upslope Brewing, Backcountry Magazine, Breckenridge Distillery, Wilderness Sports, Mountan Outfitters, RMU, Teton Gravity Research, Deuter, Orotvox, New Family Dog, Neptune Mountaineering, Big City Mountaineers, Mountain Chalet, CUFST, CU Boulder, Gravity Girl Graphics, REI, Protect Our Winters, AIARE, and Friends of CAIC.

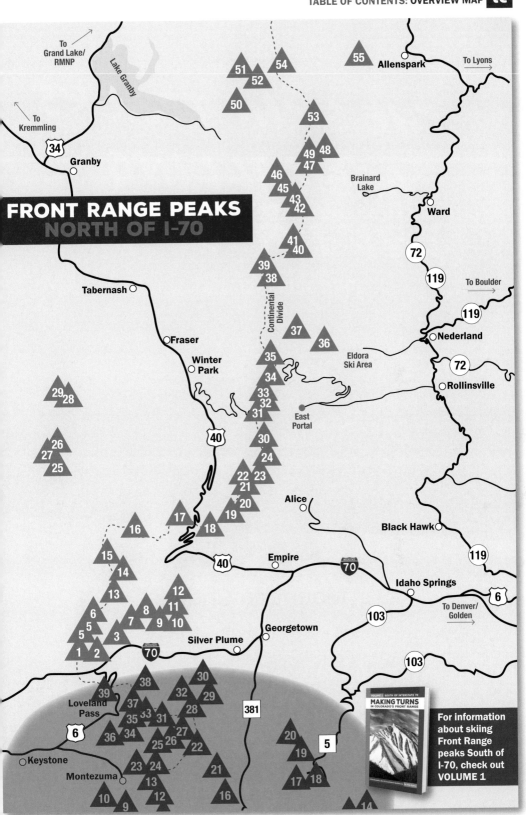

FRONT RANGE PEAKS
NORTH OF I-70

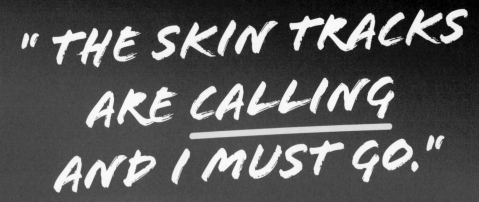

INTRODUCTION

Introduction 1
Camping and Permits 2
Avalanches 4
Lightning and Weather 8
Mountain Craft 9
Cornices 10
Rockfall 10
Moats 11
Tree Wells 11
Wildlife 11
Marijuana 13
Communication 13
Etiquette and Philosophy 14
Using This Guidebook 15

TRAILHEADS

Eisenhower Tunnel West Portal North 19
Loveland Ski Area Chair 8
          Backcountry Access Gate 19
Dry Gulch 20
Herman Gulch 20
Berthoud Falls 21
Ruby Gulch 21
Jones Pass 22
Berthoud Pass South Corner 22
Berthoud Pass Stanley Slidepath Access ... 23
Berthoud Pass Pump House 23
Berthoud Pass Summit 24
Berthoud Pass Current Creek 24
Berthoud Pass Second Creek 25
Berthoud Pass First Creek 25
Berthoud Pass Zero Creek 26
Parry Creek Trail 26
Jim Creek Trail 27
Fall River Reservoir 27
Steuart Road 28
St. Mary's Glacier 28
Deadhorse Creek 29
Iron Creek/Byers Peak Road 29
Upper Tipperary 30
Moffat Tunnel East Portal 30
Rollins Pass Road East Side 31
Rollins Pass West Side 32
Eldora Backcountry Gate 33
Hessie Winter Closure 33
Fourth of July Road 34
Devil's Thumb Pass 34
Monarch Lake 35
Roaring Fork 36
Brainard Lake Winter 36
Brainard Lake, Long & Mitchell Lake 37
Coney Flats Road 38
Camp Dick/Middle St. Vrain Road 39
Meadow Mountain 40

HAND-CRAFTED BEER

BEER RUN

SKI ROUTES

1 **"Golden Bear" – 13,010'** **41**
1a West Chute.........................41
1b Northeast Bowl.....................42
2 **Mount Trelease – 12,477'** **45**
2a South Bowl and Trees 45
2b North Face 47
2c North Gullies & Trees....................49
3 **Mount Bethel – 12,705'** **51**
3a Interstate Gully 51
3b North Saddle Gully 53
4 **Hagar Mountain – 13,195'**...........**55**
4a Southeast Face.......................55
5 **"The Citadel" (Snoopy) – 13,294'**...**57**
5a North Collar Couloir........................57
5b South Bowl and South Collar..........58
5c The Tail and East Bowl 60
6 **Pettingell Peak – 13,553'** **63**
6a South Slopes.........................63
6b 418 Chutes 64
6c North Face 65
7 **Mount Machebeuf – 12,805'**.......**67**
7a Y - YNot - YYes Gullies 67
7b East Bowl and Slopes.................69
8 **Woods Mountain – 12,940'** **73**
8a Watrous Bowl 73
8b Urad Bowl..............................74
9 **Mount Parnassus – 13,574'**........**77**
9a Northeast Face........................77
9b The Drainpipe 78
10 **Bard Peak – 13,641'**...................**81**
10a North Face 81
11 **Robeson Peak – 13,140'**.............**83**
11a Northwest Gully 83

12 **Engelmann Peak – 13,362'** **85**
12a West Gully 85
12b Lightning Gully 87
12c Breakfast Chute......................89
13 **"Hassell Peak" – 13,215'**............**91**
13a Lake Bowl...........................91
14 **Butler Gulch – 12,109'** **93**
14a Halfpipe Gully.......................93
14b Hourglass Gully.....................94
14c South Side – Hassell Lake.............96
14d Divide Chutes........................97
14e Jones Brothers Chutes 98
15 **Jones Pass – 12,451'** **101**
15a Pass Bowl...........................101
15b UN12700 East Bowl.................102
15c Bobtail BM 104
15d UN12118 (First Corner) 105
16 **Vasquez Peak – 12,939'**............**107**
16a Southwest Bowl and Gully 107
16b South Peak (UN12900) SE Bowl... 108
17W **Berthoud Pass – 11,315'** **110**
West Side
17Wa Stanley Slide Path 112
17Wb No Name - UN12424 113
17Wc Russell Peak - UN12391 114
17Wd Mainline to The Roll.....................115
17We 80s/90s/100s 117
17Wf Current Creek.....................119
17Wg Second Creek 120
17Wh First Creek.......................123
17Wi Zero Creek 124
East Side
17Ea Floral Park Zone 126
17Eb Hells Half Acre Zone 127
17Ec Seven Mile Trail 128

18	**Colorado Mines Peak – 12,493'...**	**129**
18a	Mines 1 and 2	129
18b	East Cirque	131
19	**Mount Flora – 13,132'**	**133**
19a	Flora Creek Bowl	133
19b	Northeast Bowls	135
19c	South Chute	137
20	**Witter Peak – 12,884'**	**139**
20a	Welcome Couloir	139
21	**Mount Eva – 13,130'**	**141**
21a	Southeast Bowl	141
22	**Parry Peak – 13,391'**	**143**
22a	South Face	143
22b	The Bear Claw	144
23	**Mount Bancroft – 13,250'**	**147**
23a	Caroline Bowl	147
24	**James Peak – 13,294'**	**149**
24a	SE Slopes & St Mary's Glacier	149
24b	East Cirque	151
24c	West Couloir	154
24d	North Slopes	157
25	**UN12393 – 12393'**	**159**
25a	UN12393 – Iron Creek Couloirs	159
26	**Byers Peak – 12,804'**	**161**
26a	East Bowl	161
26b	Southeast Gully	163
26c	West Gully	164
27	**Bills Peak – 12,703'**	**167**
27a	North Face	168
28	**Bottle Peak – 11,584'**	**169**
28a	Deadhorse Bowl	169
29	**Ptarmigan Peak – 11,772'**	**171**
29a	Crystal Bowl	171
30	**Haystack Mountain – 11,762'...**	**173**
30a	North Face	173
31	**Iceberg Couloirs – 12,160'**	**175**
31a	Iceberg Couloirs	175
32	**"Sprint Peak" – 12,110'**	**177**
32a	Crater Couloirs	177
33	**"Frosty Mountain" – 12,110'**	**179**
33a	East Side	179
34	**Radiobeacon BM – 12,072'**	**181**
34a	Northeast Cirque	181
34b	East Face	183
35	**Rollins Pass – 11,671'**	**185**
35a	Jenny Lake Bowl	185
35b	Skyscraper Glacier	186
35c	Challenger Glacier	188
36	**Eldora Backcountry**	**189**
36a	Lost Lake Bowl	189
37	**Woodland Mountain – 11,205'...**	**191**
37a	South Slopes	191
38	**Mount Jasper – 12,923'**	**193**
38a	Snow Lion	193
38b	Northeast Face	194
38c	East Ridge Flank	196
38d	Y Couloirs AKA Cabin Creek Couloirs	197
39	**Mount Neva – 12,814'**	**199**
39a	Northeast Face	199
39b	Caribou Lake Bowl	201
40	**South Arapaho Pk – 13,397'**	**203**
40a	Skywalker Couloir	203
41	**North Arapaho Pk – 13,502'**	**205**
41a	North Star Couloir	205
42	**Navajo Peak – 13,409'**	**207**
42a	Navajo Snowfield	207
43	**Apache Peak – 13,441'**	**209**
43a	Apache Couloir	209
43b	Queen's Way	211
43c	Fair Glacier	212
44	**"Hopi Peak" – 12,780'**	**215**
44a	The Kiva Ramp	215
44b	Hopi Glacier	218
45	**Lone Eagle Peak – 11,890'**	**221**
45a	Lone Rabbit Couloir	221
46	**"Cherokee" – 12,130'**	**223**
46a	North Gully	223
47	**Mount Toll – 12,979'**	**225**
47a	Southeast Slopes	225
48	**Mount Audubon – 13,233'**	**227**
48a	Crooked Couloir	227
48b	Coney Couloirs	229
49	**Paiute Peak – 13,088'**	**231**
49a	Southeast Face	231
49b	Paiute/Audubon Saddle Couloir	233
50	**Mount Irving Hale – 11,754'**	**235**
50a	West Slopes	235
51	**Watanga Mountain – 12,375'...**	**237**
51a	Watanga Lake Gully	237
51b	Southwest Slopes	238
52	**Hiamovi Mountain – 12,395'**	**23**
52a	West Slopes	239
53	**Sawtooth Mountain – 12,304'...**	**241**
53a	Southeast Bowl	241
54	**Ogalalla Peak – 13,138'**	**243**
54a	Dalkes Couloir	243
55	**Meadow Mountain – 11,632'...**	**245**
55a	East Slopes	245

BACKCOUNTRY TRAVEL
— GUIDE —

Backcountry Knowledge From
Teton Gravity Research

VISIT
TETONGRAVITY.COM/BACKCOUNTRY
FOR THE DIGITAL EXPERIENCE

TRAVERSES

Eisenhower Tunnel to Butler Gulch..........247
Berthoud Pass Super Tour 248
Berthoud Pass to Moffat Tunnel 250
Brainard Lake to Wild Basin....................251
Navajo–Apache Trifecta...........................253

TEASERS

Berthoud Pass to Wild Basin 255
Woods Creek Pinner 256
Parnassus Southwest Couloir 256
Englemann Disney Chute 257
Englemann North Ramp...........................257
UN12704 East Bowl 258
UN12696 Northeast Couloir....................258
Witter South Couloirs..............................259
James Peak Super Star 259
"Heartbeat Peak" Y Gully 260
"Old Baldy" South Bowl 260
North Arapaho North Face 261
Achonee Arrow 261
UN11893 "Pillow Peak" 262
Apache South Couloir 262
Shoshoni South Couloirs 263
Toll North Face 263
Paiute Ghost Dancer.................................264
Paiute West Couloir 264
"Blackfoot" North Couloir 265
Algonquin East Couloir..............................265
Twin Peaks East Chute 266
Hiamovi East Face 266
Marten West Couloir 267
Elk Tooth North Face 267

APPENDIX

Maps 268
Glossary..278
Sunrise/Sunset Chart 280
Gear List 281
Further Reading 282
Avalanche Education 283
Internet Resources...................................284
Retail Shops 285
Index 287

SKI ROUTES LISTED BY GENERAL DIFFICULTY

SEASON: WINTER

EASY

17Ec	Berthoud Pass/Seven Mile Trail

INTERMEDIATE

2c	Mount Trelease/North Gullies & Trees
3b	Mount Bethel/North Saddle Gully
7b	Mount Machebeuf/East Bowl & Slopes
14a	Butler Gulch/Halfpipe Gully
14c	Butler Gulch/South Side – Hassell Lake
16a	Vasquez Peak/Southwest Bowl & Gully
24a	James Peak/Southeast Slopes & St. Mary's Glacier
24d	James Peak/North Slopes
50a	Mount Irving Hale/West Slopes
51b	Watanga Mountain/South Slopes
55a	Meadow Mountain/East Slopes

INTERMEDIATE—ADVANCED

2a	Mount Trelease/South Bowl & Trees
14b	Butler Gulch/Hourglass Gully
36a	Eldora Backcountry/Lost Lake Bowl

INTERMEDIATE TO EXPERT

17Wd	Berthoud Pass/Mainline to The Roll
17We	Berthoud Pass/80s/90s/100s
17Wf	Berthoud Pass/Current Creek
17Wg	Berthoud Pass/Second Creek
17Ea	Berthoud Pass/Floral Park Zone
17Eb	Berthoud Pass/Hell's Half Acre Zone

ADVANCED

12c	Englemann Peak/Breakfast Chute
37a	Woodland Mountain/South Slopes
51a	Watanga Mountain/Watanga Lake Gully
52a	Hiamovi Mountain/Southwest Slopes

SKI ROUTES LISTED BY GENERAL DIFFICULTY

SEASON: SPRING & SUMMER

INTERMEDIATE

8a	Woods Mountain/Watrous Bowl
6a	Pettingell Peak/South Slopes
12a	Engelmann Peak/West Gully
15a	Jones Pass/Pass Bowl
23a	Mount Bancroft/Caroline Bowl

INTERMEDIATE TO ADVANCED

28a	Bottle Peak/Deadhorse Bowl
33a	"Frosty Mountain"/East Side
49a	Paiute Peak/Southeast Face

ADVANCED

1a	"Golden Bear"/West Chute
1a	"Golden Bear"/Northeast Bowl
3a	Mount Bethel/Interstate Gully
4a	Hagar Mountain/Southeast Face
5a	"The Citadel"/South Bowl & South Collar
6b	Pettingell Peak/418 Chutes
7a	Mount Machebeuf/Y – Y Not – Y Yes Gullies
8b	Woods Mountain/Urad Bowl
9a	Mount Parnassus/Northeast Face
9b	Mount Parnassus/The Drainpipe
11a	Robeson Peak/Northwest Gully
12b	Englemann Peak/Lightning Gully
13a	"Hassell Peak"/Lake Bowl
14d	Butler Gulch/Divide Chutes
14e	Butler Gulch/Jones Brothers Chutes
15b	Jones Pass/UN12700 East Bowl
15c	Jones Pass/Bobtail BM
15d	Jones Pass/UN12118 (First Corner)
16a	Vasquez Peak/South Peak (UN12900) Southeast Bowl
18a	Colorado Mines Peak/Mines 1 and 2
21a	Mount Eva/Southeast Bowl
22a	Parry Peak/South Face
22b	Parry Peak/The Bear Claw
24c	James Peak/West Couloir
26a	Byers Peak/East Bowl
26b	Byers Peak/Southeast Gully
26c	Byers Peak/West Gully
29a	Ptarmigan Peak/Crystal Bowl
30a	Haystack/North Face
31a	Iceberg Couloirs
32a	"Sprint Peak"/Crater Couloirs
34b	Radiobeacon BM/East Face
35a	Rollins Pass/Jenny Lake Bowl
35b	Rollins Pass/Skyscraper Glacier
38b	Mount Jasper/Northeast Face
38c	Mount Jasper/East Ridge Flank
38d	Mount Jasper/Y Couloirs aka Cabin Creek Couloirs
39b	Mount Neva/Caribou Lake Bowl
40a	South Arapaho Peak/Skywalker Couloir
41a	North Arapaho Peak/North Star Couloir
42a	Navajo Peak/Navajo Snowfield
43a	Apache Peak/Apache Couloir
43b	Apache Peak/Queen's Way
43c	Apache Peak/Fair Glacier
46a	"Cherokee"/North Gully
47a	Mount Toll/Southeast Slopes
48a	Mount Audubon/Crooked Couloir
48b	Mount Audubon/Coney Couloirs
49b	Paiute Peak/Paiute–Audubon Saddle Couloirs
53a	Sawtooth Mountain/Southeast Bowl
54a	Ogalalla Peak/Dalkes Couloir

ADVANCED TO EXPERT

2b	Mount Trelease/North Face
5a	"The Citadel"/North Collar Couloir
5c	"The Citadel"/The Tail and East Bowl
6c	Pettingell Peak/North Face
10a	Bard Peak/North Face
17Wa	Berthoud Pass/Stanley Slide Path
17Wb	Berthoud Pass/No Name - UN12,424
17Wc	Berthoud Pass/Russell Peak - UN12391
17Wh	Berthoud Pass/First Creek
17Wi	Berthoud Pass/Zero Creek
18b	Colorado Mines Peak/East Cirque
19c	Mount Flora/South Chute
24b	James Peak/East Cirque
25a	UN12,393/Iron Creek Couloirs
38a	Mount Jasper/Snow Lion
39a	Mount Neva/Northeast Face

EXPERT

19a	Mount Flora/Flora Creek Bowl
19b	Mount Flora/Northeast Bowls
20a	Witter Peak/Welcome Couloir
27a	Bills Peak/North Face
34a	Radiobeacon BM/Northeast Cirque
35c	Rollins Pass/Challenger Glacier
44a	"Hopi Peak"/The Kiva Ramp
44b	"Hopi Peak"/Hopi Glacier
45a	Lone Eagle Peak/Lone Eagle Finger

WARNING
READ THIS BEFORE USING THIS GUIDEBOOK

SKIING AND SNOWBOARDING ARE DANGEROUS SPORTS THAT CAN RESULT IN SERIOUS INJURY OR EVEN DEATH. BACKCOUNTRY SKIING IS EVEN MORE DANGEROUS THAN RESORT SKIING.

USE THIS BOOK ONLY AT YOUR OWN RISK.

This guidebook is intended as a reference tool for advanced and expert skiers and snowboarders. The terrain and routes it describes can be or are extremely dangerous and require a high degree of ability, fitness and experience to negotiate safely. This book is not intended for inexperienced/novice skiers and snowboarders. It is not intended as an instructional manual. If you are unsure of your ability to handle any situations that you may encounter, employ the services of a professional guide. Avalanche education is essential. There is a listing in the appendix on page 311 of Avalanche Education schools throughout Colorado

The information in this book is unverified, and the author and publisher cannot guarantee its accuracy. Assessments of the difficulty and risks associated with the terrain are based on opinions and are totally subjective. Numerous hazards exist that are not described and which are not marked on the mountains. Skiing or snowboarding any of the terrain in this book, regardless of its description or rating, may cause injury or death. The easiest runs in this book would be black diamond terrain at virtually every ski resort in the US. In the backcountry, you will encounter danger, hazards, and conditions that you won't find at any ski resort in the US. Ski areas have avalanche control teams. The backcountry does not. In addition to expert skiing ability, you must also possess at least a basic level of mountaineering and route finding skills. The ability to use a map and compass are essential. It is imperative that you own, carry, and know how to use an avalanche beacon, shovel, and probe when skiing the routes and terrain described in this book. More importantly is an understanding of avalanche assessment and safety protocols. Know what to look for, know the signs, and know when to turn around. If you don't know these then use a professional guide service. You must accept this risk.

The author and publisher make no representations or warranties, expressed or implied, of any kind regarding the contents of this book, and expressly disclaim any representation or warranty regarding the accuracy or reliability of the information contained herein. Use this book and the information contained herein at your own risk.

INTRODUCTION

Well, here we go again: another guidebook. The routes have been skied, or at least most of them, as of this writing. It seems like every time I go to a summit, I see 10 more lines I'd like to ski. That's the beauty of getting high up in the mountains—your horizons are that much farther. This section of the range presents some challenges that the routes in my previous books did not encounter; adapt to get it done.

First, if you plan on spending any time in this zone, you must learn to embrace the wind. The air pressure changes dramatically when you hit the Continental Divide. This leads to a shearing effect that can be quite powerful. One spring day, we experienced 120+ mph winds on a Front Range summit; this was the same day the fastest-ever wind speed was recorded in Colorado on Monarch Pass. It was enough to have me lying prone on the ridge for a few minutes, holding on for dear life. There were so many days when the wind went to work. One day my partner was slammed into rocks, breaking her ribs. There were wind-driven whiteouts, and wind was a factor in abandoning both of my Front Range traverse attempts. Again, you must learn to embrace the wind if you want to succeed here.

Second, you must embrace the approach if you want to enjoy all that the Indian Peaks have to offer. The southern portion of the range provides easy access to long lines—at

Old Man of the Mountain

least we can be thankful for something that Interstate 70 has to offer. As you get farther north and into the Indian Peaks, the winter trailheads become farther and farther from the skiing near the divide. This makes for winter epics, hence the very spring nature of skiing the Indian Peaks. Even with summer trailheads, you're looking at substantial distances to get to the goods. I tried a couple times to do a complete traverse of the Indian Peaks and got weathered out. Embracing the approach fast and light, but with the gear you need should something go wrong, is the way to go. Suck it up, buttercup, and get those legs and lungs in shape.

Third, you must embrace the impact of the lenticular cloud. Winds and pressure changes create lenticular clouds, also known as mountain wave clouds. These are very common on the east side of the Sierra where the same dynamics are at play. These high clouds can block the solar energy needed for our slopes to soften. Skiing rad lines on ice is pretty dumb and dangerous. I know more than a few people who have broken bones trying to ski icy steeps. On days impacted by lenticular clouds, you also get a flat light situation, making it difficult to see those frozen chicken-heads as well. You have to learn to get it in the right conditions. It's worth coming back when the snow and light are good.

This section of Colorado is amazing. I encourage everyone to get out into these great mountains. The area around Lone Eagle Peak is the most beautiful place I've ever seen. The mountains feel like they are still alive and forming, and the scale is amazing. Over the course of three days, I heard five rockslides. You get a sense of being really small and insignificant amongst the giants of the surrounding landscape.

Winter and spring are the best times to enjoy the mountains of Colorado. When you get away from the usual ski destinations like Berthoud and Loveland Passes, you really can get away from the masses. On most of the tours I did, especially in Grand and Clear Creek counties, I saw no one. In the Boulder zone, you will see more people, but this is the busiest wilderness in the country—what do you expect? It's still mostly peaceful in the winter.

I wasn't able to get all that I wanted into this book. There will be another edition chock full of many of the Teaser Section lines. Spring 2016 was amazing, but there are so many more options to get done. I just didn't have enough time this year with how warm it got in June; when it's 100 degrees in Denver, the snow doesn't stick around too long in the mountains. It has been a pattern of late: heavy snows in the high country through spring, late, even through May. The weather patterns are changing. Perhaps we should try harder to Protect Our Winters.

CAMPING AND PERMITS

I love camping; as I write this, I'm currently living in my 4Runner and getting ready to shoot a time-lapse of the stars. The camping experience is integral to the backcountry experience for many. Some people like to experience the rigors of winter, while others prefer car camping. From KOA and Forest Service campgrounds to dispersed roadside sites and the trailhead bivy, getting a night in the outdoors is where it's at. From June 1 through the summer, there are strict regulations, and permits are required for camping in the Indian Peaks Wilderness, as well as the less stringent rules and permit-less camping in the James Peak Wilderness. Leave No Trace is the rule of the land. Take care of this place; it's beautiful, so let's keep it that way. Pack it in, pack it out. Leave only footprints, take only pictures.

This is bear country, so keep food in a bear canister. Bears have been known to open vehicles to get food. Keep a clean tent site with no food. Wash dishes away from the sleeping zone. No perfumes or colognes please; leave that stuff in the city. Bears are especially attracted to the scent of toothpaste; get ready for bed away from where you're most vulnerable. If you need to clean fish, do it at the water—you're not supposed to camp closer than 200 feet from bodies of water. This is good, though, since water means mosquitos. Obviously, don't camp near berry patches; this would be inviting a confrontation.

From the U.S .Forest Service:

> *"Indian Peaks Wilderness spans 76,711 acres and became part of the National Wilderness Preservation System in 1978. It is bordered by the James Peak Wilderness to the south and Rocky Mountain National Park to the north. Elevations range from 8,300 to just over 13,500 feet. Indian Peaks is one of the most visited Wilderness areas in the United States."*

Overnight permits are limited and must be obtained in advance from the Boulder or Sulphur Ranger District by submitting an Indian Peaks Wilderness Permit Application Form. Camping is prohibited in the Four Lakes Backcountry Zone (Blue, Mitchell, Long, and Isabelle) from May 1 through November 30.

Permits are required for camping between June 1 and September 15. Large groups (8 to 12 people) and/or organized groups such as scouts, schools, internet outdoor groups, and hiking clubs require permits year round for day and overnight trips. Reservations can be made for the summer months as early as January 2. Download a wilderness permit application form from the Forest Service website.

> *Group size is limited to 12 people and livestock combined.*
>
> *Permits are required for all overnight campers 6/1 to 9/15.*
>
> *Permits are always required for organizational groups such as scouts, churches, schools, and hiking clubs.*
>
> *Camping is prohibited in the Four Lakes Backcountry Zone (5/1 - 11/30).*
>
> *In the Diamond, Jasper, Crater, and Caribou Lake Zones, camping is allowed only in designated campsites.*
>
> *Camping is prohibited within 100 feet of lakes, streams, and trails.*
>
> *Campfires are prohibited in most areas. Temporary fire restrictions can prohibit campfires in all areas.*
>
> *Pets must be on a hand-held leash at all times.*
>
> *Motorized or mechanized equipment including chain saws and mountain bikes are prohibited.*

Livestock (horses, llamas) are prohibited in the Four Lakes Zone, in the Cascade above Cascade Falls, the Diamond Lake Zone, and on the Diamond Lake Trail.

Permits can be picked up at the following offices: Granby, Colorado; Boulder, Colorado; Nederland, Colorado; Ward, Colorado; or online. Download and complete the Wilderness Permit Application Form and mail or bring to the office as far in advance as possible.

Decide which zone you are camping within for each day of your trip by viewing the Indian Peaks Wilderness & Backcountry Zones Map at http://www.fs.usda.gov/Internet/FSE_DOCUMENTS/fseprd502324.pdf. You will need a separate permit for each zone you plan to visit if you are visiting multiple zones. *Each backcountry zone is limited to between four and 16 permits depending on zone location and size. Day hiking trips are free of charge.*

AVALANCHES

Avalanches are the most daunting element for most backcountry users, both inexperienced and expert. There's an old adage: "There are no avalanche experts because they're all dead." This may seem extreme, but with the concepts of spatial variability, it's difficult to ski backcountry without risk. Accepting this risk and trying to work within it is the path I choose to follow.

Let's break an avalanche down to its most base level. The elements of a winter slab avalanche are 1) a slope steep enough to slide, 2) a failure plane/weak layer, 3) a slab of snow, and 4) a trigger. All four of these elements must be present for a slide to occur. If one is missing, a slide will not occur.

Typically, slopes over 30 degrees are steep enough to slide, though shallower angles have been known to slide as well, and steeper slopes have been known to pull down lower-angled slopes from below. The majority of slides occur on slopes between 35 and 45 degrees, with 38 to 40 degrees as the sweet spot. Unfortunately for us, this is also the prime angle for powder skiing. One way to eliminate the avy issue is to ski mellow slopes with no steeper slopes

Remote Trigger →

Aspect can be everything. This slide released at the trees and rock line. These dark objects acted as heating wands, undermining the snow from within.

above you. There are routes like this in this guidebook; I like to ski them during winter's higher danger days.

The failure plane is a weak layer within the snowpack. In Colorado, the usual culprit for this is a hoar frost layer. Surface hoar is essentially winter dew. Delicate crystals grow at night; they look like crystalline feathers. The angular nature of these crystals makes bonding between the crystals and subsequent layers or slabs of snow difficult. Other failure planes could be rain and sun crusts and basal facets. The rain crust issue is common in coastal zones and occasionally causes issues later in the season in Colorado; we generally don't get rain events in the winter. Sun crusts form on solar aspects when these slopes melt and refreeze; add a new layer of snow on top of these and you could have problems. Basal facets are to be expected in the higher elevation zones common in Colorado. They are caused when there is a temperature differential between the snowpack and the ground. The conditions for this are prime in Colorado's shallow early season snowpack, when the snowpack is too thin to insulate the temperature differentials from occurring. When we get early season storms like those that occur in most Octobers, expect that snow to rot into facets, then get buried by subsequent storms and become weak layers for future snow to slide on.

Slabs can be soft or hard. They can be barely cohesive or so hard it would be difficult to get a knife to penetrate them. When the new snow gets compacted by the wind during or just after a storm, you get a storm slab; more wind velocity and duration usually equals harder slabs. The wind in Colorado, especially on the Front Range, produces a lot of hard slabs. Once they get buried by future storms, these slabs become a minefield. The ones that don't fail with the new load but are still ripe for triggering are called persistent slabs. Hard slabs can be very deceptive and give a false sense of security; they may appear stronger than they are. Let's think back to that spatial variability concept and how wind-loading can differ over very close distances. This phenomenon can lead to hard slabs of differing thickness over short spans; those thinner areas are trigger points, and with a hard slab, the entire slab can come down on top of you.

A trigger can be a skier or snow-machiner, new snow load, or even heavy wind. Sonic booms don't start avalanches, but the Colorado Department of Transportation uses howitzers, gasex control systems, and even helicopter-placed bombs to trigger them

Risk can be mitigated by eliminating an element. The ability to read into the snowpack takes education and practice. The American Institute for Avalanche Research and Education (AIARE) has a great series of courses that helps explain the nuances of the avalanche puzzle. Avy I, II, and III are designed to follow along a progression of learning. Avy I is essentially an introduction, Avy II explores the snowpack, and Avy III is for guides and pros looking to forecast, as well as serious amateurs. These courses are an invaluable investment into your own preservation. Learning doesn't stop here, though. I've been at this game now for 30 years and I read *Staying Alive in Avalanche Terrain* by Bruce Tremper before every ski season. There's always something to be reminded of. Be sure to check out the bibliography for great reading selections to take your knowledge further.

There are also great professional resources available at www.avalanche.org, including videos on how to do snow tests. Consistent tests on representative slopes will provide the information needed to make the right decisions. That information, combined with other observations and the current avalanche forecast, will allow you to make informed choices.

Point releases, one of which had a minor step-down.

As you'll learn in your courses, it is imperative to be prepared with rescue gear and the skills to use it should a member of your group get buried by a slide. Essential gear includes an avalanche transceiver, shovel, and probe pole. This is not safety gear, it won't keep you safe, it is rescue gear to help make up for your mistakes in the decision-making process. Practice with this gear whenever there is snow on the ground— the faster the recovery of a burial victim, the better the chances for survival.

The chance of getting caught by an avalanche isn't reduced by carrying this rescue gear. Rather, the chances are reduced by making decisions about the lines you plan to ski based on the evidence you gather, and being able to see and understand the signs. You should be able to back up your decisions to ski or not to ski with evidence. However, I will say that if my gut is telling me not to ski, that is all the "evidence" I need to back away from a line. During a, close call in the Tenmile Range a few years ago, I just felt like I didn't want to ski it—a minute later, the cornice failed and I watched the line I would have been in get rocked. Don't ignore your inner voices.

You can supplement the above rescue gear with an avalanche airbag or an avalung. There is some argument over whether these tools increase your risk by changing your perception of the risk. Statistics show that the airbags can reduce the chance of burial by keeping you on the surface. With a significant percentage of fatalities attributed to asphyxiation, reducing burials should lead to a reduction in deaths. I use my airbag in the winter, in alpine zones outside of Colorado. As a general rule, I stay out of Colorado's alpine terrain in winter. When I do visit it on that rare occasion, I bring my BCA Float pack.

I'll let you in on my main formula to success when it comes to avalanches: trees in the winter, alpine in the spring and summer. Fall is when it gets the diciest. I spend most of the winter in Colorado skiing the trees. There are great, long tree runs that see less slab development than their neighboring alpine slopes. This is due in part to less wind, and the wind that does get through is dithered by the trees. That's not to say that there aren't wind slabs in the trees. However, there is less slab development overall. Stacking the deck for success is paramount.

If you have options that will be successful, utilize them. Skiing powder in the trees is awesome—you rarely run across other people or tracks, and with one of the elements lessened in the avalanche puzzle your risk is lower. Risk mitigation is what it's all about—well, that and face shots. Of course there are exceptions to this rule. When I do venture into the alpine occasionally in the winter, I do so with suspicion that there are persistent slabs around every gully and at the start of every couloir apron.

Progression is a key element to venturing into more slide-prone terrain, but you can push it too far very easily. You might start with a ski of a mellow slope to see what the snow is like. Then you ski a steeper line and have success. That might persuade you to push to an even steeper line, but spatial variability comes into play and you get slid. The aspect might have been the same, but the wind-loading patterns could be slightly different. Was the line free of terrain hazards? Human bodies don't fare well against trees and cliffs. Progress into terrain that won't kill you due to terrain traps if you're wrong.

I like to save hazardous lines for the spring and summer season. Let me state very clearly that I am referring to spring snow conditions and not spring on the calendar. Spring snow conditions mean that the melt freeze stabilization process has set in on the snowpack. This usually occurs on east-facing slopes first, and then works its way around the southern/solar aspects. North-facing slopes are the last to stabilize. The stabilization occurs when the sun warms the slope, causing the snow at the surface to melt. In the evening, once the solar radiation has subsided, the slope freezes. Moisture percolates down into the snowpack and freezes as well, further locking up the snowpack.

Early starts are a must when skiing spring snow. You are trying to ski on the barely melted snow's surface while getting support from the still frozen, underlying snow. If the snow gets too wet from the sun's rays, you could cause a wet slide to release. Timing is the key to avoiding this. I generally try to be off the snow by noon, but that is just a generalization—in the real world, the conditions will dictate when you need to be off the hot snow. This varies greatly by aspect. For example, if you skied a west-facing slope at 9 a.m., you would be dealing with hard ice; a north face may be powder all day. Nine a.m. could be too late on an east face. You also may not get any decent heating if the clouds that frequent the Front Range are present. These massive lenticular clouds have spoiled more than a few of my outings in the range. Ironclad rules really don't have a place in an environment as dynamic as the mountains.

By summer, the snowpack has usually turned to a rock-hard mass; I've referred to summer snow as "rock hard, egg carton, with dirt on top." Waiting for some softening is really important if you want to keep the fillings in your teeth. The avy issue is usually gone by summer, but there have been fatalities every month of the year in Colorado. So, that being the case, later starts are ideal for summer skiing. This can run into conflict with the development of near-daily convective thunder storms that develop in the afternoons. Be sure to keep an eye on the weather throughout your day in the hills and don't be sad if you have to abort your plans.

LIGHTNING AND WEATHER

Lightning is scary—very scary. The concept of not even knowing that it's over—bam, you're just dead—is very unsettling. Generally you can tell when it's coming, but there have been some crazy reports of people getting struck up to 10 miles from the storm's edge. I've had more than a couple close calls with lightning and they all leave me shaking my head and feeling lucky. My scariest experience was near the summit of Blanca Peak in the Sangre de Cristo Range, which has a very similar position to the Front Range in terms of geography. It was mid-March and there was a snowstorm raging. As we neared the top of the peak, the skis started to crackle and you could see little arcs of electricity going from edge to edge. We immediately got low on the snow and the buzzing and humming stopped. I kept going over in my mind how it was a good life and I was going to miss my kids; I was certain that this was it. The energy passed and we got down to safety, but it was a rough night. Check my blog at www.MakingTurns.com for the whole story.

Lighting kills in Colorado every year and is one of the leading hazards in the mountains behind avalanches and accidents. Colorado is second on the list behind only Florida in lightning incidents for the United States. You have to figure lightning into your risk assessment if you want to succeed; making it home is your goal, correct?

Lightning usually isn't an issue in the winter; you just don't get enough heating to drive inner-cloud convection. When planning a trip in the spring and summer, be sure to take a look at the point forecast for the day of your trip. In the spring, many of these forecasts state something along the lines of "20 percent chance of thunderstorms in the afternoon." This is telling me that there will be the necessary heating for lightning to occur, and I'd better plan on being down low before that happens.

Typically, lightning is created by convective circulation of ice particles throughout the cloud. The solar radiation that causes the evaporative effect that creates the clouds also heats the clouds, resulting in convective currents. The agitation of the ice particles causes static charges to build within the cloud. Lightning is the result. Grauple is the best indicator that the conditions for lightning are present. You don't want to be up high when the grauple or rain or thunder snow starts. When you get a chance to look in the direction the clouds are coming from, be sure to assess how much time you have for your objective. Note whether the clouds are coalescing; if so, this can decrease the time it takes for the clouds and the threat to reach you.

Under a monsoonal flow, which is basically a southwesterly flow pattern that streams moisture off the Gulf of California, you can expect the lightning to develop earlier in the day. If this happens early enough in the season there is a good possibility you will see snow at altitude; lightning is a strong possibility, too. If you get a closed low and the storm wraps around the low cyclonically, then you'll have an upslope storm. These are great for the Front Range, and the Indian Peaks typically get the most snow from these storms; they are the reason we can ski so late in the year. If the monsoonal flow is out of the southeast and the Gulf of Mexico, then we have the potential for the same scenario as the Boulder and Big Thompson Canyon floods. The flow out of the southeast is generally warmer, so you won't get snow out of this; it will just rain the snow away, and there will be lightning.

You may find yourself up high with lightning flashing. Ideally, get to lower ground. If you can't get to lower ground, be sure to separate your group and drop as much of your metal gear as you can. You aren't safe until you're in a vehicle or a building with grounded wiring. In the event of a strike, begin CPR immediately. Lightning typically stops the heart. The body of a strike victim does not hold a charge.

As a general rule, when I see the puffy cumulus clouds developing on the near horizon, I turn around. I try not to get up into the clouds to push on for my goal. The lightning issue is enough for me to deem this an unnecessary risk; not to mention the fact that low visibility usually means low quality skiing, so why push on for mediocrity? The mountain will be there when the weather is better. Generally, If I hear thunder, then the upward progress usually ends; an example of an exception to this rule would be if I'm hearing thunder from storms over Denver or Boulder.

MOUNTAIN CRAFT

Traveling through the mountains takes some acquired skills. The best places to get this information are from skilled guides, mentors, reading materials, and the vast resource that is the internet. Starting with local guides and mentors is a great way to go. You can peruse the appendix for great guide services all over Colorado. Mentors are harder to find. The Teton Gravity Forums are a great place to hook up with some partners. An avalanche course, preferably an AIARE 1 or upward, can be a good place to meet partners, too. Backcountry clubs at colleges and the Colorado Mountain Club are also great places to meet up with partners. You can also check in with your local shops to find partners.

You need to learn to use the specific gear for ski touring and mountaineering. Skins, AT bindings, splitboards, ice axes, crampons, whippets, winter camping gear, ropes, and rock gear all may be put into play to get the lines you want to accomplish. Using this gear correctly is crucial to you and your team's safety and survival. Having expert skiing skill isn't enough when you're planning a climb up steep snow and you slip. How do you perform a self-arrest with an ice axe? How do you protect that line with a rope and climbing gear?

Mountaineering Freedom of the Hills is the bible for mountain craft questions. This resource will provide the answers when you need them and don't have your guide or mentor around. You can usually search YouTube and the internet for videos that put the techniques you read about in play. How do you do a Munter hitch? Well, it's a lot easier for some things to see on a video than by reading a book. Be sure the videos are taught by certified guides.

One basic question I try to keep in mind is, "Will my friends make fun of me if I make this mistake?" The choices you make in the backcountry have consequences; some of those can be fatal. Use your brain when you're in the backcountry. Help is a long way away. This isn't a ski movie where there is a team of EMT mountain guides on standby, flying around in the other helicopter waiting to save your ass if you make a mistake. The hospital isn't a quick 10-minute flight. A rescue is a long way away, if you can get cell reception at all.

Traveling safely through the mountains is all about mitigating risk. If you don't know what the risks are, then you can't minimize the chances of those risks killing you.

CORNICES

This spring, while finishing up the skiing for this book, I had one of the closest calls of my backcountry career. While ascending the apron of Shooting Star Couloir, we were taking a rest and having a regroup moment before entering the actual harm's way portion of the couloir. We were using the cliffs above us to keep us out of the fall line of any snow slide action we might face. Suddenly all hell broke loose and multiple cornice chunks came careening down the East Face of James Peak and Shooting Star Couloir itself. We're not talking about small chunks by any means; these were school bus-sized. We moved quickly, though we didn't really have to and the debris passed by us about 15 feet away. I always say it's better to be good than lucky—in the mountains, sometimes you need both. If you push your goals without factoring all the elements of danger, then you cannot mitigate that danger. Our complacency regarding the cornice could have killed us. Always try and stay out of the fall line of chutes; stick to the edges and the cover of the cliff walls, though this does increase your risk of rockfall. This may not help if the chute has multiple doglegs, but it's better than nothing. Wait for cornices to drop before attempting lines with cornice hazard.

Another element of the cornice picture is the trap door effect. If you get too close to the edge, you may actually be on overhanging, friable snow. Boom—the trapdoor is where you fall through the cornice and onto who knows what below. Give the edge respect. Try to see where the edge is from down below the ridge before venturing to it. Overhanging cornices are dangerous and unpredictable.

If you plan on managing or cutting the cornice, be sure to rope up to nearby rock anchors. Cornices are hard slabs and they have a tendency to rip out further back than one might expect. Never use snow connected to the cornice as an anchor.

ROCKFALL

If there are rocks above you and it is steep, wear a helmet; don't be stupid. But hey, if you don't, at least if you get hit in the head you probably won't remember. The melting and freezing process is perfect for breaking down rock. As the water freezes, it expands; then in the morning the sun melts the water, releases the icy bond that holds the rocks together and boom, you have rockfall. One time while climbing up a popular 14er couloir, I had a rock whiz between my legs at about 100 mph. If it had hit my head without a helmet on, I would have been a goner. I was wearing a helmet though, so I probably would have only gotten a concussion. When you're climbing your line, take note of whether there is rock debris on the snow. This is a good indication of the rock quality and whether you need to have a spotter while climbing; this is when you take turns watching for rockfall while the rest of the group climbs, then you switch off.

MOATS

Moats are Colorado's version of crevasses. They form around heat wands—primarily rocks, but also trees. They are created when the temperature gradient snow that is formed here melts before the rest of the deeper snowpack that isn't affected by the temperature differentials; when you see some of these moats you begin to question the concept of bridging. Use caution at the snow rock interfaces. In some cases lines can  be undermined by these moats. All thinner areas should be approached with ample caution. Moats can be pretty deep; I've seen them up to fifteen feet deep.

TREE WELLS

Tree wells are a significant hazard to keep in mind. Here's the issue: the branches of the trees prevent the snow from building up under them, leaving a space near the trunk of the tree. If one were to fall into a tree well, the snow above could fall in on the victim, cutting off oxygen. Unlike an actual avalanche where the snow sets up like concrete, the snow remains loose and can keep falling in on you as you struggle to get free. These non-avalanche-related snow deaths (NARSDs) happen every year. This isn't the ski area. "No friends on a powder day" isn't cool. Powder days are for friends in the backcountry. Keep in contact with your partners and never get too far ahead of them. I stay in contact with a "Woop!" noise. Have skins with you to go back uphill if your partner needs a rescue. If you go into a tree well, try to make an air pocket. Skiing with an avalung can reduce the risk of suffocation in tree wells.

WILDLIFE

Give wildlife respect; you are a visitor in their home. Numerous species may be encountered in your travels. All should be viewed as a threat. Never approach wildlife and never feed them. Moose are of greatest concern from a safety standpoint, with more injuries to humans than from bears, cougars, wolves, and coyotes combined. They are just plain unpredictable and territorial. Spring big mountain season is prime time for mother moose and calves to be on the approaches. Be aware of what's going on around you, especially around willows and water areas. Just because they don't have claws doesn't mean they are harmless. Be calm around them and back away slowly if they seem to be aggravated by your presence.

Bears are also rising from their winter hibernation during big mountain season. Aren't you hungry when you wake up? Well, so are they. This past spring at the Montezuma campsite, I

was charged at by a yearling black bear. I scared it off, but it was a good lesson. That site was dirty and too many people had left food out. Be sure to bring a bear canister with you. Never clean fish around camp and cook separately as well. Mothers will defend cubs to the death. Do your best to fight back if they attack. These aren't grizzlies; do not play dead. Most likely, yelling at a bear will be all it takes to make it run away.

Mountain lions have seen a resurgence in their numbers and there have been incidents. If there are deer in the zone, then there may be mountain lions. Generally a cat that attacks humans is sick or malnourished. Fight back if they attack. They are pounce attackers and like to attack the neck from above, so be mindful around rocky outcrops, especially at twilight. Never run if you encounter a predator—you will trigger the animal's prey instinct. Try to appear bigger and make metallic sounds, such as banging your ice axes. I always carry a weapon when I travel in the backcountry.

Mountain goats like salt. They licked all the salt off my truck one day, denting the roof after climbing on it. They are goats, so they are also ornery and territorial. They will charge you if they feel threatened. That would hurt a lot. Give them space. The same goes for bighorn sheep.

Marmots like to eat shoes and anything else they can get their teeth on. I lost a pair of shoes to marmots on South Arapaho. Never get separated from your shoes by leaving them at the base of the line. Marmots look fat on the east side of the divide, like someone has been feeding them. Remember: never feed the animals.

You may also encounter coyotes, fox, deer, elk, and ptarmigan. There are reports of lynx in the area as well. Bobcats are found along the approaches as well as weasels, chipmunks, pikas, eagles, squirrels, beavers, and martens. This is their home, so please act like a guest and treat them with respect.

MARIJUANA

Marijuana is legal in Colorado and therefore needs to be addressed here. All of the lines in this book are on federal land. According to the state constitutional amendment that legalized marijuana, you may only partake in private. On federal land, their rules apply. This means that if you smoke in the forest and a ranger or USFS law enforcement officer catches you, then you can be punished under the federal law. This hasn't happened very often, although I can think of the feds getting involved when other rules have been broken. The smoke shack cabins around Breckenridge and Vail come to mind. The Forest Service blew up these "over the top" shacks that were illegally built on federal land, which was a bummer for all involved for sure. This isn't the place for a policy debate; I'm just here to state the rules as they are. If we want weed to stay legal, we need to show some restraint and discretion.

Full disclosure: back in the 90s, I had a very bad skiing accident where I suffered a spiral fracture of my tibia and fibula. I was up at Loveland Pass and was stoned. I fell doing a trick and could have saved it. I feel like my state made me a little lazy. Our choices have consequences. That being said, I do currently partake while skiing and find that the modern day strains can be more targeted for sports. The sativas now available are more conducive to getting into that flow state. But in the back of my mind, I still think about that day at the Pass. Still, I have to say it's really nice to have the freedom to make that choice after so many years of prohibition.

Many people choose to use before, during, and after. Do as you wish, but know the rules and don't make backcountry skiers look bad by getting caught breaking those rules.

COMMUNICATION

Back in the day, we used to appreciate getting away from the world. Today we feel we need to be connected to civilization at all times. These mountains are tough to stay in contact in. Cell coverage is spotty at best. You can get coverage in the southern and central parts of the range when you're on top of peaks and ridges. You need line of sight with the towns and the plains to have a signal. The northern part of the range is harder to make contact in. This can make for some dicey situations should you have an accident. Use a Spot satellite GPS messenger or an InReach personal satellite communicator to keep in touch. You could also carry a satellite phone. If you don't have these options, you will need to ascend to the ridge to make contact if you need a rescue; leaving an injured partner is never a good idea. Bear this in mind when you want to get rad on that cliff jump.

ETIQUETTE AND PHILOSOPHY

Backcountry skiing is the only segment of the ski industry that is still on the rise. With the onslaught of new users in the backcountry, it's important to broach the subjects of etiquette and philosophy. Some might find this information preachy, but considering how many times over the past few years I've seen confrontations, it seems necessary. With uninitiated newbies and crusty old-timers having negative interactions in the hills, there are a few subjects that really should be addressed.

Skin tracks are a pain in the ass to put in, especially after a big new storm. I look at the route of the skin track as a safe exit option as well as an ascent route for what you're hoping to ski, should the avy stability allow it. When two groups come together while a trail is being broken, they really need to work together. If one group works for it and the other group hangs back, tail riding if you will, the group doing the work will resent the lazy moochers at the back of the line. This can escalate if the well-rested moochers rip skins and snake the fresh tracks. People need to work together and show each other respect in the mountains.

On the subject of skin tracks: never ski down a skin track, ever! Like I've already stated, they are hard to put in. Why would you ruin all that work by skiing or riding down it? Are you afraid you're going to get lost? Then just keep the track in sight and ski the fresh snow next to it. The skiing will be better and you won't piss off as many people.

When putting in a skin track, don't go directly up the line you want to ski. If there are hard slabs and avy danger, then you're a sitting duck for the most dangerous slides there are: slides from above. Set the track out of the way of your intended line. Nothing disrupts flow like hitting a skin track on your descent, and hitting a zig-zagging skin track is even worse. In the spring, approach your couloir via skinning up the apron out of the couloir's fall-line. Then switch to booting to have less of an effect on the turns. It is about the turns, isn't it?

The mountains can be a dream or a nightmare; it's what you make it. They do not care that you are there. You are beyond insignificant. Perhaps that's the allure of them. We visit them to get perspective on our lives. We escape the office cubicles, the cities, and our homes; it's nature therapy. Bringing conflict to the hills makes no sense. Likewise, bringing our manmade goals and objectives makes no sense, either. Mountains are never conquered and it's an illusion to think they are. They merely let you pass. To me, the main goal is to get home safely; putting your objectives at the forefront of your decision-making process gets away from that main goal. It's funny: with so many objectives in each of my books, one would think that I'm only objective-oriented. You would be surprised at how many times I've walked away from lines because the conditions didn't merit pushing forward. No matter how well you plan your missions in the hills, you will still fail. The conditions might not be what you planned for, the weather may be bad, or the snowpack stability might not be what you'd hoped for. Only the bold will push on through such scenarios; there are old backcountry skiers and bold backcountry skiers, but not many old, bold backcountry skiers.

Remember, the mountains will still be there should you choose to bail on your objective. Enjoy the visit while you are among them. If you don't get your line, know that you'll have another shot. The snow you return to may be the run of your life. If you choose to push bad conditions in the hills for your objectives, you may have the last run of your life.

USING THIS GUIDEBOOK

A guidebook is ineffective if you don't understand the information being presented. It's also important to know where to look for the information you want. Sometimes you really need information quickly, so knowing where it is can be really important. I've had the pleasure and pain of using many guidebooks over the years. Starting with the trailhead descriptions, I've added trailhead photos to each description as seen in the Upper Tipperary Trailhead, pictured below. To further aid in getting you to the correct location, I've included longitude and latitude coordinates. Tech-savvy folks with a GPS unit can hone right into where to leave their vehicles and start the adventure. For those who like to read directions and push odometers, I've included a mileage-based set of directions. The peaks associated with the trailhead are listed in the blue box. Elevation height is also noted. Almost all of the trailheads can be reached by car. Some offer a bit more challenge. A few offer intense, bone-jarring, and technical four-wheeling, where rollovers are actually a pretty common occurrence. If there are any trespass issues, I point them out. Forest Service openings are pretty variable year to year, due to snowfall. You begin the journey of many miles with one step, but if you can't get to the trailhead, you can't take the first step.

TRAILHEAD LOCATION		PEAKS ACCESSED
Upper Tipperary		**Ptarmigan**
Elevation: 9,000'	Lat/Long: 39°56'13.37"N 105°53'57.80"W	

At the gas station in central Fraser on US Highway 40, aka Zerex St, turn west on to Eisenhower Drive and start your measure; this is the only street that crosses the railroad tracks. Drive 0.2 mile and turn left onto Norgren Road. Drive 0.1 mile to its end and turn right onto Grand County Road 73. At the 1.3 mile mark you will come to the right turn for Grand County Road 50. You will reach the actual Tipperary Trailhead at the 5.7 mile mark. For our purposes, drive up the road another 0.3 mile and you will come to another, larger parking lot. This is the winter closure of Grand County Road 50, and the access for the North Face of Ptarmigan.

The peak and route section headers are shown below. At the start of each peak section, I include the summit elevation, and a number. Numbering starts in the south and works its way north. Some peaks have more than one route, so to distinguish them I mark the route letter. Then there is the peak description. If it's one of the higher peaks, there is usually a state height ranking. I try to include history here. Sometimes I include geologic information.

Other times I will wax poetically about getting away from the high peaks for solitude. Some peaks have naming history. Many of those records are unavailable, lost history. If there are more routes than one, I will speak to the differences of the routes.

---

7 MOUNT MACHEBEUF – 12,805'

From the website of Bishop Machebeuf High School, "a mountain just east of Loveland Pass was named Mount Machebeuf in honor of the first Bishop of Colorado. The mountain is 12,805 feet tall and can be seen from Interstate 70. A dedication Mass was celebrated at the summit by Rev. Richard Ling and Rev. Ed Hoffman in June 1991 using one of Bishop Joseph P. Machebeuf's chalices that he used in the 1880s." He was named bishop of the Colorado diocese in 1887. The peak does not rise 300' above its higher neighbor Woods Mountain, so it's not an officially ranked summit, but its elevation is tied for 777th highest and its name is official.

7a – Mount Machebeuf	Y – Y Not – Y Yes Gullies	
DIFFICULTY: Advanced	DISTANCE: 3.6 Miles Roundtrip	VERTICAL: 2,500'
SUNHIT: Sunrise + 1 Hour	ASPECT: Southeast and South	SEASON: Spring
TRAILHEAD: Herman Gulch	MAP: Page 268	PHOTO: Page 67, 68, 69

Coming eastbound out of the East Portal of the Eisenhower Tunnel and making the first corner, this line comes into view. It's the obvious swath cut out of the shoulder of Machebeuf, just to the north of the interstate. It looks like a ski run and it is—but it's also an avy path, like so many great ski runs. You can also get a great look at this line from Loveland Pass. The cross-loaded nature of this line and the near-perfect start zone angle of 40 degrees makes this a dangerous winter undertaking, and you might need an undertaker if you get it in unstable conditions. Save this line for after the melt-freeze cycle starts. Be mindful of these lines above you if you are going under them for other objectives up-valley.

DIFFICULTY: The table has information that I find to be the most useful for planning. It's important to understand the difficulty of what you're getting yourself into. I like to think in terms of stress level when considering difficulty. It's all about your comfort zone.

Intermediate: For backcountry skiing, this means black diamond ski area-grade terrain with minimal avy hazard. If skiing in winter, you should be able to skin most, if not all, of these routes. This doesn't mean there is no hazard of avalanches. Always be on guard in the wild.

Advanced: The stress level goes up a notch here. With more exposure to avalanche hazards, these lines are just more intense experiences. Safe travel is advised at times, one at a time. Timing can be an issue on these lines. There may be hard bootpacks to negotiate. Terrain traps may be present, but most of these features won't be of lethal proportions. These lines are generally in that primetime avalanche zone of around 35-45 degrees. There may be serious exposure to avalanches from above. Route finding can be an issue on the way up or the way down. The skiing, minus all these factors, will be in the double black diamond ski area grade. Remember that there isn't a ski patrol setting off bombs and cutting slopes for you.

Expert: These are top-flight ski mountaineering lines. Some may even be considered extreme, where a fall would be fatal. There will be avalanche hazard. Timing will most likely be essential. No-fall skiing ability is mandatory. Slope steepness in some places may even approach 60°. Steep snow climbing skills will be needed. Ice axe and crampons will probably be used. Terrain traps may be fatal. Some lines dogleg into rock walls. Cornices may need to be dealt with. The actual skiing will be on the level with the most demanding ski area terrain, again minus the avalanche control by the ski patrol. Hopefully some of these classics will test you. A few of the lines in this category only get skied every few years.

DISTANCE: This may seem obvious, but many books out there list mileage and then fail to explain whether the distance is one-way or round-trip. All distances are round-trip unless otherwise stated. Some trailheads are in different locations due to season.

VERTICAL: Backcountry skiing begins when you hit the trail. The vertical listed here is full route vertical. I like to start with this number to assess what the day will entail. The route description for the line of your choice will usually have line vertical. Otherwise check the contour lines on the map.

VERTICAL UP AND DOWN: For areas in the book that offer mechanical assistance, such as Berthoud Pass or the Traverses, I provide a vertical gain measurement and a vertical descent measurement.

SUNHIT: This is a general estimate of the time after sunrise that the sun will hit the line. It's important to know this because the sun will warm the snow, potentially raising the avalanche hazard. The appendix includes a sunrise calendar. Use this to plan your start time in conjunction with the route distance and vertical. Factor in your pace and you can time for perfect corn snow.

ASPECT: Easily knowing the aspect at a glance can speed planning for your day in the hills. It can also aid in planning multi-line days. If you know it's an east-facing line, you know you have to get an early start; not so much with a west-facing line.

SEASON: Generally the choice here is winter or spring. Spring will usually mean to include summer. Winter lines are generally safe in powder conditions. Always be aware of avalanche hazards. The spring lines usually have higher avalanche danger and should be skied after spring consolidation begins.

TRAILHEAD: This is where you start from. A few routes have multiple choices.

MAP PAGE: In the appendix, you will find full-color, marked USGS topo maps. These are the best maps available from the U.S. government.

PHOTO PAGE: Each route has multiple pictures. Find them here. There may also be line photos included with other peaks or routes.

COLORADO'S
PREMIER
BACKCOUNTRY
SNOWBOARDING
GUIDE SERVICE

CSG COLORADO
SNOWBOARD
GUIDES

GUIDED TOURS & BACKCOUNTRY EDUCATION

- AMGA & AIARE
  Professionally Trained Guides
- Avalanche Education
- Splitboard Courses
- Snowboard Mountaineering
- Overnight Hut Trips

coloradosnowboardguides.com ▪ **info@coloradosnowboardguides.com**

TRAILHEADS

TRAILHEADS LOCATION		PEAKS ACCESSED
Eisenhower Tunnel West Portal North		"Golden Bear"
Elevation: 11,157'	Lat/Long: 39°40'43.26"N 105°56'16.73"W	

Located on the west side of the Eisenhower Tunnel, this trailhead is only accessible for westbound travelers. If you are traveling eastbound, you will need to drive through the tunnel, exit I-70 at Loveland Pass, and return westbound, back through the tunnel. Due to Homeland Security issues, the turnaround on the west side of the tunnel is closed. Once through the tunnel, take your first chance for escape through the barriers into the rest stop. About 100 yards from the entrance, park to the right along the plow-line near the road-cut. CDOT doesn't mind if you park here; closer to the highway, not so much. Eastbound users will need to drive all the way down to Silverthorne to get back home; do not use the turnabout above the tunnel.

TRAILHEAD LOCATION		PEAKS ACCESSED
Loveland Ski Area Chair 8 BC Access Gate		"Golden Bear," Trelease, "The Citadel," Hagar
Elevation: 11,800'	Lat/Long: 39°41'30.43"N 105°54'19.81"W	

For this trailhead, you will need a valid Loveland Ski Area ticket, either for riding the lifts or for uphill only. Make your way up the hill to the top of Chair 8. Follow the rope line east to the gate. The position changes a little every year. Be sure to exit and enter ski areas only through the backcountry access gate. Not doing so is a violation of the Skier Responsibility Code and is a finable offense. Coordinates are a position estimate based on previous years' placements.

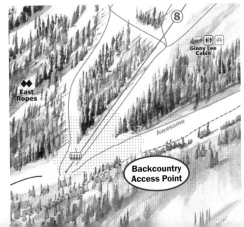

TRAILHEAD LOCATION	PEAKS ACCESSED
Dry Gulch	**Trelease, "The Citadel," Hagar, Bethel, "Golden Bear"**
Elevation: 10,700'	**Lat/Long: 39°41'9.45"N 105°53'10.36"W**

Located at the end of the Loveland Pass westbound exit ramp and across the road from the westbound entrance ramp, this trailhead offers access to many classic descents, both winter and spring. The Loveland Pass exit is number 216 and is based on Interstate 70 mile markers. Early in the season, you can drive east along the north frontage road to a gate, saving yourself some approach. By the time the lines on Trelease are in condition for skiing, the frontage road option is too deep to drive.

TRAILHEAD LOCATION	PEAKS ACCESSED
Herman Gulch	**Bethel, Parnassus, Woods, "Machebeuf," "The Citadel," Pettingell**
Elevation: 10,310'	**Lat/Long: 39°42'8.86"N 105°51'15.42"W**

The Herman Gulch exit is located at Exit 218 on Interstate 70. Like all exits on Interstate 70 the number corresponds to the closest mileage marker east from Utah. The trailhead is north of the exit ramps along a "frontage road" going east. The trailhead turn is marked. There is ample parking as well as restroom facilities here, though they are currently under repair. Behind the info kiosk is the Herman Gulch Trail.

TRAILHEAD LOCATION	PEAKS ACCESSED
Berthoud Falls	**Englemann**
Elevation: 9,800'	Lat/Long: 39°46'15.18"N 105°48'26.61"W

From the gas station in Empire begin your measure. Drive west for 7 miles to this trailhead. On the north side of the road is the CDOT shed/garage. On the south side of the road just west of the sheds is a parking pull-off located under some power lines. This trailhead is at the bottom of a slide path so this isn't the best zone for high danger days. Be sure to cross the creek to the east side of the path as the west side of the path is private property. Once the snow bridges over the creek are gone, please don't use this trailhead, or just wade. Either way, respect private property or we could lose this access.

Park off the tarmac!!!

TRAILHEAD LOCATION	PEAKS ACCESSED
Ruby Gulch	**Parnassus, Englemann, Robeson, Bard, Woods**
Elevation: 10,250'	Lat/Long: 39°45'17.14"N 105°49'27.13"W

This trailhead was closed for a couple years while Urad Mine was under construction. It has reopened and offers great skiing options on some great 13ers and a fun 12er. From the center of Empire, begin your measure. Drive west on US Highway 40 for 7.3 miles and turn left onto Clear Creek County Road 202. At the 7.8 mile mark you will turn left onto Clear Creek County Road 203 and drive to a pull-off at the 9.1 mile mark. Be sure to pull all the way off the road. This lot is small and can't accommodate many vehicles. Do not park on the road or you could be towed. The actual trail is a short distance up the road behind a closure gate.

Woods Mountain

Gate

Not much space here for parking.

21

TRAILHEAD LOCATION	PEAKS ACCESSED
Jones Pass	**"Hassel," Jones Pass, Butler Gulch, Vasquez**
Elevation: 10,480'	Lat/Long: 39°46'16.42"N 105°51'17.69"W

From the gas station in Empire, begin your measure. Drive 7.3 miles west of town to the turnoff for Jones Pass Road. Alternately this turnoff is 5.8 miles from the summit of Berthoud Pass, if traveling eastbound. From the turn, drive an additional 1.8 miles to the right turn that continues Jones Pass Road. Going straight here is blocked by the gate to the entrance to the Henderson Mine. The road becomes dirt at the turn and you will go another .5 mile to the winter trailhead. This is the end of plowed maintenance. Early in the season it's possible for 4x4 vehicles to make it all the way up to the summit of the pass and over into the Bobtail Creek drainage, though the upper section is usually covered with snow and is impassable by the time there's enough snow to ski. The lower lot is for snowmobiles and their trailers.

TRAILHEAD LOCATION	PEAKS ACCESSED
Berthoud Pass South Corner	**Berthoud Pass**
Elevation: 10,730'	Lat/Long: 39°47'28.02"N 105°46'48.27"W

This is more of a pickup spot than a trailhead. Telegraph, Floral Park, and the Fairway empty out at this corner and it's a great spot to pick up hitchhikers, earning some karma points for your own day of hitchhiking. I've noticed that this corner is harder to get rides at than the other similar spot on Loveland Pass. If you do pull over to pick up hitchhiking skiers, be sure to pull over all the way, out of the roadway or you'll risk getting a ticket from highway patrol or an even worse result like causing an accident on the snowy roads. The corner is located on the westbound side, 10.7 miles from the gas station in Empire and 2.6 miles from the summit of Berthoud Pass.

TRAILHEAD LOCATION	PEAKS ACCESSED
Berthoud Pass Stanley Slidepath Access	**Berthoud Pass**
Elevation: 10,960'	Lat/Long: 39°47'16.79"N 105°47'41.26"W

This is the access point for the Stanley Slidepath. The ideal parking spot for this is on the eastbound side of the road, at the corner. On heavy snow days when there is a lot of plowing activity this isn't the best place to park. Above the corner on the eastbound side, there is a small pullout that is a better option. One can also park on the westbound side of the highway just below the apex of the corner. Be sure to park as far from the roadway as possible. The corner is located 11.7 miles from the gas station in Empire and 1.6 miles from the summit of the pass.

TRAILHEAD LOCATION	PEAKS ACCESSED
Berthoud Pass Pump House	**Berthoud Pass**
Elevation: 11,200'	Lat/Long: 39°47'47.46"N 105°47'6.07"W

This is an underused trailhead that provides access to Russell's Waterfall and No Name's Oatmeal Bowl. One could also approach Stanley Slidepath from here if the lower lots are full. This spot offers more parking on those days when Berthoud gets really busy on a big winter pow day. The trailhead is located 12.7 miles from Empire's gas station and 0.5 mile from the summit. On those heavy-use days, you can park here and access Russell's East Ridge to connect with Current Creek lines.

TRAILHEAD LOCATION	PEAKS ACCESSED
Berthoud Pass Summit	**Berthoud Pass, Colorado Mines, Flora, Witter, Eva**
Elevation: 11,306'	Lat/Long: 39°47'52.77"N 105°46'36.91"W

This is the main access to Berthoud Pass and is the starting point for most of the classic Pass lines. The base area of Colorado's first ski area has been removed and replaced with a warming hut with bathrooms. There are three rows of parking available here. There is no snowmobiling allowed in the Berthoud Pass zone. Snowmobiling is allowed at Jones Pass down the road. The people who use the station on top of Colorado Mines Peak sometimes access via snowcat and snowmobile, but they only use the access road. Sledding is also forbidden at the Pass due to multiple accidents involving kids, snowbanks, and cars in the parking lot, but people don't seem to be able to read the signs. The turnoff is located 13.3 miles from the gas station in Empire and 8.5 miles from the turnoff for Mary Jane Ski Area. Of note, there are pullouts on either side of the highway at the summit. Be sure not to unload hitchhikers here—pull into the actual parking lot to unload your riders.

TRAILHEAD LOCATION	PEAKS ACCESSED
Berthoud Pass Current Creek	**Berthoud Pass**
Elevation: 10,820'	Lat/Long: 39°48'36.86"N 105°46'42.17"W

This is the first trailhead on the Winter Park side of the pass. Although the Hell's Half Acre lot at the first corner could be considered a trailhead, it's more of a pickup zone as well as overflow parking for the summit lot. The Current Creek trailhead is located 1.9 miles from the summit of the pass and 6.6 miles from the Mary Jane entrance intersection. Pick up skin tracks for Peter Rabbit and Tea Cup here. It is also a popular pickup area for those lapping the 80s, 90s, and other Current Creek lines from the Pass Summit.

TRAILHEAD LOCATION		PEAKS ACCESSED	
Berthoud Pass Second Creek		**Berthoud Pass**	
Elevation: 10,600'		Lat/Long: 39°49'21.69"N 105°46'10.89"W	

This is the primary access for Broome Hut and the classic Frankenstein as well as some great, too infrequently skied lines on Second Creek Ridge. Located 3 miles from the summit on the Winter Park side and 5.5 miles from the Mary Jane entrance, there is a good sized parking lot here.

TRAILHEAD LOCATION		PEAKS ACCESSED	
Berthoud Pass First Creek		**Berthoud Pass**	
Elevation: 10,450'		Lat/Long: 39°49'39.40"N 105°46'5.53"W	

The access for First Creek is located 3.6 miles from the summit of the pass and 4.9 miles from the Mary Jane turn-off. This trailhead provides easy access to the Chimney and a safer approach to Zero Creek. One could also access Winter Park's Panoramic Express Lift summit. This also provides another access point for Broome Hut if the parking is full at Second Creek.

TRAILHEAD LOCATION	PEAKS ACCESSED
Berthoud Pass Zero Creek	**Berthoud Pass**
Elevation: 10,150'	Lat/Long: 39°50'37.91"N 105°45'26.60"W

Located 4.9 miles from the summit of the pass and 3.6 miles from the Mary Jane turnoff, this trailhead is more of a pickup spot for those skiing out the gate at Winter Park into Zero Creek. One could park here and skin up Zero Creek, but that's not the way people usually use this zone. If you do park here, be sure to park on the inside corner of the switchback. Use care when reentering the highway as it's a bit of a blind curve.

TRAILHEAD LOCATION	PEAKS ACCESSED
Parry Creek Trail	**Parry**
Elevation: 9,420'	Lat/Long: 39°51'43.24"N 105°44'56.69"W

This trailhead provides not-so-easy access to the Bear Claw on Parry. Getting to the trailhead, though, is very easy. Drive 1 mile south along Highway 40 from the stoplight at the Winter Park Drive or drive 0.6 miles north from the Mary Jane turn-off and turn onto Forest Service 128. Follow the dirt road around a slight corner and take your first right onto Forest Service Road 128.3. Drive to its end at 0.5 mile from the turn. If Forest Service 128 is gated, you can park at the entrance of the Midland Campground.

TRAILHEAD LOCATION	PEAKS ACCESSED
Jim Creek Trail	**James, Parry**
Elevation: 9,390'	Lat/Long: 39°52'50.22"N 105°44'30.41"W

Drive 1 mile south along Highway 40 from the stoplight at the Winter Park Drive or drive 0.6 mile from the Mary Jane turnoff and turn onto Forest Service 128. Follow the dirt road around a slight corner and then continue straight past the turn for 128.3. Measuring from here, follow the road 1.2 miles to the Jim Creek trailhead. This access usually opens in early May. There is year-round access to this trailhead via the Lakota neighborhood. The access point is at 39°53'28.04"N 105°45'38.11"W on US 40, 0.7 mile north of the main entrance to Winter Park Ski Area. Turn onto Arrow Trail and take the first right at 0.1 mile, staying on Arrow Trail. Go up the hill and join the Denver Water Road at the 0.5 mile mark from the highway, then take a right. From this point drive 1.6 miles to the Jim Creek Trailhead.

TRAILHEAD LOCATION	PEAKS ACCESSED
Fall River Reservoir	**Eva, Witter, Bancroft, Parry**
Elevation: 10,760'	Lat/Long: 39°49'10.18"N 105°41'20.97"W

Get off Interstate 70 at Exit 238 and begin your measure from the bottom of the westbound exit ramp. There is a parking lot here for carpooling to the actual trailhead if you'd like to save some gas. Drive 0.2 mile and turn right onto Clear Creek County 275, aka Fall River Road, at its intersection with the westbound entrance ramp. Follow the road to the 6.7 mile mark and turn left onto Rainbow Road, aka Forest Service 174.1. The road is now dirt and can get a little rough, especially in the spring. It is also fairly shaded so there tends to be

ice on the road. Follow the road to its end at the Fall River Reservoir Dam and find a parking spot; I like to park above the dam. Most of Rainbow Road crosses through private property to the dam, so hold off on camping until you get to the end of the road.

TRAILHEAD LOCATION		PEAKS ACCESSED	
Steuart Road		**Bancroft, James**	
Elevation: 10,380'	Lat/Long: 39°48'44.74"N 105°39'40.49"W		

You may be able to get past this point.

From Interstate 70's Exit 238, begin your measure at the bottom of the westbound exit ramp. There is a parking lot here for carpooling to the actual trailhead if you'd like to save some gas. Drive 0.2 mile and turn right onto Clear Creek County 275, aka Fall River Road, at its intersection with the westbound entrance ramp. Follow the paved road to the town of Alice and turn left onto Alice Road at the 8.4 mile mark. Drive along Alice Road to the 9.3 mile mark and turn right onto Steuart Road. Right after the road leaves the city limits, you enter Forest Service land and there is usually a spot to pull off the road at the 9.6 mile mark. The road continues past this point and is also your trail into Loch Lomond drainage; drive the road as far as you can to save on the approach.

TRAILHEAD LOCATION		PEAKS ACCESSED	
St. Mary's Glacier		**James**	
Elevation: 10,400'	Lat/Long: 39°49'30.81"N 105°38'40.67"W		

Take Exit 238 off Interstate 70 and begin your measure at the bottom of the westbound exit ramp. There is a parking lot here for carpooling to the actual trailhead if you'd like to save some gas. Drive 0.2 mile and turn right onto Clear Creek County 275, aka Fall River Road, at its intersection with the westbound entrance ramp. Follow the paved road through the

The upper lot.

town of Alice to the 8.9 mile mark. The lot on the left is the trailhead. This lot was also the former parking for the now defunct Saint Mary's Glacier Ski Area, which closed in the mid-1980s. This trailhead gets crowded, especially on weekends. There is additional parking 0.2 mile up the road past the actual start of the St. Mary's Trail. There is a fee to use this lot of $5 per calendar day. Be sure to have exact cash or a check to pay the fee as there aren't any stores in Alice to give you change.

TRAILHEAD LOCATION		PEAKS ACCESSED	
Deadhorse Creek		**Bottle, Byers, Bills**	
Elevation: 9,060'	Lat/Long: 39°54'24.75"N 105°52'59.39"W		

At the gas station in central Fraser on US Highway 40, aka Zerex St, start your measure and head west on Eisenhower Drive; this is the only street that crosses the railroad tracks. Drive 0.2 mile and turn left onto Norgren Road. Drive 0.1 mile to its end and turn right onto Grand County Road 73. At the 4.7 mile mark you will come to the right turn for Deadhorse Creek Trailhead. There is no camping allowed in the Experimental Forest except at the St. Louis Creek Campground. The Byers Creek Campground is permanently closed due to beetle kill.

TRAILHEAD LOCATION		PEAKS ACCESSED	
Iron Creek/Byers Peak Road		**Byers, Bills, Iron Creek Couloirs**	
Byers Peak Trailhead Elevation: 9,900'	Lat/Long: 39°53'0.80 N 105°55'30.94"W		
Iron Creek Trailhead Elevation: 9,530'	Lat/Long: 39°51'37.61"N 105°54'29.30"W		

Park here on the left of the road.

At the gas station in central Fraser on US Highway 40, aka Zerex St., head west on Eisenhower Drive and start your measure; this is the only street that crosses the railroad tracks. Drive 0.2 mile and turn left onto Norgren Road. Drive 0.1 mile to its end and turn right onto Grand County Road 73. At the 4.7 mile mark you will come to the junction for Deadhorse Creek Trailhead. The road continues up St. Louis Creek once the melt is done and the gates open. At the 7.4 mark is the turn for the road leading to Byers Peak Trail; start a new measure and turn right onto the trailhead road. At the 1.9 mile mark, bear left and continue upward. Stay right at 2.3 miles; at the 3 mile mark you will reach the trailhead. You used to be able to drive farther up the road but the Forest Service moved the trailhead to this lower location. Some people like to bike this before the gate opens; it's faster and easier to go from the Deadhorse Creek Trailhead and use the Lower Byers Peak Trail.

For the Iron Creek Trailhead, start a new measure at the Deadhorse Creek/St. Louis Creek Junction and drive south up St. Louis Creek Road. At 2.4 miles stay right; at 2.7 stay left. At the 3.9 mile mark you will come to the diversion project for Iron Creek. There is parking just past this on the left.

TRAILHEAD LOCATION		PEAKS ACCESSED
Upper Tipperary		**Ptarmigan**
Elevation: 9,000'	Lat/Long: 39°56'13.37"N 105°53'57.80"W	

At the gas station in central Fraser on US Highway 40, aka Zerex St., turn west on to Eisenhower Drive and start your measure; this is the only street that crosses the railroad tracks. Drive 0.2 mile and turn left onto Norgren Road. Drive 0.1 mile to its end and turn right onto Grand County Road 73. At the 1.3 mile mark you will come to the right turn for Grand County Road 50. You will reach the actual Tipperary Trailhead at the 5.7 mile mark. For our purposes, drive up the road another 0.3 mile and you will come to another, larger parking lot. This is the winter closure of Grand County Road 50, and the access for the North Face of Ptarmigan.

TRAILHEAD LOCATION		PEAKS ACCESSED
Moffat Tunnel East Portal		**James, Haystack, "Sprint," Iceberg Couloir, Radiobeacon, "Frosty"**
Elevation: 9,220'	Lat/Long: 39° 54' 10.83"N 105° 38' 36.77" W	

From the intersection of Colorado 72 (Coal Creek Canyon Road) and Colorado 119 (Peak to Peak Highway), the intersection is located 2.8 miles south of the circle in Nederland; set your measure and head south on Colorado 119 to Rollinsville. At the 1.8 mile mark, take a right going west, onto Gilpin County Road 16 (Tolland Road). Drive 9.8 miles to road's end and the parking lot on the south side of the road.

TRAILHEAD LOCATION		PEAKS ACCESSED	
Rollins Pass East Side		**Radiobeacon, "Sprint," Iceberg Couloir, "Frosty"**	
Upper Elevation: 11,050'	Lat/Long: 39° 55' 25.42"N 105°40'6.89"W		
Lower Elevation: 10,430'	Lat/Long: 39°55'24.38"N 105°38'54.37"W		

This can be a tough trailhead to get to early in the season; even in early July I've been turned around by snow. If you can't make it all the way, there is a lower trailhead that requires some bushwhacking but shortcuts the road by about 3.2 miles; it also adds about 500' of vertical. From the intersection of Colorado 72 (Coal Creek Canyon Road) and Colorado 119 (Peak to Peak Highway), the intersection is located 2.8 miles south of the circle in Nederland; set your measure and head south on Colorado 119 to Rollinsville. At the 1.8 mile mark, take a right, going west, onto Gilpin County Road 16 (aka Tolland Road). Drive to the 9.1 mile mark and turn onto Rollins Pass Road. This is where the winter closure is. It's not a reasonable option for access during the winter; use the Moffat Tunnel Trailhead in the winter. Finally at the 16.9 mark, you will reach the lower trailhead. There are a couple of decent campsites by the road here, or just head up the trail a little ways for some cool open spaces. At the 20.3 mile mark, you will get to the switchback and the upper trailhead. The lot is small, fitting about seven cars. Sometimes it can be hard to get past the snow at the road cut sections above Yankee Doodle Lake. If this is the case, just park and walk the road to the trailhead.

TRAILHEAD LOCATION	PEAKS ACCESSED
Rollins Pass West Side	**Radiobeacon, "Skyscraper," "Challenger Glacier," "Sprint," Iceberg Couloir, "Frosty"**
Iceberg Couloir Elevation: 11,100'	**Lat/Long: 39°53'55.81"N 105°42'28.25"W**
Sprint/Radiobeacon/Frosty Elevation: 11,285'	**Lat/Long: 39°54'21.07"N 105°41'53.89"W**
Summit Elevation: 11,700'	**Lat/Long: 39°56'4.31"N 105°40'58.42"W**

Rollins Pass is the actual name of the pass that crosses the Continental Divide at Corona townsite; the town was used by railroad workers to service the trains over Rollins Pass from 1904 to 1928, according to Dale Rohrback from ghosttowns.com. With the Forest Service's decision not to repair the Needles Eye Tunnel, the only way to drive to Rollins Pass Summit is from the Winter Park side. From the stoplight at the entrance of Winter Park Ski Area and US Highway 40, drive north 1.4 miles, or 1.8 miles from the south stoplight on Highway 40 in the town of Winter Park. Turn onto Grand County 80, pictured, and set your measure here. At the 2.3 mile mark, you'll come to an intersection. Take the center path and continue on. At the 3.6 mile mark, you will come to a five-way intersection. Take right forward, staying on Grand County 80. At the 10.4 mile mark, you will arrive at the very cool old trestle ruin at Riflesight Notch. This is the trailhead for Iceberg Couloirs. At the 10.8 mile mark, you will come to a handy pullout for Sprint Peak's Crater Couloirs, Frosty and Radiobeacon. You can hike 0.6 mile east-southeast to the summit of Radiobeacon from here. Continuing on, you will reach the terminus of the Rollins Pass Road at the Corona Townsite on top of Rollins Pass at the 13.7 mile mark.

TRAILHEAD LOCATION	PEAKS ACCESSED
Eldora Backcountry Gate	**Eldora Ski Area Backcountry**
Elevation: 10,640'	**Lat/Long: 39°56'29.88"N 105°36'33.42"W**

From the top of the Corona Quad, hike or skin about 500' west across the cat track to the backcountry access gate. BCA has provided a beacon check station here; use it. Hike along the ridge to access goods past the radio station.

TRAILHEAD LOCATION	PEAKS ACCESSED
Hessie Winter Closure	**Eldora Ski Area Backcountry, South Arapaho, Neva, Jasper, Skyscraper Glacier**
Elevation: 8,830'	**Lat/Long: 39°57'4.64"N 105°34'58.23"W**

From the circle in the center of Nederland at the junction of Peak to Peak Highway and Boulder Canyon, start your measure and drive 0.6 mile south on Colorado 119 (Peak to Peak) to the right turn onto Eldora Road (Boulder County 130). At the 2 mile mark, you will come to the fork for Eldora Ski Area; stay right here and continue on County 130. After 3.8 miles, you will reach the town of Eldora. Drive through it. Finally at the 4.6 mile mark, you will arrive at the winter trailhead and the end of plowing. Park on the south side of the road.

TRAILHEAD LOCATION	PEAKS ACCESSED
Fourth of July Road	**Neva, Jasper, South Arapaho, North Arapaho**
Elevation: 10,135'	Lat/Long: 39°59'42.62"N 105°38'3.39"W

From the circle in the center of Nederland at the junction of the Peak to Peak Highway and Boulder Canyon, start your measure and drive 0.6 mile south on Colorado 119 to a right turn onto Eldora Road (Boulder County 130). At the 2 mile mark, you will come to the fork for Eldora Ski Area; stay right here and continue on County 130. After 3.8 miles, you will reach the town of Eldora; drive through it. At the 5.8 mile mark, you will come to the fork for the Hessie Townsite. Stay right here as the road turns into Fourth of July Road (Boulder County 111). Drive this to the 9.3 mile mark and the right turn for trailhead parking just up the hill. They call it Fourth of July for a reason; this area sees a lot of snow during the winter and opens late in the spring most years.

TRAILHEAD LOCATION	PEAKS ACCESSED
Devil's Thumb Trail	**Jasper**
Elevation: 9,600'	Lat/Long: 39°59'11.53"N 105°44'33.46"W

Start your measure at the Shell gas station in Fraser. Drive north 0.4 mile on US Highway 40 to the right-hand turn onto County Road 8. At 0.7 mile bear left around a corner at an intersection to stay on County Road 8. Stay left at the fork at 2.2 miles and left again at 3.2 miles. At the 4.8 mile mark you will reach the Denver Water Road; take a left here. This road is open earlier than the road on US 40 with the sign to Devil's Thumb Trailhead, north of Fraser. Denver Water opens it to vehicles as soon as they can't access it via snowmobile. At the 8 mile mark, turn right and arrive at the trailhead parking at the 8.4 mile mark.

TRAILHEAD LOCATION	PEAKS ACCESSED
Monarch Lake	**Neva, North Arapaho, Caribou Bowl, Hopi, Apache**
Elevation: 8,360'	Lat/Long: 40° 6'38.75"N 105° 44'45.81"W

Begin from the intersection of US Highways 40 and 34 at the west end of the town of Granby. Start your measure here and turn onto US 34. Drive 5.4 miles to Grand County 6 and turn right. This is the Arapaho National Recreation Area (ANRA), which is a fee area; at the 5.5 mile mark you will come to the automated pay station. After paying (if you need to; fee details below), continue on Grand County 6 around Lake Granby to the 14.3 mile mark and the winter closure at the last driveway. Of note, along the way the road crosses three dams, all of which lack guardrails; the dirt on this road can be especially slippery when wet, such as after a wet spring storm. If the road has been plowed past the winter closure, continue on to the summer trailhead at the 15.1 mile mark.

If venturing into the Indian Peaks after June 1, you will need an Overnight Camping Permit. They are $5 and supersede the ANRA fees. What this means is that if you're going in for an overnight, you should buy your camping permit first so you don't have to pay the fee twice. Permits can be picked up at the Forest Service offices in Granby, Boulder, Nederland, and Ward.

If in the zone for the day, the below information applies. ANRA fees are covered under valid annual federal interagency passes (aka National Parks Pass, America the Beautiful Pass, Golden Eagle Pass, Senior Interagency Pass, Access Interagency Pass), which must still be properly displayed on the vehicle dashboard or from a mirror hangtag with the signature side visible to enforcement personnel.

Otherwise, ANRA fees for vehicle passes are as follows: $5/day, $10/3 days, $15/7 days, $30/annual pass (includes ANRA access for up to four vehicles, boats, RVs, or snowmobiles), $50/annual pass for ANRA and Rocky Mountain National Park (includes ANRA access for up to four vehicles, boats, RVs, or snowmobiles)

Passes can be purchased at automated machines in most areas of ANRA or at the Sulphur Ranger District office in Granby.

TRAILHEAD LOCATION		PEAKS ACCESSED	
Roaring Fork		**Twin Peaks, Watanga, Hiamovi**	
Elevation: 8,300'	Lat/Long: 40° 7'46.10"N 105° 45'51.16"W		

From the intersection of US Highways 40 and 34 at the west end of the town of Granby, start your measure and turn onto US 34. Drive 5.4 miles to Grand County 6 and turn right. This is the Arapaho National Recreation Area (ANRA) and is a fee area; at the 5.5 mile mark you will come to the automated pay station (see the Monarch Trailhead section for a breakdown of fee details, including camping permits). After paying (if you need to), continue on Grand County 6 to the 14.2 mile mark and turn left onto Grand County 637 and into the Arapaho Bay Campground. Drive through the campground to the 14.7 mile mark and bear right at the fork. At the 15 mile mark, you will come to the right turn for the trailhead.

TRAILHEAD LOCATION		PEAKS ACCESSED	
Brainard Lake Winter		**Apache, Navajo, Toll, Audubon, Paiute**	
Elevation: 10,070'	Lat/Long: 40° 4'48.62"N 105° 32'0.04"W		

From Estes Park or Lyons, head east or west respectively on Colorado 7 to its junction with Colorado 72 (Peak to Peak Highway); begin your measure here. Drive 9.7 miles to the right turn for Brainard Lake Road (Boulder County Road 112). From Nederland, measuring from the circle, drive west on Colorado 72 for 11.6 miles to the left turn for Brainard Lake Road. Reset your measure here and drive 2.5 miles to the trailhead parking on the right. If you get to the toll gate, you went too far. No fee is charged when the seasonal gate is closed; summer fee details are in the next section.

TRAILHEAD LOCATION		PEAKS ACCESSED	
Brainard Lake, Long & Mitchell Lake		**Apache, Navajo, Toll, Audubon, Paiute**	
Brainard Lake Elevation: 10,370'		Lat/Long: 40° 4'42.65"N 105°34'16.22"W	
Long Lake Elevation: 10,530'		Lat/Long: 40° 4'41.21"N 105°35'2.82"W	
Mitchell Lake Elevation: 10,500'		Lat/Long: 40° 4'58.63"N 105°34'52.59"W	

Begin measuring from the Winter Trailhead parking entrance. Drive or ride through the toll booth and pay your fee. Details of the fees are listed below. Drive to the 2.1 mile mark and turn right at the stop sign. The turn is located a few yards before the gate that closes the lake loop road and the upper trailheads. Brainard Lake operators no longer open the upper trailheads. To reach the upper trailheads, hike past the kiosk and bathrooms to the loop road and take a right, going over the bridge and the dam. About 0.4 mile from the parking lot, you will come to the Mitchell/Long Lake trail at an intersection; this can be difficult to follow under a winter coat of snow. Take this trail, if you can follow it, to the fork for Mitchell and Long Lake trailheads. If it's covered, follow the well-signed road to the trailheads of your choice.

Brainard Lake Recreation Area fees apply during the summer operating season (typically mid-June through mid-October). These services generally aren't available until the Brainard Lake Campground is open.

- Passenger Vehicles & RVs (per vehicle/3 days): $10
- Vans (per vehicle/1 day): $25
- Buses (per vehicle/1 day): $40
- Motorcycles (per cycle/3 days): $5
- Hiker/Biker/Walker (per person/3 days): $1
- Short-term Bicyclist: 30 minute free pass
- American Land & Leisure Season Pass (passenger vehicles): $55
- American Land & Leisure Season Pass (hiker/biker/walker): $20
- Interagency Annual, Military, Senior or Access passes, Golden Age and Golden Access passes are accepted; this includes National Parks passes. No fee is charged when the seasonal gate is closed (winter season).

TRAILHEAD LOCATION	PEAKS ACCESSED
Coney Flats Road	**Sawtooth, Audubon**
Lower Elevation: 9,185'	Lat/Long: 40° 7'16.65"N 105°31'26.29"W
Low Clearance Elevation: 9,520'	Lat/Long: 40° 7'31.88"N 105°32'27.31"W
Upper Elevation: 9,800'	Lat/Long: 40° 7'49.68"N 105°34'38.08"W

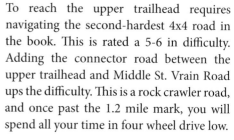

To reach the upper trailhead requires navigating the second-hardest 4x4 road in the book. This is rated a 5-6 in difficulty. Adding the connector road between the upper trailhead and Middle St. Vrain Road ups the difficulty. This is a rock crawler road, and once past the 1.2 mile mark, you will spend all your time in four wheel drive low.

To get to the fun, head north from the circle in Nederland on Colorado 72 for 14.2 miles to the left turn for Boulder County 96; this turn is 7.3 miles from the north, from the junction of Colorado 7 and 72. Reset your measure here and stay left at the 0.3 mile mark. Stay right at the 1.3 mile mark as well. The signs mention Beaver Reservoir being private property; this is true, but the road is an easement so you're fine to get to the Coney Flats Trailhead. Drive around the lake, using care at the dam spillway if there is water flowing across the road, to the 2.7 mile mark and park if you have a low clearance vehicle. If you have a Subaru-type all-wheel-drive vehicle, you can make it another 1.2 miles before things start to get difficult. There are a few spaces to park here. Past this point you will need good clearance, four wheel drive low, and some driving skills. At the 1.5 mile mark of Coney Flats

Road, you will come to a trail junction; the road goes left and hikers go right. The road gets tough from here with multiple problem sections to deal with. At the 3.3-mile mark, the trail and the road rejoin each other. At the 3.8 mile mark, you will come to the pond crossing. There is a bridge around this if you don't want to drive through the water. Of note, there are some fairly large rocks under the water that I hit my differential on. Caution should be exercised going across the pond. The actual trailhead is on the other side of the crossing.

Coney Flats Road continues on past the trailhead and links with the Middle St. Vrain Road. This is the hardest section of 4x4 road in the book. I got my lifted 4Runner stuck here twice, which is a rare occurrence. Middle St. Vrain road is 0.7 mile from the Upper Coney Flats Trailhead. Combining this trip with an exit via Middle St. Vrain works well to save mileage.

TRAILHEAD LOCATION		PEAKS ACCESSED	
Camp Dick/Middle St. Vrain Road		**Ogalalla, Sawtooth**	
Lower Elevation: 8,585'	Lat/Long: 40° 7'54.18"N 105°30'33.46"W		
Upper Elevation: 8,585'	Lat/Long: 40° 7'54.18"N 105°30'33.46"W		

To reach the trailhead, this is the hardest road in the book; the connector between Middle St. Vrain Road and the Upper Coney Flats Trailhead is more difficult, so combining trips isn't easy. From the circle in Nederland, drive north 17.5 miles on Colorado 72 to the Middle St. Vrain Road and turn left. Alternatively, from the junction of Colorado 72 and 7, drive south 4 miles and turn right onto the road. Reset your measure at the turnoff and head up Middle St. Vrain Road past the campgrounds. At the 1.2 mile mark, you will reach the low clearance trailhead. Park your vehicle here if you don't have four wheel drive low and good clearance.

If you have some skill and a worthy vehicle, continue up the road. Almost immediately you will come to a difficult problem. If you can't get through this initial section, then you are toast and won't be able to make it to the upper trailhead. At about the 4.7 mile mark, you will reach the turn for Coney Flats Road. Continue straight to the end of the road and the trailhead at the 5 mile mark.

Most of the vehicles I've seen here have been heavily modified 4x4s. I did see a stock Toyota FJ Cruiser making it with minimal metal crunching. The connector road from Middle St. Vrain Road to the upper Coney Flats Trailhead is the hardest road in the book. I got stuck twice on its hardest problem. Keep this fact in mind if you are trying to combine trips and save some driving. The Upper Coney Flats Trailhead is 0.7 mile from the Middle St. Vrain Road junction.

TRAILHEAD LOCATION		PEAKS ACCESSED
Meadow Mountain		**Meadow Mountain**
Elevation: 8,700'	Lat/Long: 40°10'25.05"N 105°31'37.43"W	

From the Business Loop 7, turn off for Allenspark on Colorado 7, southeast of Estes Park and west of Lyons, to begin your measure. This road is also called Washington Ave. Drive one block and turn left. Drive one more block and turn right onto Ski Road, aka Boulder County Road 107. Drive this road to the intersection at 1.7 miles. There is no parking lot here, so do your best to pull off to the side of the road.

1 "GOLDEN BEAR" – 13,010'

This unassuming peak is the highest point of Loveland Ski Area and also marks the area's northern boundary. The Southeast Chute used to be a fun backcountry line, but was incorporated into the ski area; since then it is rarely open. It is the 634th highest in the state and there are only four lower 13ers. The Loveland Ski Area master plan has snowcat skiing proposed for the Northeast Bowl as well as on the slopes of neighboring Mount Trelease.

1a – "Golden Bear"	West Chute	
DIFFICULTY: Advanced	DISTANCE: 3.2 Miles Roundtrip	VERTICAL: 1,900'
SUNHIT: Sunrise + 4 Hours	ASPECT: West-Southwest	SEASON: Spring
TRAILHEAD: Eisenhower Tunnel West Portal North	MAP: Page 268	PHOTO: Page 41, 49, 247

Here's an easy access line from the West Portal of the Eisenhower Tunnel. Descending off the Continental Divide, this west-facing line offers the chance to get up high a little earlier than most. The windward position of this route usually offers compacted, "bridged," or supported snow. You can get a good sense of this route's stability by noting any recent activity on slopes above the tunnel, some of which are controlled.

Looking up at the line from the trailhead at the tunnel.

From the trailhead, skin east and then north up the Straight Creek drainage. There's usually a skin track that ascends into the trees above and to skinner's left; don't follow this. Instead, stay near the creek bottom and follow its course upward. After rounding the corner of the trees, the line will come into view. Work your way through the willows and up the line or to the side of it. At the ridge top, you will be entering Loveland Ski Area if you cross under the rope line. There isn't a rope out this far, but there may be after this book is published. Hike north along the ridge to the actual summit of "Golden Bear."

Gary Fondl enjoying spring powder in the central steeps of the line.

Make your way back to the line and enjoy 35-40 degree slopes. About halfway down, there is a choke that is the steepest point on the line; this is also a wind-loaded pillow so use caution. Below this it opens up and you can let 'em rip.

1b – "Golden Bear"	Northeast Bowl	
DIFFICULTY: Advanced	DISTANCE: 2.1–7.7 Miles Roundtrip	VERTICAL: 1,500'–3,200'
SUNHIT: Sunrise	ASPECT: East	SEASON: Spring
TRAILHEAD: Loveland Chair 8 Backcountry Gate or Dry Gulch	MAP: Page 268	PHOTO: Page 42–43, 49, 247

This is a fun, quick tour from Loveland Ski Area. From the Chair 8 backcountry gate, it's easy to get this one done with minimal effort. This zone, however, is on the Loveland Ski Area master plan to be developed for snowcat skiing, so this area may be closed or you may have a substantial amount of company in the near future. Accessing this route from Dry Gulch is also possible, but at 7.2 miles and 3,200' of gain, this is a long trip for minimal excitement. It would be more beneficial if you combined it with the lines on Hagar, Citadel, or Trelease. Going into the Southeast Bowl of "Golden Bear" is forbidden and could land you in jail. Skiing in closed areas is illegal. Stick to the north side of the Trelease/"Golden Bear" ridge.

From the gate, skin northwest to the saddle of the Trelease/"Golden Bear" Ridge and then make your way west to the summit of "Golden Bear". This is an easy 1,100' ascent and is covered in a brief 0.7 mile. At the summit, ski north along the Continental Divide to the bowl north of the Trelease/"Golden Bear" Ridge, and enjoy east-facing slopes for about 1,100'. At the bottom, you can either repeat or head south back to the Trelease/"Golden Bear" Saddle and a descent back to the gate you left from. Be sure to re-enter the ski area through the gate as entering anywhere else is against Colorado law.

From Dry Gulch, you're looking at a much bigger day and much higher hazard. From the parking lot by the I-70 exit or down by the gate, skin along the road up past the Loveland

Plenty of options in the Northeast Bowl.
Since it's short you can get laps in.

storage sheds. Make your way up Dry Gulch and around to the west. You will pass under Trelease's North Slopes and a fair number of avalanche paths. These paths have taken skiers in the past and I had a close call here a few years ago. Use caution. There are also slide paths to the north on the flanks of Citadel. Once up in the basin, head for the summit of "Golden Bear"; the actual summit is just to the south of the Trelease/"Golden Bear" Ridge where it meets the Continental Divide. For the descent and egress, follow your ascent. This route is a good combination with Hagar, "Citadel," and Trelease's North Face.

Hagar   "Citadel"   Pettingel

Looking down at the
bowl from just north of
the actual summit.

#speedup
www.dynafit.com

Location: Rocky Mountain National Park

2   MOUNT TRELEASE – 12,477'

This unassuming hump should not be underestimated. For winter glissé, there are multiple options for fun here. As things get more stable, usually later in the season, one can get an early taste of steeper lines with easy access. There are plenty of options for getting into the air here as well; if you doubt that, check out the back cover photo, shot on Trelease. The only downside can be the access road and having to walk uphill at the end of the day. With a negligible rise above its saddle with its higher neighbor "Golden Bear," this named peak doesn't attain an official rank. According to the decision card from the USGS, the peak was named in 1933 in honor of Dr. William Trelease, an American botanist born in 1857 who shared in the botanical labors of Gray and Engelmann, for whom peaks in this vicinity have also been named.

Mount Trelease as seen from Loveland Pass.
Super easy access from Interstate 70.

2a – Mount Trelease	South Bowl and Trees	
DIFFICULTY: Intermediate—Advanced	DISTANCE: 1.2 Miles Roundtrip	VERTICAL: 1,000'
SUNHIT: Sunrise + 2 Hours	ASPECT: Southeast	SEASON: Winter
TRAILHEAD: Dry Gulch	MAP: Page 268	PHOTO: Page 45–47

This is one of my go-to routes for quick powder laps during the winter. Access is super easy and you can ski it even when Loveland Pass is closed, which seems to be fairly often. The angle of the slope rarely causes concern for avalanches unless you would be foolish enough to ski the upper bowl. Every year the upper bowl slides huge and should be given a wide berth. Just stay below treeline and you should be fine; it would take a 100-year avalanche event to get past treeline, but remain vigilant as low danger doesn't mean no danger. There

Nothing to ski here, move along.
athlete: Gary Fondl

are a few mini bowls above the lower woods that can and do slide occasionally. These are marked on the topo photo.

From the lot closest to the exit ramp for Interstate 70, skin up the shallow gully just east of the lot. It gets pretty steep just as it heads into the trees, but mellows out after a hundred feet or so. Work your way through the trees in a northeasterly direction. This is a very popular line so there is usually a skin track; if not, choose the line of least resistance that starts at the top of the shallow gully and follows it. This is a summer trail and you can tell by the depression in the terrain. Switchback up to where the trees begin to thin and head for where the slope eases as you approach treeline. Try not to set the skin track right up the meadow—that's for skiing, people. The trees on climber's right of the meadow are a great place for setting your switchbacks.

To the east of the meadow are some fun sets of cliffs to jump off. The exit below these jumps isn't very much fun, so head back to the zone you ascended through the woods to skier's right for your exit. Also below the

Getting into that happy place.
athlete: Gary Fondl

cliffs, but not in the landings, are a couple of small slide zones; be on your game here. Good lines extend from the meadow to skier's right. It's a straightforward exit from these options. The road cut can wreck a pair of skis with ease; use care at the bottom getting through the final pitch to the parking lot.

2b – Mount Trelease	North Face	
Difficulty: Expert	Distance: 4.9 Miles Roundtrip	Vertical: 2,100'
Sunhit: Sunrise + 1 Hour	Aspect: North	Season: Spring
Trailhead: Dry Gulch	Map: Page 268	Photo: Page 48–49

Gentle Mount Trelease harbors some steep lines; you just have to check out the north side. The North Face of Trelease offers about 700' of quality steep skiing. Once you're back there, hit it a few times, or you could combine it with Hagar or Snoopy.

From the Dry Gulch lot, follow the South Bowl ascent up from the parking lot, right at the westbound Loveland Pass exit from Interstate 70. This route is steep at first, then it mellows as it enters denser trees. There is a trail here. Follow it on a northeasterly course and then upward to treeline. Here is where you need your spring stability as you ascend the South Bowl. The line of least resistance is to climber's right of the bowl. Follow the ridge over and past the false summit and on to the actual summit.

This short face reminds me a little of the Palisades at Squaw. Lot's of fun options.

Steep, short and fun. The author drops in while his partner looks on.
photo: Joe Brannan

West of the summit, the North Face offers wild to wilder slopes. The first line is a fairly steep chute. Farther west the entrance gets extreme. Some of the shots don't go through cleanly, so you will either have to shut down your entry speed or prepare for some airtime. An ascent of Citadel or Hagar prior to coming to this line is a good idea as you will be able to preview conditions. On the exit at the valley floor, below the flanks of Citadel and Trelease's North Trees, you will be in a terrain trap. Be aware of the snow above you and use safe travel protocols here. There have been fatalities in this area.

A skier puts the size of the routes in perspective.

2c – Mount Trelease	North Gullies & Trees	
DIFFICULTY: Intermediate	DISTANCE: 4.7 Miles Roundtrip	VERTICAL: 1,500'
SUNHIT: Sunrise + 1 Hour	ASPECT: North	SEASON: Winter
TRAILHEAD: Dry Gulch	MAP: Page 268	PHOTO: Page 49–50

The South Trees of Trelease can get a bit crowded with their super easy access. This option is a bit farther and sees a little less traffic. There are multiple lines as well, so multiple groups can get their fill. This zone has seen a fatality, so be careful when the winds are cross-loading the steeper shots to the west of the main zone. The lines to the east of the main zone also get fairly scoured; watch out for slabs on facets here.

Multiple lines to choose from but more serious avalanche terrain lurks at both margins and in the steeper trees.
inset photo: Jason Killgore

Mount Trelease

"Golden Bear"

Northeast Bowl

North Gullies and Trees

DANGER

DANGER

DANGER

Plenty of mellow, meadow skipping here.
athlete: Gary Fondl

I usually hit this route earlier in the season when you can drive the frontage road the short distance to the closure gate. This may change in the future as Loveland Ski Area has plans to develop this zone for snowcat skiing. I'm not sure how that's going to play out. I don't think access would close because Citadel and Hagar aren't part of the operating plan. We'll have to see what happens; stay tuned to www.GiterdunPublishing.com for more information. From the gate, head up the road past the fenced storage zone for Loveland Ski Area about 0.4 mile from the closure gate. Head up-valley to the base of the zone pictured. If there isn't a skin track, follow a line that zigs and zags up through the trees between the first two gullies. Save the gullies for skiing and spend less time in harm's way; these gullies are treeless due to slides. In considerable and high danger, this is not a good place to ski.

Pick your line and have at it. The main line in the center is really fun with low 30 degrees slopes and a few rollovers that are steeper and should cause concern if the danger is high. Traverse to skier's right to link another short section back to the skin track. The lines to the skier's left of the central gully start out tight and then open to steeper shots that are tight enough to remain somewhat protected from slab development.

These lines are shorter and you've put in a bit of effort to get there, so be sure to put in a few laps. For the exit, follow your approach and be sure that you waxed for the correct temperature; the out goes a lot faster if you can glide.

There are also steeper pitches.
athlete: Gary Fondl

3   MOUNT BETHEL – 12,705'

When I first moved to Colorado, I was immediately taken with this mountain. The season I moved here, A-Basin was open until July 4 and it had been an epic year. When I got here a few days after Killington closed on June 1, the line down to the highway was still chock full of snow. How cool would it be to get this classic done? It would be a few years before I got it, and now I think about that day every time I pass under it on the way to other mountains. The snow fences to control loading into Interstate Gully are the best way

You get a great look at the line coming up from Denver on Interstate 70.

to identify this peak from the west and Loveland Pass. The peak was named in 1926 for Ellsworth Bethel, a pathologist for the U.S. Forest Service and director of the University of Colorado Museum in Boulder, according to USGS documents.

3a – Mount Bethel	Interstate Gully	
DIFFICULTY: Advanced	DISTANCE: 3.5 Miles Point to Point	VERTICAL: 2,200'
SUNHIT: Sunrise	ASPECT: Southeast	SEASON: Spring
TRAILHEAD: Dry Gulch to Herman Gulch	MAP: Page 268	PHOTO: Page 51–52

This is one of the coolest lines along the I-70 corridor. It's downright surreal to ski right down to the interstate. Unlike the Sisters on Loveland Pass, this is not a closure. However, if you slid the interstate I'm certain you would get into serious trouble, like felony trouble. You need to be absolutely certain that the line won't slide if you plan on skiing it. Spring is the best time, without a doubt. Get an early start and ski it with the corn thaw early in the day. It will always be in your mind when you drive by it and now you'll be able to tell your friends about that day.

From Mt Sniktau you get a nice view of the line and it's alternatives.

The safest way to get up to the line would be from Dry Gulch. You could go from Herman Gulch right up the line but this would be more dangerous and should only be done early in the morning on frozen snow. From Dry Gulch make your way down the frontage road and then up to the Loveland Ski Area shed. From here, skin or hike up the Southwest Slopes of Bethel—the

Hiking past the avalanche control fences.
photo: Miriam Green

Lower down the line.
photo: Miriam Green

Just below the entrance.
photo: Miriam Green

wind fence slopes. This aspect is windward, so expect less snow. Make your way up the slope past the wind control fences, which are put in place to help reduce loading in the Interstate Gully. The top of the line is at the terminus of the southeast side of the summit ridge. You can drop your gear here and make for the summit if you'd like.

From the summit ridge, the entrance is steep and tight. Some years you'll need to descend the Southwest Slope a little ways to get to a skiable entrance. Even with the wind fencing, there is still a cornice up here most years. Once in the line, expect 45-50 degree sections in the upper line. Once at treeline, the angle eases. There are rowdy pillows and cliffs to skier's right; or just stay in the gut and enjoy 30 degree terrain to the highway below.

The easy out is to skier's left, but this puts you at Herman Gulch. Perhaps utilizing a car shuttle is the best way to go for this route as it's a long walk along the interstate to get back to Dry Gulch if that was your ascent route.

3b – Mount Bethel	North Saddle Gully	
DIFFICULTY: Intermediate	DISTANCE: 5.1 Miles Roundtrip	VERTICAL: 2,000'
SUNHIT: Northeast	ASPECT: Sunrise +1 Hour	SEASON: Winter
TRAILHEAD: Herman Gulch	MAP: Page 268	PHOTO: Page 53–54

Finding safer winter options can sometimes be a bit of a challenge. One of the goals of the books is to reduce the densities of users at the more popular places to ski in the winter, like Berthoud Pass, Loveland Pass, and Butler Gulch This is a nice option but does have some threat of sliding—it is an avy path, after all. The slopes coming directly off the saddle are steep enough to slide, as is the skier's left side of the top of lower gully. There are, however, well-spaced trees to skier's right in the lower gully and above there is a nice bench to make skinning to below the saddle slope worth the effort.

Looking up the line from Herman Creek.

From the Herman Gulch trailhead, skin up the trail. At 0.2 mile you will come to the junction for Herman Gulch and Watrous Gulch. Take the left option. About 0.5 mile from the junction you will come to the Y Gully deposition zone. Remember that the snow is all connected so travel one at a time across this hazard. After the next stand of trees you will come to the Y Not Gully's deposition zone; treat this one with respect as well. At this point you will get a look at a steep, rocky zone on the North Flank of Bethel. If you are an expert group and the stability is good, this is worth a lap when you're done with the saddle line. Continue up the valley, keeping an eye on the slopes of Machebeuf to your right. This line has a lot of hazard from above. At about 1.2 miles in, you will come to the third avy path, the Y Yes Gully. Use care and continue on up the valley through mostly open terrain. At about 1.9 miles in, you will reach the base of the line. A skin track is usually in on the climber's right side of the gully; access this by entering the trees on the far side. You can keep this ascent route safe while deciding if the gully itself is safe to ski; if it's not, you can use the up for the down and mitigate your risk.

Climb as high as you wish and switch over. The upper section is straightforward and offers nice powder as its lee position provides plenty of loading. Below the bench, be sure to aim to skier's left to get into the correct line. The gully coming off the bench to skier's right leads to a different gully, a shorter, steeper one that leads to tight trees; getting slid here could be catastrophic. Once at the top of the correct gully, be aware of the pillow that develops to skier's left, as this can be a cap of fragile hard slab. The trees on the other side of the gully, to skier's right, offer a safer option without the threat from the pillow above. The valley back to the trailhead is pretty flat but is usually skiable if you remembered to wax 'em before your tour.

Just below the steep roll.
photo: Allison Seymour

Justin Ibarra slashes a turn in the steep tree shots lower down the valley.

Summit

Boomerang
Couloir

You get a great view of the Southeast
Face from Mount Trelease.

4 HAGAR MOUNTAIN – 13,195'

At the back of Dry Gulch resides this fine and aesthetic skier's peak. The 413th highest peak in the state sits in concert with its higher neighbor "The Citadel" to the east. Though lower, this peak's normal route is steeper than "The Citadel's". You can get a great look at conditions for this peak by the Herman Gulch Exit on Interstate 70, or you can see it well from the Ridge at Loveland Basin Ski Area, which is a great place to access it.

4a – Hagar Mountain	Southeast Face	
DIFFICULTY: Advanced	DISTANCE: 3.3–7.5 Miles Roundtrip	VERTICAL: 2,000–2,800'
SUNHIT: Sunrise + 1 Hour	ASPECT: Southeast	SEASON: Spring
TRAILHEAD: Loveland Ski Area Chair 8 BC Access Gate or Dry Gulch	MAP: Page 268	PHOTO: Page 55–56

This route offers a European-style peak tour, utilizing lift service and the USFS backcountry access gate near the top of Chair 8 at Loveland Ski Area. Much like the touring available at Arapahoe Basin, you can ride the lift, leave the gate, tour into Dry Gulch, get your objective done, and then ski back the way you came. For those without a pass at Loveland, you can always access this peak the hard way, via Dry Gulch. This line combines well with Trelease's North Face Direct and "The Citadel's" South Bowl.

From the Loveland gate, skin north up to the "Golden Bear"/Trelease saddle and drop into a short gully past a rocky rib on your left. Once past this obstruction, begin a contour around the head of Dry Gulch. Aim for the saddle to the west of Hagar; this will provide easier access to the peak and won't mar your tracks on the face, while still offering the chance for representative assessments.

Alternatively, you can go from Dry Gulch. Skin east up the frontage road; by the time the line is safe to ski, you may be able to drive to the gate. Pass the Loveland shed and head up the

valley as it turns north and then west. Use care in the valley as it's threatened by many slide paths. Near the end of the trees, look to your right for a gully that will lead you to the bench below the actual face and the bottom of the South Bowl of "The Citadel". This is a good route to higher ground. At the bench, aim for the left side of the South Face; there is a gully that leads to just west of the summit.

Directly off the summit, enjoy 45+ degree slopes for about half of the 800' face. Another option is the Boomerang Couloir at the east end of the peak's summit ridge; to find it, hike or ski across the summit ridge to the east to the first "saddle." Drop in to skier's left of a rocky rib to access the top of the couloir.

If you start at Chair 8 and want to re-enter the ski area, you will need to go back to the gate to follow the rules. If you decide to exit via Dry Gulch, you will have a short walk along US Highway 6 to get back to the ski area.

Steep slopes directly off the summit.
athlete: Jeremy Dobish

Jeremy in Boomerang Couloir

5 "THE CITADEL" (SNOOPY) – 13,294'

For many old-time locals, this peak will always be Snoopy. This name is due to the classic view of the peak from Loveland Pass. The summit is the belly, and the north peak is the snout. There's also the collar and the tail, all resembling Snoopy on his back, on the doghouse. The name Citadel appears in *Guide to the Colorado Mountains* by Robert M. Ormes, originally printed in 1952, so the "The Citadel" name has a history as well. This is the 406th highest peak in the state.

5a – "The Citadel"	North Collar Couloir	
DIFFICULTY: Advanced–Expert	DISTANCE: 8 Miles Roundtrip	VERTICAL: 3,150'
SUNHIT: Sunrise	ASPECT: East–Southeast	SEASON: Spring
TRAILHEAD: Herman Gulch	MAP: Page 268	PHOTO: Page TOC, 57–58, 64

This line would be a classic if it wasn't for the long, flat approach. It does offer great skiing, though in a very cool zone. The East Face of "The Citadel"/Snoopy is a dramatic one, reminiscent of the spires in Europe, though on a much smaller scale. The approach and exit can be a bit of a pain in the butt. Be sure to wax the night before your planned tour; you'll be glad you did.

From the Herman Gulch Trailhead, hike up the trail by the kiosk about 0.2 mile to the Herman/Watrous junction. Hang a left here and skin up a good trail. You will come to a succession of avy paths cascading down "Machebeuf." The first one is Y Gully, the second is Y Not, and the third is Y Yes. Basically from the first gully to the last you need to be on your guard; however, this aspect of the mountain faces southwest so the danger will be greatest on your departure from the zone, after it's been heated by the day's sun. It is about 4 miles to the summit from the trailhead if you take the direct route up the couloir. The easier option is to climb up to the South Ridge at the low saddle to the southeast of the summit. Then you would want to climb the Tail. This route is usually locked up better than the North Collar,

There's a short downclimb to get to the Notch for the Collars.

Looking down the North Collar from the Notch.

which gets way less of a sun hit and can hold pow surprisingly long after a spring storm. Climbing the North Collar directly can be a wallowfest due to this fact. Later in the spring, the North Collar line gets the earliest sunhit on "The Citadel."

Drop in off the top, make your way down to the Collar Saddle, and drop in; this is the expert portion, where there's a short down climb or short exposed huck. Slope angles reach the high 40s near the top and stay steep for most of this 1,000' line. There are a few more options in the zone so you should look at skiing a few laps since you walked so far to get here. With good waxing, you can kick and glide most of the way back. Watch those avy slopes above you on the way out—they may be hot.

5b – "The Citadel"	South Bowl and South Collar	
DIFFICULTY: Advanced	**DISTANCE: 3.9–7.4 Miles Roundtrip**	**VERTICAL: 2,300'–2,850'**
SUNHIT: Sunrise + 3 Hours	**ASPECT: South**	**SEASON: Spring**
TRAILHEAD: Loveland Ski Area Chair 8 Backcountry Gate or Dry Gulch	**MAP: Page 268**	**PHOTO: Page 59–61, 247**

This is a classic spring descent and the line that earned the nickname Snoopy. You can easily check conditions on this line from the top of Loveland Pass or the top of Loveland Ski Area. The best view, of course, is from the summit of Trelease.

Like Hagar's Southeast Face, this route offers a Euro-style tour from Loveland Ski Area. For those without a pass at Loveland, you can always access this peak the hard way via Dry Gulch.

The South Face of "The Citadel."

This line combines well with Trelease North Face Direct and Hagar's Southeast Face; this one is the last of the three to get sunhit.

From the Loveland gate, skin north up to the "Golden Bear"/Trelease saddle and drop into a short gully past a rocky rib on your left. Once past this obstruction, begin a contour around the head of Dry Gulch. Work your way around to the base of the South Bowl. The safest route is to climb the South Ridge to climber's right, as this option will have less time exposed to rock fall than ascending the bowl directly.

Alternatively, you can go from Dry Gulch. Skin east up the frontage road; by the time the line is safe to ski, you may be able to drive to the gate. Pass the Loveland shed and head up the valley as it turns north and then west. Use care in the valley as it's threatened by many slide paths. Near the end of the trees, look to your right for a gully that will lead you to the bench below the actual face and the bottom of the South Bowl of "The Citadel." At the bench, head right to the South Ridge.

Looking down the South Collar from the Notch.

"The Citadel" from Loveland Pass.

Once at the summit cliffs, you can either summit via the Tail—directly in front of you if you took the ridge—and then ski and down-climb to the South Collar. Option two would be to skirt the summit cliffs and climb the collar directly. The collar is short and offers narrow, high 40 degree turns for about 200'. The bowl itself is mellower and offers high 30 degree turns. Watch out for your sluff in the choke. If descending into Dry Gulch, you'll get the added bonus of the gully below the bench. Remember to wax to make the Dry Gulch exit bearable. If going back to the ski area, don't forget to re-enter via the gate—you wouldn't want to get your pass pulled by ski patrol.

5c – "The Citadel"	The Tail and East Bowl	
DIFFICULTY: **Advanced - Expert**	DISTANCE: **8 Miles Roundtrip**	VERTICAL: **3,150'**
SUNHIT: **Sunrise**	ASPECT: **East–Southeast**	SEASON: **Spring**
TRAILHEAD: **Herman Gulch or Dry Gulch**	MAP: **Page 268**	PHOTO: **Page TOC, 57, 60–62**

You have a couple options for this one as with all the "The Citadel" routes. I prefer the approach from Herman Gulch. It's mostly skiable and doesn't have the dreaded uphill walk-out next to the interstate. Talk about ruining the mood by choking on fumes. The last thing I want to do is spend any extra time on that highway. Plus if you go the Herman Gulch route, you're in position to add lines on Bethel, Machebeuf, or Pettingell.

From the trailhead, hike up the Herman Trail about 0.2 mile to a junction for Watrous Gulch. Turn left here and skin or hike up into Herman Gulch. The trail is your exit, so make note of conditions for the descent. It reminds me a little of those tight East Coast trails but not quite as twisty. At the first opening you enter harm's way with the potential for slides from above; first from Y Gully, then Y Not, and Y Yes. Though slides are rare in spring, some of you might not follow my advice and find themselves back here in winter, so talk of threats is important. Triggering paths from below isn't uncommon in our snowpack; an example would be Sheep

Skiing the East Bowl with
The Tail in the background.
photo: Allison Seymour

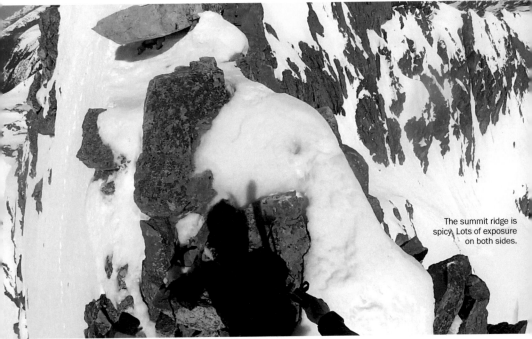

The summit ridge is
spicy. Lots of exposure
on both sides.

Creek on Loveland Pass, just across the interstate. Use care and be aware of what's above you. Keep heading up-valley, following the path of least resistance along the creek. "The Citadel" will come into view just past Bethel's North Gully. This route is the bowl to viewer's left of the summit, along with the strip or Tail of snow that connects the bowl to the summit. The upper tail is barely visible along the ridge extending leftward from the summit; yes, over

Dropping in off the ridge.
athlete: Gary Fondl

the giant cliff. Ascend the bowl to the notch and the entrance to the Tail. Crampons are useful here as the angle steepens to around 50 degrees getting in from the notch. Follow the Tail to the top. Use care along the ridge as you are over cliffs on both sides and a fall from the summit would probably be fatal.

Click in at the summit and lock them down. The upper snow of the South Face, aka the Belly, links up to the Tail in most years; use extra care getting into the Tail, as a slip to your left will garner you 150' of air, at least. After the initial entry, the Tail benches out slightly and divides; have fun down to the bowl and on down into the valley. Just above the valley there is a short, fun chuted section to ski as well. Don't forget to tune and wax for the exit. You can break it up by adding other lines—just be aware of how warm it is if you're going to add Pettingell's south facing lines, as they may be cooked by the time you're getting on them.

Exiting the Tail.
photo: Gary Fondl

6   PETTINGELL PEAK – 13,553'

This is one of the highest peaks in the volume. Measuring as the 217th highest, this peak sees way fewer visitors than any 14er; even though you can see it from the highway, I've never seen anyone on it when the trail has been snow covered, though you will see people down low since the access from the interstate is so easy. Now this is a completely different story when it is summer and the cars at the trailhead are parked down to the on-ramp to the interstate, but by then the ski lines are usually gone. The peak was named in honor of the late J. N. Pettingell of Hot Sulphur Springs in 1942. According to county records he was a Grand County judge and a proprietor of the Grand Hotel.

The South Slopes from just above Herman Lake.

6a – Pettingell Peak	South Slopes	
DIFFICULTY: Intermediate	DISTANCE: 7.6 Miles Roundtrip	VERTICAL: 3,300'
SUNHIT: Sunrise + 1 Hour	ASPECT: South–Southeast	SEASON: Spring
TRAILHEAD: Herman Gulch	MAP: Page 268	PHOTO: Page 63–64

Surprisingly, completing this simple line took multiple tries. Two times I underestimated the day's weather and it got too hot to ski. I also had a gear issue another time. 3,300' for a pretty mellow line is still a decent day in the hills. Couple that with not charging for the gnar, and your pace might be slower than usual. This is a good first-summit ski as the route finding and most of the slope's angle are easy. The area just above the lake to get to the upper face is steep enough to slide as is the upper face. Be sure to ski it in stable conditions.

From the Herman Gulch Trailhead, skin or hike up the trail to the Watrous junction. Turn left here and head up Herman Gulch along the aspen-lined trail. Use care at Y, Y Not, and Y Yes. If you're in here early enough and there are persistent slab issues, you could trigger these lines from above, like Sheep Creek a few miles away. Continuing past Bethel's North Gully, you round a bend in the valley. I find it's easiest to just angle up to Herman Lake from here. I try to aim for the flattening of the shoulder, then descend to the lake and head for the chute

UN13418's options with
Citadel in the background.

on the north side of the lake to access the upper face of Pettingell. There are steeper options
coming off the East Ridge of Pettingell. If this is your speed, have at it. Once at the upper
ridge, be sure to use care as the drop-off into the north side is pretty rowdy.

For the ski, just follow your ascent route. No need to hike out of the lake's basin; just contour
around and keep up your speed. Ski a descending traverse of the trees back into the valley
bottom; this will keep you moving and it's much better than skiing the valley bottom itself.
The lower trail is fast and fun to ski, but watch out for other users; you are on Interstate 70,
so use is higher than for most zones.

6b – Pettingell Peak	418 Chutes	
DIFFICULTY: **Advanced**	DISTANCE: **8 Miles Roundtrip**	VERTICAL: **3,500'**
SUNHIT: **Sunrise**	ASPECT: **South and East**	SEASON: **Spring**
TRAILHEAD: **Herman Gulch**	MAP: **Page 268**	PHOTO: **Page 63–65**

These lines are really an off-shoot of Pettingell's South Face as they return to the same
drainage and can even be accessed from the summit. But since they have a different aspect
and are steeper, I thought they should have their own section. They drop in farther west of
Pettingell and flow southeast to easterly off the south ridge of UN13,418. The actual summit
of UN13,418 is a tower not really connected to the main lines by snow, but it is a cool perch

to check out. You'll see the condition of these lines along your ascent of Pettingell's South Slopes. These lines are a step up in steepness over the South Slopes route.

Follow the South Slopes route for the approach; take it to the summit of Pettingell. Be sure to choose your ski line on the way up. You won't get another view until the top, so get a look below the lake and think about it along the way.

UN13418 looks less steep from the side.

Once you're ready to drop in, ski west along the ridge from the summit. After a rollover, you'll get another look at the options and can choose from the 700' vertical options. Some are a little longer and some are a little shorter. This vertical refers to the meat of the lines; above and below is fun skiing too, just not as steep. Follow the valley bottom back to the car.

6c – Pettingell Peak	North Face	
DIFFICULTY: Expert	DISTANCE: 8.7–9.3 Miles Roundtrip	VERTICAL: 4,400'–6,300'
SUNHIT: Sunrise + 2 Hours	ASPECT: North	SEASON: Spring
TRAILHEAD: Herman Gulch or Butler Gulch	MAP: Page 268	PHOTO: Page 65–66, 248

If it wasn't for the approach, this would be a classic line for the Front Range. It's still a great line and, however you get to it, you are guaranteed two lines to ski. Therein lies the difficulty—you must commit to dropping into another valley and then return to your trailhead. Weather is the most important factor to consider when making this decision in the spring, but also don't forget afternoon avy conditions on your second line. Will the

The entrance is just off the ridge.

Keep an eye on the cornice.

thunder and lightning hold off until you can return? You can best preview conditions along Pettingell's East Ridge or along the Continental Divide from "Hassel Peak" to Jones Pass. Considering the difficulty of getting this one, you might consider finding that perfect weather day and combining it into the Eisenhower Tunnel to Butler Gulch Traverse. This is a great way to ski this line and is the best line of the traverse itself. See the Traverse section for more information about this classic trip.

The easiest and shortest way to get this done is from the Herman Gulch Trailhead. Follow the South Slopes route up the valley and up the south side of the peak. At the ridge, make a note of the conditions in the line. The goods are accessed by an uncorniced entrance; you can't see the entrance from the ridge. You can keep the cornice from being a fall-line threat for the entire line. Some years you'll have to walk down to the entrance of the chute. The apron of the line has variable wind-loading patterns. It's often difficult to piece together the vertical at the bottom.

For your return to Herman drainage, hike due south from the unnamed lake at the bottom of the line. You're aiming for the saddle that starts the East Ridge. You'll get an additional 600' shot of fun, moderate snow, then rollers down to Herman Lake and an easy ski out to the Herman Trailhead. You could add the Woods Creek Pinner to this line. Be aware that the Pinner is southeast facing and could be cooked.

Alternately, one could go at this route from Butler Gulch. Ascend to the Continental Divide and ski the west-facing gully into the basin below Pettingell's North Face. Contour around to the base of the line and ascend it. Those cornices at the top will be a threat for this route. Summit, ski, and follow your approach for the exit. This would be a big day.

The entrance is steep– in the low 50s.

Seen from Mount Sniktau in its entirety. You can also check it out from I-70 east of the tunnel

7   MOUNT MACHEBEUF – 12,805'

From the website of Bishop Machebeuf High School, "a mountain just east of Loveland Pass was named Mount Machebeuf in honor of the first Bishop of Colorado. The mountain is 12,805 feet tall and can be seen from Interstate 70. A dedication Mass was celebrated at the summit by Rev. Richard Ling and Rev. Ed Hoffman in June 1991 using one of Bishop Joseph P. Machebeuf's chalices that he used in the 1880s." He was named bishop of the Colorado diocese in 1887. The peak does not rise 300' above its higher neighbor Woods Mountain, so it's not an officially ranked summit, but its elevation is tied for 777th highest and its name is official.

7a – Mount Machebeuf	Y – Y Not – Y Yes Gullies	
DIFFICULTY: Advanced	DISTANCE: 3.6 Miles Roundtrip	VERTICAL: 2,500'
SUNHIT: Sunrise + 1 Hour	ASPECT: Southeast and South	SEASON: Spring
TRAILHEAD: Herman Gulch	MAP: Page 268	PHOTO: Page 67–69

Coming eastbound out of the East Portal of the Eisenhower Tunnel and making the first corner, this line comes into view. It's the obvious swath cut out of the shoulder of Machebeuf, just to the north of the interstate. It looks like a ski run and it is—but it's also an avy path, like so many great ski runs. You can also get a great look at this line from Loveland Pass. The cross-loaded nature of this line and the near-perfect start zone angle of 40 degrees makes this a dangerous winter undertaking, and you might need an undertaker if you get it in unstable conditions. Save this line for after the melt-freeze cycle starts. Be mindful of these lines above you if you are going under them for other objectives up-valley.

Looking up at the peak from the bottom of Why Not.

The choke of Why Not.
athlete: Justin Ibarra

From the Herman Gulch Trailhead, hike or skin up the Herman Lake Trail. After 0.2 mile you will get to the junction for Watrous Gulch and Herman Lake; take the left and stay on the Herman trail. About 0.8 mile in you will get to the base of the Y Gully. In order to minimize your exposure to hazard, ascend the trees to either side of the gully. This is a far safer approach than going right up the gully. Stable slopes down low can trick you into getting under unstable slopes above. The east or climber's right side of the gully offers the safest ascent because it avoids exposure to the upper bowl and its cross-load. The trees here are tight and steep. Top out on the summit ridge to the side of the gully's entrance so you can just follow your footprints back to the line.

If your destination is the Y Not Gully, the safest way is to climb Machebeuf via Watrous Gulch. Go 0.2 mile up the trail from the parking lot and take the right turn onto the Watrous Gulch Trail, and skin or hike up into Watrous Gulch. Just past the Southwest Gully of Parnassus, look for a clearing in the trees and turn off the trail

The choke of Why Gully.
athlete: Jason McGowin

to the west-northwest. Skin up the mellow East Slopes to the East Ridge of Machebeuf. Getting up to the actual ridge takes you across some avy start zones. Follow the ridge up to the summit. The line is to the southwest of the summit. Y Not Gully is steeper than Y Gully and offers a short chuted section with a rock-walled choke. The choke offers a short section of 45 degree snow. Past Y Not is the Y Yes Gully. This route is a little mellower than Y Gully and tops out west of the summit of Machebeuf.

For either line, ski the Herman Gulch Trail back to the lot. This is a tight trail through the aspens so watch your speed. This trail sees a lot of use since it's so close to the interstate.

7b – Mount Machebeuf	East Bowl and Slopes	
DIFFICULTY: Intermediate	DISTANCE: 5.1 Miles Roundtrip	VERTICAL: 2,700'
SUNHIT: Sunrise	ASPECT: East	SEASON: Winter
TRAILHEAD: Herman Gulch	MAP: Page 268–269	PHOTO: Page 70–71

This is a great option for winter turns with mellow tree laps and an upper bowl you can progress to should the avy stability merit. From the Herman Gulch Trailhead, start skinning up the Herman Lake Trail. At 0.2 mile you will reach the Watrous Trail junction; take a right here. The trail does a rising contour through a beautiful stand of aspens up to the base of the East Slopes and Parnassus' Southwest Gully at about the 1.1 mile mark. Here you will look for a break in the forest to your left and head up the East Slopes of Machebeuf. Set a skin track that meanders through the trees to save the open slopes for turns. Near treeline you have the option to go higher on the ridge. This bowl leading to the ridge is an avalanche start zone, so use caution. The other option is to head for the East Bowl coming off the actual summit of Machebeuf; this is lower angled than the ridge options.

Stay clear of the runout of the Southwest Gully of Parnassus.

Ski what the conditions merit and return via the Watrous Gulch trail. This route combines well with the Watrous Bowl of Woods. You could even add in the Urad Bowl on Woods if you don't mind climbing back to the summit of Woods to get back to the Watrous drainage. Or you could combine this route with Parnassus' Southwest Gully, but I've never seen that line in very good condition. It's so far east of the divide that it doesn't get the best coverage, which is why it's not in this edition.

Lots of mellow skiing in the trees. Watch out for the steeper terrain near the ridge.

Fun meadow skipping.
athlete: Jason McGowin

The aforementioned
start zones at the ridge.

The path less traveled begins here.

Mountain Outfitters

———— • Est. 1985 • ————

Sales. Service. Rentals.

112 S. Ridge Street
Breckenridge CO 80424
(970) 453-2201
mtnoutfitters.com

DYNAFIT
COMPETENCE
CENTER

8 WOODS MOUNTAIN – 12,940'

The 681st highest point in Colorado is obviously not a 14er. You won't see this peak on many lists; the summit will not be crowded and the trailheads won't be packed. You will, however, find some great lines to ski. The north side of this peak dominates the view coming down US Highway 40 below the Floral Park corner and the base of Stanley Chute. This is the best spot to get a sense of conditions. On the south side, the peak is set back too far to get a good, easy view from the interstate.

8a – Woods Mountain	Watrous Bowl	
DIFFICULTY: **Intermediate**	DISTANCE: **6 Miles Roundtrip**	VERTICAL: **2,800'**
SUNHIT: **Sunrise + 2 Hours**	ASPECT: **Southwest through Southeast**	SEASON: **Spring**
TRAILHEAD: **Herman Gulch**	MAP: **Page 268-269**	PHOTO: **Page 70, 73–74**

This can be a fun, early-season venture into the alpine. With a southern exposure, you can get the development of melt-freeze conditions on this route fairly early in the spring or even late in the winter. Some years, however, this might not be the case, so evaluate the snowpack on the way. Access from the interstate is easy. Start at the Herman Trailhead, head up the Herman Lake Trail 0.2 mile to the Watrous Gulch Trail, and take a right. The line will come into view as you get to the base of Parnassus' Southwest Gully. Give the base of the gully a

The chutes between the two summits offers mid 40 degree terrain

Dropping in off the west summit.
athlete: Justin Ibarra

wide berth to avoid avalanche hazard from above. Keep working your way up the valley to treeline. The safest way to get this one is to ascend the Southwest Ridge of Woods. This will give you the chance to assess the stability while minimizing your exposure to harm's way. Follow the ridge to the west summit of Woods and then connect to the actual summit via the summit ridge. This is a pretty cool ridge with some exposure.

The direct line off the actual summit is windward and doesn't get the best coverage without the benefit of strong upslope storms and loading from the east. These storms usually occur in April and May, so coverage on this line may be better later in the spring than at the end of winter. The line descending off the west summit usually holds great snow. This is also the case for the lines descending off the Southwest Ridge. The shot coming right off the West Summit is the steepest measuring about 40 degrees at the slight choke through the rocks.

For the exit, follow your ascent down the Watrous Gulch Trail. Be mindful on the way up of any logs that might be down. Also be aware of the fact that this is a very busy trail due to its proximity to the interstate. This route combines well with all the lines of Machebeuf and Urad Bowl on Woods. If the Southwest Gully of Parnassus is in, go for it.

8b – Woods Mountain	Urad Bowl	
DIFFICULTY: Advanced	DISTANCE: 5.1 Miles Roundtrip	VERTICAL: 2,900'
SUNHIT: Sunrise	ASPECT: North to Northeast	SEASON: Spring
TRAILHEAD: Ruby Gulch	MAP: Page 269	PHOTO: Page 75–76

These days it feels like there's no time for greatness. This line can resolve those issues by providing great skiing, and lots of it, for very little effort. At only 5 miles roundtrip, you can get a nice steep line and nearly 3000' of vertical. This line is really close to Denver and now that the trailhead has reopened, we can take advantage of it once again; it was closed due to construction at the Urad mine. Be sure to check GiterdunPublishing.com for updates regarding closures.

Follow the trail up Ruby Gulch as it winds its way through the woods. After about 1.5 miles you will see the North Face of Parnassus and the Drainpipe. At this point, begin working your way west, across the drainage. This will put you on Wood's East Slopes. Follow the line of least resistance. There are some steeper slopes here that can and do slide. The high point

Woods Mountain
Summit

West
Summit

You can get a good look at
coverage from Berthoud Pass.

There's a nice view of the line just
below the last pitch to the true
summit along the Northeast Ridge.

The lines to my left are threatened by a big cornice.

is to the left even though it doesn't look like it from below. Once on the summit, you need to cross the summit ridge extending west to get to the drop-in zone for Urad Bowl.

There are a couple of options for the descent. The main line drops in from the end of the summit ridge. Average angle for the meat of the line is in the low 40 degree range. There are other options past this along the bowl's northwestern ridge. These have corniced entrances; use care around cornices. Always have a partner watching your back if descending below a cornice, as their failure can be hard to predict.

At the bottom of the chute of your choosing, there are two exit gullies. They meet up and take you to the same place, so select the one with the freshest snow. Follow the road back to the trailhead. This road is a Forest Service easement that leads to the Hassel Lake trailhead. Follow the road east back to the Ruby Gulch trailhead.

9   MOUNT PARNASSUS – 13,574'

The 208th-highest point in the state is in plain view to the millions of people who drive Interstate 70 east from the Eisenhower Tunnel. However, the Southwest Gullies, the lines seen from the interstate, don't fill in very well and therefore the best ski lines are on the other side of the mountain. That's fine though—the Bard/Parnassus cirque is beautiful and worth the visit. The mountain is named for Mount Parnassus in Greece, which was home to the Muses of Greek myth. Find your muse in the form of steep turns on its great ski routes.

The entrance is steep in the mid-50 degree range.

9a – Mount Parnassus	Northeast Face	
DIFFICULTY: **Advanced**	DISTANCE: **5.8 Miles Roundtrip**	VERTICAL: **3,400'**
SUNHIT: **Sunrise**	ASPECT: **Northeast**	SEASON: **Spring**
TRAILHEAD: **Ruby Gulch**	MAP: **Page 269**	PHOTO: **Page 77**

This is the most direct line off the summit of Parnassus. It's not the most aesthetic, though—that title goes to the Drainpipe. This line is a little steeper than the Drainpipe with slopes right off the top at about 50 degrees, depending on the season's loading patterns. With minimal consequences and terrain traps, this is a good place to get your feet wet on some steeper terrain without the hazards of no-fall zones. Access is easy, but be sure to get this one early. The sun hits this line early in the morning, as soon as the sun's angle gets over the Robeson/Bard Ridge.

From the Ruby Gulch Trailhead, skin up Ruby Gulch. There is a great trail up through the trees here. At about the 1 mile mark, you'll reach a junction. Some years, the sign is covered completely. Take the left trail to make for the Bard Parnassus Cirque and your objective. At treeline, follow the valley bottom up and around to the base of the Northeast Face. This is where you should decide if your timing is right. This is also a good spot to switch to crampons and pull out the ice axe; though this line doesn't have many terrain traps, falling down it would suck, so having an axe for self-arrest is a good idea. The face proper offers 1,500' of vertical with the very upper section being the steepest. The top-out is almost right on the summit. Since this is a spring line, ascending the route is the proper way to go. When ascending the line, be sure to stay to climber's right out of the direct fall-line to avoid being in the path of potential other groups dropping in on top of you; you don't want to get sluffed or slid. One could also ascend via the saddle between Woods and Parnassus; this can be a better choice if there are multiple groups on the mountain. You don't get the hands-on assessment of the snow if you go this route, but you will minimize your time in harm's way.

From the summit, drop in and enjoy the steep entrance. Half the face is over 45 degrees and the lower portion is in the high 30s. Things mellow out after about 1,400'. The exit is usually 100 percent skiable down the Ruby Gulch Trail; it's tight like an old New England trail. This route combines well with Bard's North Face, Robeson's Northwest Gully, and Englemann's West Gully. You could also combine it with Wood's Urad Bowl and have a completely different exit; see that route for a description of the ski and egress.

9b – Mount Parnassus	The Drainpipe	
DIFFICULTY: Advanced	DISTANCE: 5.3 Miles Roundtrip	VERTICAL: 3,400'
SUNHIT: Sunrise + 2 Hours	ASPECT: North	SEASON: Spring
TRAILHEAD: Ruby Gulch	MAP: Page 269	PHOTO: Page 78–80

This line can be inspected from the road leading to Ruby Gulch Trailhead, just after it rounds the corner below Red Mountain's East Ridge. You can't see the lower portion of the chute, but if the upper bowl is in, then the lower section is usually in as well. This is one of the more aesthetic couloirs in the southern portion of this book. The route has two distinctive sections: the upper bowl and the lower, twisting couloir, the Drainpipe portion. Head up

the Ruby Gulch Trail for about a mile and bear right, following the creek. This will lead you to the base of the Drainpipe. Skin to the base and switch to boots and ice axe. Please don't skin up this line; nobody wants to ski over your skin track as it switchbacks up the line, destroying all the good snow. If you must skin, go to the Woods/Parnassus Saddle and skin up the ridge.

The drop-in for the upper bowl is about hundred feet north of the summit and you can usually ski windswept snow along the ridge to make it a summit descent. The upper bowl approaches 50 degrees in steepness and

Approaching The Drainpipe.

The Drainpipe's namesake chute.
athlete: Allison Seymour

Looking down the
Drainpipe's chok
athlete: Luke Worl
photo: Jake Foj

may be even steeper depending on loading patterns that year. One issue with going around for this line is that it can be difficult to tell which gully to ski if you don't have your boot-pack to follow. Ski the gully to skier' left if in doubt. You'll get about 1,000' of wide open, steep bowl skiing before the walls close in and the turns get tight and twisty. The narrowest section is a few ski lengths wide. The Drainpipe lower section offers about 700' of vertical.

For the descent, follow the Ruby Gulch Trail. This is a fairly busy trail, so be sure to stay in enough control to avoid other groups using this zone.

From Mount Robeson you get a sense of the steepness. This was shot in May '16—a big snow year.

10 BARD PEAK – 13,641'

This is the highest peak in the book. The 176th highest peak in Colorado is a far cry from a 14er. The entire zone is bordered by 14ers: i.e. Grays, Torreys, Evans, Bierstadt, and Longs, but the lack of 14ers in the zone is a good thing. Can you imagine how many people would be crawling all over these mountains if there were 14ers here? In the summer, the Indian Peaks are a bit of a circus; the trailheads on Interstate 70 are filled to overflowing. Winter is less crowded, but even in winter the 14ers see traffic, especially in the Front Range. The peak has been known as Bard Peak for many years with references in the local newspapers going back to 1877.

10a – Bard Peak	North Face	
DIFFICULTY: Advanced to Expert	DISTANCE: 5.9 Miles Roundtrip	VERTICAL: 3,450'
SUNHIT: Sunrise + 2 Hours	ASPECT: North	SEASON: Spring
TRAILHEAD: Ruby Gulch	MAP: Page 269	PHOTO: Page 81–82

This is one of the more difficult lines in the book with very steep skiing over the massive lower cliff's exposure to a narrow exit ramp. This is true no-fall skiing at its finest. You want to be certain of stability when dropping in over so much exposure. This line isn't always in, however; you will need to wait for a strong series of upslope storms that will load the face with enough snow over the spring. One storm usually isn't enough to cover the upper talus

The summit line has major consequences for any mistake.

slope, so wait for the right conditions on this one. You can get a good look at the coverage of the face from the saddle at Butler Gulch or on the way up Mount Parnassus or Woods Mountain. If you go without looking at it first and it's not covered enough to ski, you could ski Parnassus' Northeast Face or The Drainpipe as a consolation prize.

From the trailhead, skin up the Ruby Gulch Trail for about a mile to the trail junction. If you can't find the junction sign, just stay on the east side of the river. At treeline, you'll get a good view of the face. I suggest climbing to the saddle between Bard and Parnassus instead of going up the line for this route. Skin and boot up the moderate snow to the ridge and then on to the summit.

You can still get a summit ski via mellower slopes descending from the Bard/Parnassus Ridge.

Be sure to take a picture of the face in its current condition to use for route finding from the top, then drop in. The upper section is usually pretty scratchy due to partially buried rocks. Do not fall here! Ski about 400' of the upper slopes to the exit ramp going to skier's right. Once at the lower face, you can breathe again.

A less consequential line is to follow your ascent route and ski off the ridge to the saddle. This allows you to get that summit ski, as the ridge usually has enough coverage to link it up. There are multiple chutes along the ridge to choose from.

The exit follows Ruby Gulch Trail; as always, be aware that there may be people on the trail. This zone usually isn't as busy as the routes on the interstate.

The first of many doglegs.

11 ROBESON PEAK – 13,140'

This unranked peak is a bump on the ridge extending from Bard Peak to Englemann Peak. I wasn't planning on putting this mountain in the book, but had such a fun descent this past spring that I felt adding it was the way to go. The point is named after the successful local miner Solomon Robeson. The Robeson house, built for his son Jacob in 1899, still stands at 811 Rose Street in Georgetown. Jacob K. Robeson was the mayor of Georgetown and a Colorado House Representative.

11a – Robeson Peak	Northwest Gully	
DIFFICULTY: Advanced	**DISTANCE: 4.3 Miles Roundtrip**	**VERTICAL: 3,000'**
SUNHIT: Sunrise + 3 Hours	**ASPECT: North – Northwest**	**SEASON: Spring**
TRAILHEAD: Ruby Gulch	**MAP: Page 269**	**PHOTO: Page 83–84**

This line offers a fairly mellow descent but is threatened by multiple slopes and aspects from above. The route snakes its way up Robeson from the Ruby Gulch Trail. The actual skiing is generally in the mid-30 degree range with a short section of 45 degrees halfway down the upper gully. As the gully snakes around, it crosses under west, northwest, and north facing slopes that are avalanche start zones. The gully itself is a terrain trap and if any of the slopes above slide, you will have little chance of surviving. Evidence of avalanche activity, such as flagged trees, is everywhere in the gully itself. Though low-angled, this line should only be attempted in spring with a very stable snowpack.

The upper gully offers some 40 degree fun.

To access this line, skin up Ruby Gulch. At

Use the dead tree in the center of the photo as your reference point to turn left to the access the Northwest Gully.

Main Ruby Gulch Trail

about 0.7 mile you will come to an obvious gully on your left. This isn't the line; this is the West Gully of Engelmann. The actual line entrance is about 0.1 mile past this and is pictured above. Follow the slight depression of the creek below the snowpack up through the woods; this will lead you to the gully itself. Once in the gully, look for the first "junction" on the right and take it; going straight leads to the flank of Engelmann. The gully twists its way upward toward treeline. Note how deep the gully is from millennia of slides. Once above treeline, the gully takes one more turn. Note the chutes off to the right and pick your line. It's easiest to just stay in the gully to the saddle and then head west at the ridge to the summit. We kept skins on the whole way by using this route.

Terrain trap city.

Drop in on a northwesterly course and make your way to the line you picked. The routes are mostly in the mid-30 degree range with some roll-overs approaching the mid-40s. Once back at the main gully, enjoy the halfpipe-like skiing. With so many start zones above you, be aware of what's going on around you, especially how hot it's getting. The gully peters out before reaching the trail; we found hollow snow here around the trees. Watch out for this, as the creek undermines the stability down low. The rest of the way is on the trail; be alert for people on the trail.

12 ENGELMANN PEAK – 13,362'

This mountain was known locally in Empire as Cowles Mountain prior to being named after Dr. George Engelmann, a famous botanist who worked extensively cataloging the flora of the Rockies. The Englemann spruce is also named after him. Christopher Parry named the peak after him, along with Grays and Torreys. In fact, according to *Fourteen Thousand Feet: A History of the Naming and Early Ascents of the High Colorado Peaks* by John Lathrop Jerome Hart, it's believed that the USGS got the peak wrong and that Kelso was actually the peak named for Engelmann. However, the peak that did receive the name Engelmann was the collection site of the tree that would later bear his name, according to USGS documents. The peak is the 349th highest point in Colorado. The peak is a bonanza for the backcountry skier. There are more routes than I covered here; some have property issues and some have coverage issues. Lightning Gully is without a doubt one of the finest lines in the Front Range.

12a – Engelmann Peak	West Gully	
DIFFICULTY: Intermediate	DISTANCE: 3.6 Miles Roundtrip	VERTICAL: 3,050'
SUNHIT: Sunrise + 3 Hours	ASPECT: West	SEASON: Spring
TRAILHEAD: Ruby Gulch	MAP: Page 269	PHOTO: Page 85–87

This is a great quick hit once the spring snowpack stability arrives. As this line is generally windward, you may need to wait for a spring upslope storm to fill it in. Timing on this line is later than your usual spring line; since the sun hits it later, you will have to start later in the day to get a thaw of the frozen snow. The slope angle of this line is pretty similar to the Northwest Gully on Robeson; the reason for the lower difficulty rating is due to less complexity and fewer threats from above. This route also lacks the twisting nature of the line on Robeson. That doesn't mean that there isn't avalanche hazard here, so be alert.

From the trailhead, go around the gate and up the Ruby Gulch Trail. At the 0.7 mile mark you will come to the base of the West Gully. Stable spring snow is key to this line as you will be ascending the gully. Be aware that its windward nature means that there is the heightened possibility of slabs, especially up high. Slides from above are the most likely to kill, so be

Though the line is mostly mellow, there is a start zone at the top of this avy path.

The entrance to the gully from Ruby Gulch Trail.

certain of the slope's stability. Stability may change as you get higher up the line. The ascent is straightforward; you can almost see the summit from the gully's bottom. Staying out of the center of the gully can reduce risk of getting caught should a slide be triggered, but being off to the side, under the steeper walls of the gully, could trigger a slide.

The upper gully is great for skiing with angles right around 40 degrees. This is prime avalanche terrain. You may need to piece the summit descent together. The best places to check out coverage are from the Butler Gulch Saddle and from "Hassell Peak." Return via the Ruby Gulch trail, being mindful that there might be people ascending this busy trail; it's tight, so stay in control.

The top of West Gully is often wind stripped of snow.

Easy access and great vertical.

Englemann · Robeson · West Gully · Lightning · Breakfast

12b – Englemann Peak	Lightning Gully	
DIFFICULTY: **Advanced**	DISTANCE: **4.7 Miles Roundtrip**	VERTICAL: **3,700'**
SUNHIT: **Sunrise + 1 Hour**	ASPECT: **North**	SEASON: **Spring**
TRAILHEAD: **Berthoud Falls**	MAP: **Page 269**	PHOTO: **Page 87–89**

This is one of my favorite lines in the book. We got this one with about a foot of new on top of a stable spring snowpack at the beginning of June. This is the ideal situation for this route. At 3,700' of vertical, if you ski from the summit of Engelmann, this is one of the bigger lines in the Front Range. You can get a great look at almost the entire route from the turn for Urad Mine and Ruby Gulch Trailhead off of Jones Pass Road.

It looks a little like the Steal Your Face lightning bolt.

From the pull-off on US Highway 40, be sure to cross the creek while you're still in the clearing to avoid crossing the private property of Berthoud Falls. Once in the trees on the other side, look for the trail that heads west under the abrupt steeps of Engelmann's North Flank. Follow this trail to about the .5 mile mark from the trailhead and enter the steep trees. Skinning up the trees is far safer than skinning up the gully itself. The goal is to minimize your time in harm's way. Switchback your way up the steep trees, following a southerly course. This will put

The upper bowl has a giant convex.
Be sure of your decisions he

you on the lightly treed slope to the east of the gully. You can get a great look from here at the bulk of the line. Follow the margins of the trees to the summit ridge and the summit.

For the descent, follow the ridge back to the line. Be aware that there is a cornice to skier's right and give it a wide margin. On the upper slopes of the line, to skier's left of the wind lip that develops yearly, the angle is fairly mellow. This slope rolls over as you get to treeline. Be sure of your stability here if entering the gully proper. The tighter trees offer some degree of safety should things get dicey. Once in the gully, the line twists and turns its way downward. Near the bottom you will reach the crux, a short 45+ degree section. Follow the gully to the flats and then head to your right to meet up with your ascent trail through the trees.

Powder in May—thanks to a
spring upslope storm.

At the lower choke there is a
nice short steep section.

The larger chute to the left of Breakfast Chute has heinous trees at the bottom.

12c – Englemann Peak	Breakfast Chute	
DIFFICULTY: Advanced	**DISTANCE: 2 Miles Roundtrip**	**VERTICAL: 1,900'**
SUNHIT: Sunrise + 3 Hours	**ASPECT: North**	**SEASON: Winter and Spring**
TRAILHEAD: Berthoud Falls	**MAP: Page 269**	**PHOTO: Page 87, 89–90**

This is a great option for quick winter turns, granted you have stable snow. Locals call it the Breakfast Chute because they like to ski it before breakfast. Conditions can best be checked on US Highway 40 just past the Jones Pass switchback.

From the pull-off on US Highway 40, cross the creek while you're still in the clearing to avoid the private property of Berthoud Falls. Once in the trees on the other side, look for the trail that heads west under the abrupt steeps of Engelmann's north flank. About 0.3 mile from the trailhead, you will come to the base of the Breakfast Chute. The very base of the chute is the steepest section; it's very abrupt and could be considered a terrain trap. The slope is around 45 degrees here. Skin with caution if you must; the trees on either side of the chute are just as steep but much safer. However, you will get an immediate assessment of

Tight trees but enough space to lay out some carve[s]
athlete: Otina F[o]

stability should you ascend the steep gully. Once past the steep section, move to the west side of the gully and skin up the margin of the gully. About three-quarters of the way up the gully you will get to a slight bench. Above here the trees get sparser and the avy hazard can change due to a slight shift in the aspect; there will be more slabs above you. Should the conditions merit, continue to treeline and get ready to ski. This route isn't a summit ski.

Ski the gully with care. There are a lot of small Christmas trees in the line. If you get slid here you will get hurt. It's much like the base of Mines at Berthoud in that respect. Follow your up track on the way out and remember to stay on the mountain side of the creek to the clearing.

The bottom of the line is steep, in the 40s and it ends at a terrain trap.

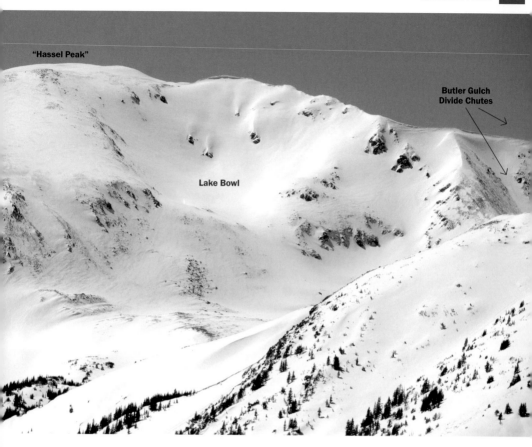

"Hassel Peak"

Butler Gulch
Divide Chutes

Lake Bowl

13 "HASSELL PEAK" – 13,215'

This peak is unnamed on the map. Locals commonly refer to it as "Hassell Peak" in reference to its position above Hassell Lake. Typically, one accesses lines via the drainage below the line they're going for. This isn't the case with "Hassell Peak," as the access above the Urad Mine is closed for mining. If you want to get this line, go for it from Butler Gulch. I didn't include this peak in the Butler Gulch section because you leave Butler Gulch and it's a 13er, so I figured it deserved its own description.

13a – "Hassell Peak"	Lake Bowl	
DIFFICULTY: Advanced	DISTANCE: 6 Miles Roundtrip	VERTICAL: 3,200'
SUNHIT: Sunrise	ASPECT: East and North	SEASON: Spring
TRAILHEAD: Jones Pass	MAP: Page 269	PHOTO: Page 91–93, 96

From the winter Jones Pass parking lot, skin up Jones Pass Road to the gated turn for Butler Gulch. Take this trail about 1.5 miles to the first big switchback at the base of the Halfpipe Gully. Take the next switchback and leave the trail at the third switchback. Follow the east side of the Halfpipe Gully up to treeline. Aim for the ridge to your south that forms the southern boundary of Butler Gulch and extends west to the Continental Divide. This is your route; follow the ridge to the divide. Once at the divide, you will head south for about 0.2 mile.

Low tide, early season conditions.
You can make it spicy or mild.

For the ski, just drop in on an easterly heading. This is Lake Bowl and you get roughly 800'
of quality turns before the line crosses a long, flat section. After another short section, you'll
want to make your way back to the ridge separating Butler Gulch from the Hassell drainage.
Once at the ridge, pick a line to reenter Butler Gulch and ski it back to the Butler Gulch Trail;
use the Halfpipe Gully as your guide or just follow your skin track. Butler Gulch Trail is fairly
busy so be on the lookout for hikers and other skiers ascending.

14 BUTLER GULCH – 12,109'

Butler Gulch is a non-motorized backcountry zone accessed from the winter Jones Pass Trailhead. It is a very popular area despite the long, flat approach on the access trail. This isn't surprising given the easy access provided by US Highway 40 and the Jones Pass Road; it is, after all, closer to the masses than Berthoud Pass and much less crowded on a weekend. Lines are generally short, with maximum continuous vertical of around 1,000'; you can get more vertical by ascending above treeline, but the windward nature of these slopes yields hollow snow and wind slabs all too often. There are two big lines called the Jones Brothers Chutes; however, these are spring lines. Despite this zone being so close to the very busy snowmobile zone of Jones Pass and the very active Henderson Mine, noise is barely noticeable. Given the mild nature of the zone, one can expect to see less experienced users here learning the ropes, or should I say skins.

14a – Butler Gulch	Halfpipe Gully	
DIFFICULTY: Intermediate	DISTANCE: 3.8 Miles Roundtrip	VERTICAL: 1,400'
SUNHIT: Sunrise + 2 Hours	ASPECT: Northeast	SEASON: Winter
TRAILHEAD: Jones Pass	MAP: Page 268	PHOTO: Page 93–94

This is a great intermediate line with a very short section that can slide and a few zones to either side that offer a little more challenge and risk. Above the Halfpipe Gully, you can connect other destinations like the Divide Chutes or "Hassell Peak." There is also lower angled meadow skipping terrain to play in as well.

From the winter Jones Pass Trailhead, follow the Jones Pass road about .1 mile to the Butler Gulch trail, past the gate and up the trail. After about 1.5 miles you will come to an abrupt switchback; this is the base of the Halfpipe Gully. Take the switchbacks, and at the third switchback leave the trail and head up the open slope that parallels the Halfpipe Gully. Follow the Halfpipe Gully until you get to its top and cross the open slope above it; the angle is low here. This is where you want to start.

A look up at the Divide Chutes from near the top of Halfpipe Gully. Early season conditions.

Ski the Halfpipe Gully to the first switchback and repeat as necessary. Of note: about three-fourths of the way down, the gully does get steep enough to slide. It would take a seriously weak snowpack, but it should be in your mind that it's possible.

Alternatively, there are other lines on either side of the Halfpipe Gully. To skier's right are a few lines with less avy hazard, but there is still a hazard. To skier's left is a more open bowl with higher danger that leads to trees; this is a terrain trap. The line to skier's left has a convex roll above the trees. I have seen a crown here only once in 10 years. It's all about the options.

14b – Butler Gulch	Hourglass Gully	
DIFFICULTY: **Intermediate to Advanced**	DISTANCE: **4 Miles Roundtrip**	VERTICAL: **1,800'**
SUNHIT: **Sunrise + 3 Hours**	ASPECT: **West through North**	SEASON: **Winter**
TRAILHEAD: **Jones Pass**	MAP: **Page 268**	PHOTO: **Page 94–95**

This is the classic Butler Gulch line. From the winter Jones Pass trailhead, follow the Jones Pass road about 0.1 mile to the Butler Gulch trail, past the gate and up the trail. After about 1.5 miles you will come to an abrupt switchback at the base of the Halfpipe Gully. Take the switchbacks (there are three) and keep following the trail as it makes a rising contour through the woods. About 0.1 mile from the switchbacks, the trail steepens as it hugs the trees; the zone is in harm's way of slides from above. Once it relents, you are back to the rising contour that reaches the base of the Hourglass. Do not skin up the Hourglass, as this would ruin it for everyone who came after you. Instead, skin up the slope toward the saddle of UN12109 and UN12317. After the bank of trees to your left ends, go left above the trees. This is the more moderate lower entrance to the Hourglass. There is a trail here to reach the Hourglass' upper entrance;' this is the advanced zone due to the need to assess avalanche stability. If you deem the snow stable, then the upper entrance is yours. The lower entrance offers lower angle turns, but remember that the snow is all connected so you may be able to trigger the upper snow from below.

Past the upper Hourglass entrance, you can contour to a couple more lines. These are shallow gullies that aren't as open as the Hourglass. All the lines in this zone ski down to the Butler Gulch trail so there's no getting lost, as long as you ski downhill. Skin, ski, and repeat until all the freshies are gone.

Doug Mock drops a knee
in Hourglass Gully.

The North Slopes of UN12109 offer some nice options
and hold good snow. Beware of lurking slabs as the slope
gets cross loaded. Check conditions above the skin track.
athlete: Doug Mock

14c – Butler Gulch	South Side – Hassell Lake	
DIFFICULTY: Intermediate	DISTANCE: 5 Miles Roundtrip	VERTICAL: 2,500'
SUNHIT: Sunrise + 2 Hours	ASPECT: South and North	SEASON: Winter
TRAILHEAD: Jones Pass	MAP: Page 268	PHOTO: Page 96

This is a fun little tour that puts you in the Hassell Lake drainage. Since this is south-facing, the snow can get a little hot and can be crusty if it hasn't snowed for a while. From the winter Jones Pass trailhead, follow the Jones Pass road about 0.1 mile to the Butler Gulch trail, past the gate and up the trail. After about 1.5 miles you will come to an abrupt switchback at the Halfpipe Gully. Take the switchbacks (there are three) and keep following the trail as it follows a rising contour through the woods. About 0.1 mile from the switchbacks, the trail generally steepens as it hugs the trees. Once it relents, you are back to the rising contour that reaches the base of the Hourglass. Skin up the slope leading to the saddle of UN12109 and UN12317. At the saddle, you can head for the "summit" of UN12109.

From here, ski south to Hassell Lake. This is an 800' drop. If you drop in from the "summit" you will avoid the road cuts that break up the skiing directly south of the saddle. Utilize the road cuts for your skin back to the saddle. From there, ski directly down from the saddle or combine with the Hourglass. You can also head to skier's left from the saddle to other treed chutes. Just be careful not to undercut the avy slopes that are above these tree shots.

Looking north from where the Continental
Divide and the west ridge of UN12109 meet.
Early season conditions.

14d – Butler Gulch	Divide Chutes	
DIFFICULTY: Advanced	DISTANCE: **5.9 Miles Roundtrip**	VERTICAL: **2,900'**
SUNHIT: **Sunrise**	ASPECT: **East to Northeast**	SEASON: **Spring**
TRAILHEAD: **Jones Pass**	MAP: **Page 268**	PHOTO: **Page 91, 93, 96–97, 102**

From the winter Jones Pass parking lot, skin up Jones Pass Road to the gated turn for Butler Gulch. Take this trail about 1.5 miles to the first big switchback at the base of the Halfpipe Gully. Take the next switchback, leave the trail at the third switchback, and follow the east side of the Halfpipe Gully up to treeline. Aim for the ridge to your south that forms the southern boundary of Butler Gulch and extends west to the Continental Divide. This is your route; follow the ridge to the divide. Climbing the ridge exposes you to harm's way for much less time than ascending the line. Do not skin up the chutes.

Alternatively, there are more mellow lines coming off the divide to the northwest of the Halfpipe Gully. These are skinable and present lower avalanche hazard. Lower hazard doesn't mean no hazard. With the amount of wind that this zone sees, always use caution in the alpine.

For the ski, just drop in on an easterly heading. If ascending the ridge you can get a good look at your line on the way up. If going up the northern option then you know where to ski—just follow your skin track. Some of these lines may be corniced. The lines to viewer's left reach 50 degrees at their steepest. Use the Halfpipe Gully as your exit route. Don't miss the trail at the switchbacks, as it's pretty flat past the switchbacks.

UN 12085

14e – Butler Gulch	Jones Brothers Chutes	
DIFFICULTY: Advanced	DISTANCE: 2.2 Miles Roundtrip	VERTICAL: 1,700'
SUNHIT: Sunrise	ASPECT: Northeast	SEASON: Spring
TRAILHEAD: Jones Pass	MAP: Page 268	PHOTO: Page 98–100, 102

This has to be one of the easiest-access 1,500' lines around. At just over 2.2 miles roundtrip, you get a 40 degree chute that holds snow late every year. The first time I skied this line was in June and it was complete from the "summit." This line should only be skied in the spring. Every year, this path slides big; it's kind of the barometer for the snowpack changing in the fall. Once Jones Brothers goes, I usually stop skiing the alpine paths around Jones Pass. You do not want to be in this path when it slides. The lower section is filled with little Christmas trees that will act as a strainer for your flesh and bone. The upper start zone is in prime position for wind-loading and slab development, and with the amount of wind this zone gets, you can be almost certain there is plenty of slab development. Save it for spring!

From the winter trailhead, skin up Jones Pass road to the turn for Butler Gulch. Go past the gate to the very first switchback and enter the trees on the other side of the creek. Skin up through the trees, staying between the two Brothers. This is extreme skinning at times, with slopes reaching the low 40 degree range. It can be very tight in here, so although it's steep, it's most likely not going to slide. If the pack is at all hollow, then bail on the line. Do not skin up the line. The Christmas trees mentioned above can act as heating wands, undermining the snowpack from within; the slope actually may not be bridged but may just be capped,

Vasquez Peak

"South Vasquez Peak"

UN 12118

The upper section of Jones Brothers is in the low 40s.

Allison Seymour drops into the lower part of Jones Brothers Main Chute. The trees are nicely spaced in this avy path.

waiting for a trigger. Once near treeline make for the treed rib, closest to the edge of the main Jones Brother Chute, to climber's right. Follow these trees to the summit, using extra care once above treeline. Once on top of UN12085, enjoy the commanding view of Jones Pass and Butler Gulch.

The very top of the line is the most dangerous from an avalanche perspective. Use care getting into the line; if you suspect issues, ski the other Jones Brother Chute which may have better stability, though tighter skiing. In the main Brother, the steepest section is about 45 degrees and is right under the top start zone. Past this there is a nice open section before you hit the trees. Staying to skier's' right offers the most open path for turns through the trees. Lower down after the roll there is a section on the middle of the path that is most open for turning.

At the bottom of the line, resist the urge to ski all the way to the creek. Instead, enter the trees above the creek and look for a faint trail that leads back to the initial switchback on the Butler Gulch Trail. It's pretty cool when you pop out here and there are other people there. The look on their faces is pretty awesome.

Looking up from the bottom of the main Jones Brothers Chute. I've seen skin tracks going up this line; skinning this line dramatically increases your time in harm's way.

15 JONES PASS – 12,451'

John S. Jones, of Empire, proposed building a wagon road to Middle Park in 1866, as reported in the Rocky Mountain News. He went ahead and built it and now the pass is named in his honor. This route to Middle Park was longer than Berthoud Pass, its competing road. Berthoud Pass also had the backing of the Pony Express. According to Clear Creek County documents, Jones Pass was only used a few times as a wagon road. According to *Powder Ghost Towns* by Peter Bronski, the 1930s were a great time for skiing in Clear Creek, with skiers enjoying both Jones Pass and the newly opened Berthoud Pass Ski Area. Berthoud had about 26,000 skier visits in its first season. The Red Mountain Lodge sat at the base of Red Mountain, near Berthoud Falls. There was even talk of putting in lifts through the 40s, but access seemed like an issue for large numbers of skiers. The Forest Service also wanted to focus skier traffic on the Highway 6/Interstate 70 corridor.

Today the zone is one of the most popular snowmobile access zones in Colorado. There are multiple drainages around the pass that allow sled access. The Butler Gulch drainage isn't one of them. Please respect this closure or it may affect future access.

Jones Pass is the home of Powder Addiction, a guided snowcat skiing operation. They offer guided skiing on the slopes of Jones Pass and control their lines for avalanche safety. Please respect their zones.

15a – Jones Pass	Pass Bowl	
DIFFICULTY: Intermediate	DISTANCE: 1.8–5.6 Miles Roundtrip	VERTICAL: 1,100'–2,300'
SUNHIT: Sunrise	ASPECT: East	SEASON: Fall or Spring
TRAILHEAD: Jones Pass	MAP: Page 268, 270	PHOTO: Page 102, 104

This is the Jones Pass classic, direct from the summit of the pass. The angle here is lower than the other lines. This means lower danger, not no danger, as there are still threats on the margins, just below the cornice on the ridge, and from the cornice itself. Every year it seems there are avalanche incidents on the pass.

Early season conditions. Once this line gets a lot of snow I ski elsewhere, like in the trees.

UN12700

"Hassel Peak"

Pettingell Peak

Divide Chutes

UN12109

Jones Brothers Chutes

Butler Gulch Zone
No Snowmobiles

Panoramic view from "South Vasquez" in a good snow year.

From the winter trailhead, either drive or hike to the fourth switchback at treeline. Take a southwesterly route to the next gully to the south of the road; this will lead you to the base of Pass Bowl. Ascend the margin of the bowl to the summit of the pass. Don't skin up the middle as it will mess up the skiing for groups that come after you. The upper slopes approaching the cornice deserve extra caution.

The skiing is about 700' of fun. Skin, ski, and repeat the mid-30 degree bowl. Exit the way you came.

15b – Jones Pass	UN12700 East Bowl	
DIFFICULTY: Advanced	DISTANCE: 2.2–6 Miles Roundtrip	VERTICAL: 1,400'–2,500'
SUNHIT: Sunrise	ASPECT: East	SEASON: Autumn or Spring
TRAILHEAD: Jones Pass	MAP: Page 268, 270	PHOTO: Page 101–103

This is one of my favorite lines in the fall. Jones Pass is usually one of the first places to accumulate significant amounts of snow each season. At this time of year, one can typically drive up the road 1.9 miles past the winter closure and get in this line with relative ease. Once

UN12700
athlete: Justin Ibarra

UN12700
Bobtail BM
Jones Pass
Pass Bowl
UN12118
Jones Pass Zone
Snowmobiles Permitted

the snowpack starts to get more complex, usually by mid-November, I see this as the time to ski lower lines in the trees and leave the alpine avalanche slopes for spring. It seems like every year there are early season avalanche incidents here. Perhaps this is due to the easy access, or the fact that people don't have their avalanche hats on. Remember, if there is snow, the avalanche issue needs to be on your mind. Complacency can kill you. Early season slides usually involve getting dragged across the basal rocks; these are trauma-inducing slides.

From the winter lot, either drive or hike 1.9 miles to the fourth switchback, just at treeline. From here, cross the small creek and take a southwesterly course, angling uphill; this will put you below Pass Bowl. Ascend the northern margin of Pass Bowl to the last upper portion of Jones Pass Road. Please do not skin directly up the middle of Pass Bowl as this will ruin the skiing for others who come after you. Take the road the remainder of the way to the pass summit. From here, hike the ridge south 0.2 mile to the summit of UN12700; there is a trail here.

The East Bowl offers 900' of moderately steep vertical. Average angle is in the mid-

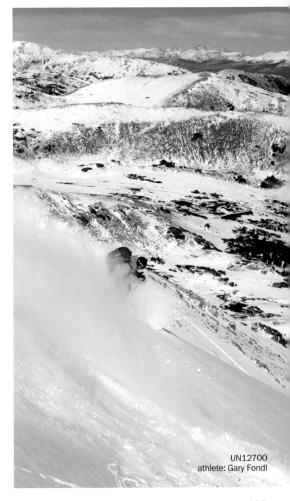

UN12700
athlete: Gary Fondl

30s and you can find sections in the mid-40 degree range on the margins and through some shallow chutes. Near the bottom of the bowl is a fun little gully. At the bottom you can do some more laps; setting a skin track on the ridge between Pass Bowl and UN12700 is the way to go. For the exit, ski to the northeast, surmounting the slight ridge and then hooking back up with your lower ascent route. Then meet back up with the road to either return to your vehicle or ski/hike back to the winter trailhead.

15c – Jones Pass	Bobtail BM	
DIFFICULTY: Advanced	DISTANCE: 1.9–5.6 Miles Roundtrip	VERTICAL: 1,400'–2,500'
SUNHIT: Sunrise	ASPECT: East	SEASON: Spring
TRAILHEAD: Jones Pass	MAP: Page 270	PHOTO: Page 103–104

This is the only named point on Jones Pass. The east face is a pretty fun ski that is steeper than both Pass Bowl and UN12700. For some reason, this line doesn't get the loading the previous lines see, at least in the early season. Therefore, I usually get this one in the spring. It seems like every year there is snow-machine avalanche incident video that surfaces on YouTube from this zone. Be smart in the alpine in winter, as the combined weight of you and your machine have a deeper impact on the snowpack.

From the winter lot, either drive or hike 1.9 miles to the fourth switchback, just at treeline. From here, cross the small creek and take a westerly course; this will allow you to avoid a switchback. Meet back up with the road and follow it to the east ridge of Bobtail BM. Ascend the ridge to the summit.

Ski slightly north and drop into Bobtail's East Bowl. There are steeper shots closer to the summit. The easy way is farther north along the ridge. Use care if there is a cornice. Ski the 900' route back to the pass road.

Jones Pass

Bobtail BM

Looking up at UN12118 from the "Corral."
Use the trees to approach the ridge.

15d – Jones Pass	UN12118 (First Corner)	
DIFFICULTY: Advanced	DISTANCE: 3.3 Miles Roundtrip	VERTICAL: 1,800'
SUNHIT: Sunrise	ASPECT: East	SEASON: Spring
TRAILHEAD: Jones Pass	MAP: Page 270	PHOTO: Page 99, 103, 105–106, 108

This is easily my favorite line at Jones Pass. Access is easy and what you get for your effort is really fun. This is a massive slide path so be sure of stability before dropping in. I like to hit this line in the spring to help minimize the snowpack issues. This also minimizes interactions with high-marking snow-machiners. If there are high markers on the line, don't ski this route; snow-machines can add a lot of weight and if the snowpack is fragile this might be all you need for a trigger.

Once you get to the ridge you get a nice view of the line. Watch the cornice at the edge.

Fun trees with great spacing.
This is a good early spring route.

From the winter trailhead, skin up the road about a mile to the "Corral," the first real opening in the forest. At the first switchback, leave the road on a westerly course and head up into the glades. These can offer up some fun powder in the winter. After about 600' of vertical, you will reach the top of the trees and a short steep section to get to the ridge proper. Ascend the ridge to the summit of UN12118. While ascending the ridge, you can check out your ski route.

The line, directly fall-line from the summit, is lightly treed and steep, but it is steep in steps. To skier's right you can enter a more open chute that leads to the steepest section; the angle here is in the high-40s. Below these top sections, the slopes open up before the small Christmas trees. These small trees are fairly open. At the base, return to the "Corral" and the Jones Pass Road.

There's a lot of snowmobile highmarking on this line.
Be aware of what's going on below you when you
commit to this route.

Looking at the options on Vasquez Peak from UN12118.

Vasquez Peak

"South Vasquez Peak"

16 VASQUEZ PEAK – 12,939'

From the U.S. Forest Service website, "Edward Berthoud named Vasquez Peak, the highest point in the Vasquez Peak Wilderness... Berthoud was the founder and engineer of the mountain pass through the Rocky Mountains into the Middle Park area of Colorado, now known as Berthoud Pass." The peak is the namesake for the Vasquez Peak Wilderness, created by Congress in 1993. At 12,000 acres, it's a fairly small wilderness area. The northern slopes of Vasquez Peak are included in the wilderness area.

16a – Vasquez Peak	Southwest Bowl and Gully	
DIFFICULTY: Intermediate	DISTANCE: 4.6 Miles Roundtrip	VERTICAL: 2,600'
SUNHIT: Sunrise + 3 Hours	ASPECT: South–Southwest	SEASON: Winter and Spring
TRAILHEAD: Jones Pass	MAP: Page 270	PHOTO: Page 107–108

Finding lines in the alpine that are mellow enough to safely navigate in the winter can be a challenge. This route on Vasquez fits the bill, as, with minimal start zones, you can keep the slope angle mellow and minimize your avalanche risk. There are a few start zones, however, so remember that low hazard doesn't mean no hazard.

Access is easy. Start skinning up Jones Pass from the winter trailhead. At about 1 mile, you will come to the "Corral," a nice opening in the forest. Hike north across the "Corral" meadow; be mindful of the avy paths coming off of UN12118 to your left. The true

Heading up the trees on the Southwest Slopes of Vasquez.

Some mellow options on Vasquez Peak.

summit of Vasquez comes into view on the other side of the Southwest Gully. Angle up on a northeasterly course and enter the gully. There are a few start zones here, so be aware of what's above you. Follow the gully to treeline and then pick the path of least resistance to the summit of Vasquez Peak. Descend the way you came.

16b – Vasquez Peak	South Peak (UN12900) Southeast Bowl	
DIFFICULTY: Advanced	DISTANCE: 3.7 Miles Roundtrip	VERTICAL: 2,600'
SUNHIT: Sunrise	ASPECT: East through South	SEASON: Spring
TRAILHEAD: Jones Pass	MAP: Page 270	PHOTO: Page 107, 109

If you've ever been up Butler Gulch, looked over toward Vasquez Peak, and wondered what it was like to ski this line, here it is. Access is easy and the skiing can be really good. Timing, however, is difficult due to the lower section being south facing. You need the upper snow to be in a spring state, but you also need the day to be cool enough to not cook the lower section in the trees. Finding these conditions can be the crux of the route. One solution can be to get it very early in the morning, skiing the East Bowl and South Slopes in the trees before the

Jones Brothers Chutes

UN12,118

The southwest slope is a little towards windward so the snow can be a little funky sometimes.
athlete: Scott Edlin

sun has a chance to heat up the lower slopes. The other is to get it after a spring storm and hope for cooling clouds.

From the winter trailhead, skin up the road. It's important to have enough coverage to skin as you'll need it down low on the South Slope exit. After about a mile, reach the meadow of the "Corral" and take a right, heading up the margin of the open slope coming off "South Vasquez Peak." Once above treeline, follow the ridge to the summit. Use care to climber's right, as there is a cornice that develops.

For the ski, do your best to discern the size of the cornice without getting too close to the edge. Checking from lower down the ridge is a good way to go. Once you know where to go, drop in and enjoy the upper bowl. Stay to skier's right at the bottom for another short, steep chute. There are a couple gullies below this; they all feed down to the Loop Trail, which connects the Jones Pass Trailhead to Berthoud Pass. This is what you're looking for. Below the trail the trees get too tight to ski. Once on the trail, the skiing gets a bit less fun but the trail brings you back to the trailhead. You can shortcut at the switchbacks if you like and there is enough coverage. This zone has a lot of deadfall so you will need the good coverage.

"South Vasquez Peak"

Looking at the options on "South Vasquez Peak".

The south facing exit gully can get hot quickly. Ski it in the morning. Too bad the chutes in the background are on Henderson Mine property.
athlete: Scott Edlin

Coming off the top of "South Vasquez"
athlete: Scott Edlin

Stanley
Slide Path
Summit

"No N

Russell

The Roll

Berthoud Pass
Summit

The 90s

The 80s

Current Creek

17 BERTHOUD PASS – 11,315'

The pass is named for Edward L. Berthoud, chief surveyor of the Colorado Central Railroad during the 1870s. On the orders of William Hepburn Russell and accompanied by Jim Bridger, Berthoud discovered the pass in July 1861 while surveying a possible route for the railroad. Berthoud concluded that the pass was suitable as a wagon road, but not as a railroad, and was then hired by the Central Overland California and Pikes Peak Express Company, the parent company of the Pony Express, to survey a route over the pass to Salt Lake, according to *The Real Pioneers of Colorado* by Maria Davies McGrath.

Berthoud Pass was also the home of Colorado's first ski lift. Berthoud beat out Glen Cove, a ski area on the flanks of Pikes Peak, for the title by a couple of months. Berthoud Pass Ski Area was also the site of the first double chair. Unfortunately the area had trouble competing with the Interstate 70 resorts and closed in 2001.

Today Berthoud Pass has returned to its backcountry roots. It has a guardian in the Friends of Berthoud Pass. This group works with the Forest Service as a liaison between avid backcountry users and the government. They also provide avalanche awareness seminars and promote safe backcountry use. They were instrumental in getting the warming hut at the pass summit built.

Berthoud Pass can be a very crowded place on the weekends in the winter. Parking can be tough to find after a big dump. There have been incidents of groups dropping in on top of each other. Other issues are people boot-packing up skin tracks and questionable

decision making regarding line selection. Sometimes it feels a bit like a race to get at the freshies. Almost every year there are avalanche incidents at the pass. According to the great book *Powder Ghost Towns* by Peter Bronski, Colorado's first recreational avalanche fatality occurred at the pass during the ski area's first day of operation on February 7, 1937; they were skiing in a different zone. *The Georgetown Courier* reported that their bodies were found in May of that year, within a half mile of the Berthoud Pass Inn, situated at Berthoud Pass Summit.

Know before you go. Follow the snowpack at the Berthoud Pass snotel site at the Natural Resources Conservation Service (NRCS) website (see Glossary for the link). The Colorado Avalanche Information Center (CAIC) website and mobile app are great places to get professional avalanche forecasts on a daily basis to help you make good decisions about the lines you choose. If you don't know, get the education—it's an investment that could save your life.

Many of the names differ between the two iterations of the Berthoud Ski Area. For instance, Pauly's Powder Stash was originally called the Fairway, and Pioneer Bowl was called the Roll. This can cause some confusion among users. Generally in this book I use the name I like the best. All routes are marked on the topo photos. Due to the short, lap skiing nature of the terrain, the route sections don't have stats. Generally speaking you're looking at about 1,300' and 2 miles to get from any of the creeks on the West Side to the ridge. Stats for the East Side are mentioned within the routes.

17W – BERTHOUD PASS WEST SIDE

The West Side of the pass, due to loading, generally gets more snow than the East Side. This is the effect of the clouds being lifted—a phenomenon known as orographic lift. Berthoud Pass and especially the West Side is perfectly positioned to benefit from this squeezing effect on the clouds.

Stanley Slide Path

17Wa – Berthoud Pass	Stanley Slide Path

Stanley Slide Path as viewed from Englemann Peak.

Despite the easy access and the fact that it sees some control work by Colorado Department of Transportation (CDOT), this route should not be taken lightly. This is a serious line with an almost ideal start zone. It has a long history of burying the road and worse. Last year was the introduction of the Gasex avalanche control system, which are the funky-looking pipes that jut out near the summit ridge, in the middle of the start zone. This system has been used successfully in Wyoming on a similar line, Glory Bowl at Teton Pass. Stats for the biggest line at the pass are 1.7 miles point to point, 1,400' up for a 2,400' descent.

From the corner of the Stanley Slidepath Access, skin west southwest into the trees. Work your way up to the Southeast Ridge of Stanley Slidepath. The ridge is a good place to check out conditions and plan your line. The very upper section of the ridge is a bit convex and usually windswept; this is the most likely place for slab issues on the ascent.

The direct line is steep, especially at the top; the angle approaches 50 degrees. This is only for about a hundred feet. The line mellows out below there to the high 30s. At the bottom, as the line approaches the highway, the line splits. The skier's right option typically has more snow. Be sure to cross the road and walk down to the pullout when hitchhiking back up the pass, below the "Avalanche Zone: No Stopping" sign. This will also allow your driver to pull all the way off the road and not be threatened by the slide path.

17Wb – Berthoud Pass	No Name – UN12424

The peak isn't named on USGS topo maps, but its elevation is. The easiest way to get this one is from Berthoud Pass Summit. You could also get it done from the Pumphouse. The east bowl of No Name is called **Oatmeal Bowl**. The southeast ridge of No Name is called No Name Bench. If avy conditions are dicey, you can safely ski **No Name Bench**. Just be sure to stay on the lower-angled ridge proper.

From the summit parking lot, cross the highway and head up the skin-track. At the trees, the skin-track and boot-pack diverge; the skin-track goes into the woods, contouring at first and then heading up a steep section. After that the angle mellows out and the slope opens up as the route heads up the ridge to the weather station at the top of UN11963. Follow the ridge west and up Mount Russell. At the top of Mount Russell, walk around the ridge, along the Continental Divide to the summit of No Name. You will have plenty of time on your ascent of Russell to choose your line.

Going from Pumphouse involves touring through the woods to No Name Bench and then ascending to the summit of No Name. From there either ski Oatmeal Bowl or return the way you came down No Name Bench.

Stanley
Slide Path

"No Name"

Oatmeal Bowl

Russell Peak

"No Name"

The Waterfall

17Wc – Berthoud Pass　　　　　　　　**Russell Peak – UN12391**

The peak is named for William Hepburn Russell, who built the first six miles of the wagon road west out of Empire to Hoop Creek. It would take several more years before the wagon road would be completed over the Pass, according to Clear Creek County documents. The peak isn't named on USGS topo maps, but its elevation is. It has been called Mt. Russell for generations by the locals who love Berthoud Pass.

There are many lines that come off the flanks of Mt. Russell. From the summit parking lot, cross the highway and head up the skin-track. At the trees the skin-track and boot-pack diverge; the skin-track goes into the woods, contouring at first and then heading up a steep

Y Chute

Z Chute

section. After that the angle mellows out and the slope opens up as the route heads up the ridge to the weather station at the top of UN11963. Follow the ridge west and up Mt. Russell's East Ridge. As you approach the steep ridge, look left to check conditions of **The Waterfall Face** or look right near the top of Mt. Russell to check out the **North Chute.**

Ski whichever route looks better. The Waterfall Face is an early-in-the-morning line. The North Chute stays cooler longer. The Waterfall Face skis down to the Pumphouse Corner and combines well with No Name via No Name Bench. North Chute skis to Current Creek Corner and combines well with **X, Y, and Z Chutes**.

17Wd – Berthoud Pass	Mainline to The Roll

When people think of Berthoud Pass, this is the terrain they think of first. Access is super easy from the summit lot and you can get a lot of laps. Those laps are pretty short, but they are so much fun. It's only 700' of vertical to the weather station at the top of UN11963, and this is where I like to start skiing these lines. From viewer's left to right are **Great Divide, Triple Rock, Mustang, The Plunge, Lift Line, Gaffney's, Rush Chute, Nitro Cliffs** and **Chute,** and **The Roll.** All have the potential for slides, except Great Divide. There have been avy incidents in The Roll and the Nitro Cliffs. Ski back to the road or the base of the face and skin back for more. Alternatively, you can combine with a quick skate across the Aqueduct and ski the **80s** or **90s** down to Current Creek Corner.

Ascending the old Quicksilver Trail on the way to Hell's Half Acre one gets a nice view of the West Side.

Powder in Rush Chute
doesn't happen very often.
athlete: Doug Mock

The Roll delivers but is
steep enough to slide.

This is another classic zone at Berthoud Pass. One typically combines these lines with the Roll or Nitro but you can also access it from the highway just north of the summit. Hike along the road north to the first bend and look for the gate. Follow the trail beyond the gate to the snotel weather station. Then take the Berthoud Pass Ditch Aqueduct to the top of the **90s**, at the turn of the aqueduct. This is also the access for the **80s**; just drop in from the aqueduct corner and stay to skier's right. There are more than a few options if you follow the Aqueduct across the top of the **90s**; choose your line and have fun. These lines end up at the Current Creek Corner.

This was our third run of the day. Mother's Day 2015 in the 90s.
athlete: Frank Bowman

The Diving Board is one of the lines in the 90s.
athlete: Unknown

Looking north across upper Current Creek from the summit of Russell Peak.

17Wf – Berthoud Pass   **Current Creek**

This zone offers plenty of options. The previous route skis into Current Creek but is accessed from the Summit. **Tea Cup, Perfect Trees, Postage Stamp, Ten Little Indians,** and the **110s** are typically accessed from the Current Creek Corner. Current Creek Bench and the **XYZ Chutes** are accessed by going over the summit of Russell from the Summit Trailhead. Between the 90s and XYZ Chutes, **Skull Bite** is right off the ridge and the **100s** and **Weebles**, lower down. All of these routes lead to the Current Creek Corner unless you stop above the corner to get more laps in.

Current Creek is also the home of the classic Peter Rabbit Cabin. Though not the cleanest, this is a cool old cabin that is available on a first come, first served basis. Though I would probably forgo sleeping on the mattresses, there is room for about eight people or more if you want to get cozy. The hut has a wood stove that can be used as a cooking stove.

The classic Peter Rabbit Cabin. Somewhere in Current Creek.

Corner Pocket

Second Creek Ridge

Frankenstein

Second Creek

17Wg – Berthoud Pass　　　　　　　　**Second Creek**

Second Creek is the home of some decent lines as well as the Broome Hut. The steep lines off the ridge to the southwest of the hut are great test pieces. There have been some slide incidents, mainly when people push the limits and try to ski these lines too early in the season. **Corner Pocket** at the top of the 110s is a fun line in the low-40 degree range. Farther east along that ridge there are some excellent chutes that descend through the trees. The ridge that forms the north side of the Second Creek drainage offers easy access to the **Chimney Chute**; that line is on the other side of the ridge and skis into First Creek.

The Broome Hut is one of the newest huts in Colorado and is a very comfortable place to base out of. With all the short laps that Current, Second, First, and Zero Creeks provide, you can easily base at the hut and ski multiple laps all over the West Side.

Corner Pocket

Broome Hut

First Creek

Blown Edge on Second Creek
Ridge—filled in for once.

17Wh – Berthoud Pass	First Creek

Some of the gnarliest treed terrain at the pass is found in First Creek. **The Pillows** and **Chimney Chute** are super easy to access, either from the First Creek corner or from the other side of the ridge as described above. The Pillows are just east of Chimney Chute and have multiple mandatory airs in the 10' range. The landings are technical, meaning they are stop and drops, much like some of the more difficult lines at Crested Butte. Both of these lines offer about 700' of fun. Chimney Chute is a nice mid-40 degree chute through two rocky towers. Do not ascend the Chimney Chute; this is a really good way to get slid by parties dropping in above you. There is a slight dogleg in the chute so parties at the top can't see the entire chute; they will have no idea you're in there. Instead skin up through the trees to the east of the Pillows. Farther up First Creek is **The Headwall**. This is a very steep headwall line with a few turns in the low-50s over cliffs. Turn to skier's right to hit a short exit ramp.

Looking back up Chimney after skiing bumps down the line. This is a popular route.

Winter Park's
Panoramic Express Lift

Zero Creek

17Wi – Berthoud Pass — Zero Creek

This zone is best accessed from First Creek or from the top of Winter Park's Panoramic Express Lift. If coming from First Creek, take the northern drainage around **The Knob** and then head for the ridge separating First Creek and Zero Creek. From Winter Park, go out the snowcat gate and head east along the rope line to the top of **Zero Creek Bowl**.

Zero Creek Bowl.

This will put you at the top of Zero Creek Bowl, where there are plenty of options. At the bottom of the bowl, be sure to stay to skier's right. There is a fairly large cliff to skier's left. Once in the trees, follow the creek to Zero Creek Corner and stick out your thumb.

The entrance to Zero Creek Bowl.

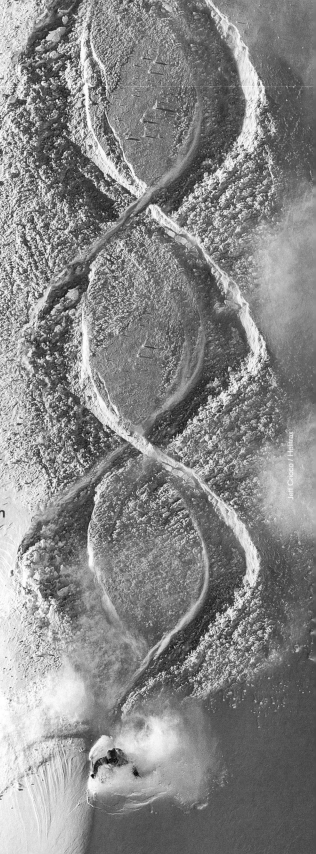

Snow Safety is in our DNA.

Snow safety is our specialty. We support all of our products with education and customer service.

Jeff Cricco / Helitrax

The most trusted name in backcountry safety.™

www.**backcountryaccess**.com

17 BERTHOUD PASS – EAST SIDE

The original Berthoud Pass Inn was located here, right in front of the current trail for Floral Park. This side tends to get a little less snow in the winter, with more wind. In the spring, the classic upslope storms typically favor this side. I prefer skiing this side, as a 450' ascent for a 1,000' lap makes me happy. You gotta love Floral Park. Ski good or eat wood. The Hell's Half Acre zone is also easy access and I like to save these lines for the afternoon when the traffic from Winter Park is returning to Denver over the pass. Mines 1 and 2 are covered in the Colorado Mines Peak section.

17Ea – Berthoud Pass	Floral Park Zone

One of my favorite zones in Colorado.

Fairway

Floral Park

Floral can be awesome.
athlete: Ellis Smith

As I mentioned in the opener of this section, this is one of my favorite zones at the pass. **Floral Park** holds loads of snow and usually starts skiing pretty well in December. It takes a fair amount of snow to cover all the buried logs so if you happen to find yourself here early in the season, use caution. The line descending to Floral Park corner from the summit lot is called **Telegraph**. The skin track starts up the Colorado Mines Peak Road and leaves the road at the first switchback. It's only 450' of vertical to get to the top of Floral Park. Once you get to the top of the trees, drop in here at the meadow. It's a 1,000' shot to the Floral Park Corner. For **The Fairway**, aka **Pauly's Powder Stash**, look to the rounded ridge past the

Floral Park meadow entrance. All of the lines coming off this ridge roll over to steep skiing. The Fairway is a chute that breaks the west aspect of this ridge. There are three entrances: the upper, middle, and lower; all see a lot of wind loading and, if they break, can cause some damage. If you get slid the length of the entire chute, you will get strained through the trees. The entrances are in the high-40 degree range, and the chute itself is in the mid 30 degree range. At the bottom, head to skier's right to avoid the masonry wall at the highway, as it's a big drop to flat.

17Eb – Berthoud Pass	Hell's Half Acre Zone

Like Floral Park, the Hell's Half Acre zone offers up about 1,000' of vertical for only 500' of gain; it's like a two-for-one sale at the mall. There is a great range of difficulty in this zone from tight intermediate trees to gnarly chutes and cliffs. Head up the old **Quicksilver Trail**, the left-most cut ski trail. Keep those boot-packs separate from the skin track, please. Get up to where the trees start to thin out—higher if it's covered—but the thinning trees are your marker for where to drop in. Drop into the northwest for intermediate lines like **Hell's Half Acre, Hanging Meadow,** and **Sentinel**. Drop in due north for advanced lines like **North Chute, The Knuckles,** and **The Fingers**. I like to save The Knuckles and The Fingers for the spring. I had an old friend get slid in The Knuckles back in the 90s, so it scares me. Whichever line you choose, ski down to the switchback to hitchhike back to the pass, or ski the Seven Mile Trail down to the lower switchback.

North Chute is steep and fun.
athlete: Allison Seymour

The west facing Knuckles can be
wind swept, faceted and rocky.

17Ec – Berthoud Pass   **Seven Mile Trail**

North of the warming hut is the longest run at the pass. The **Seven Mile Trail** isn't actually seven miles; it's only 2.2. It is almost seven miles to Winter Park, but the trail basically goes flat below the lower switchback. That's still pretty long for Colorado. This beginner-level trail reminds me of the old wooded trails of New England, the ones cut by the Civilian Conservation Corps back in the 1930s. There are usually plenty of bumps and jumps to have fun on as it twists its way through the woods. Finally it reaches the northernmost switchback of the pass. This trail is fun to ski after skiing Mines and is the exit route for Flora West.

Seven Mile is the mellowest
line in the book.

You get a great view of the upper line from the Grand County side of Berthoud Pass.

18 COLORADO MINES PEAK – 12,493'

The peak was named in honor of the university in Golden, Colorado in 1954. Colorado School of Mines students extensively studied the effects of glaciation on the peak's geography. The peak is just east of Berthoud Pass on the Continental Divide. As the access is from Berthoud Pass, one could consider this part of Berthoud Pass, although I generally like to cover peaks as peaks. The East Bowl is a serious section that doesn't really fall into the terrain that gets skied in the winter at Berthoud. Mines 1 and 2 also really shouldn't be treated as winter Berthoud Pass lines. There have been fatalities in Mines. Every year it goes big and my hope is that if it's separated from Berthoud in this book and talked about for the hazard it is, hopefully people will think a little harder before dropping into it too early in the season.

The top of the peak has multiple towers and buildings for who knows what. I wish one of them was a cell tower because it would be nice to have some coverage on the pass. I heard a rumor that one of the buildings was run by Homeland Security. Whatever the case, it's not the most wild and tranquil place, but given the right conditions, it is well worth the visit.

18a – Colorado Mines Peak	Mines 1 and 2	
DIFFICULTY: Advanced	DISTANCE: 2.8–3.4 Miles Roundtrip	VERTICAL: 750'–1,300' Up, 2,300'–2,800' Down
SUNHIT: Sunrise + 3 Hours	ASPECT: Northwest	SEASON: Spring
TRAILHEAD: Berthoud Pass Summit	MAP: Page 271	PHOTO: Page 129–130

This line was the site of a fatality back in 2005, along with numerous incidents over the years. The geography and loading patterns are basically perfect for slab formation and the grassy slopes at the top of the start zone are the perfect bed surface. Early season storms load up on even earlier season facets and bam, that's it. Once the slide gets going, you are looking at

The lower gully is a low-angled terrain trap.
Get through here quickly.

a 200 yard section of short Christmas trees just above the dogleg at the junction of Mines 1 and 2; I like to think of this section as the meat grinder. The feature that takes this line to the next level as far as threat is the easy access; if you forgo the summit it's only 750' of gain to get to the top of the line. The increased usage means that while you're in the line, you can expect groups of unknown experience levels dropping in on top of you. I save this line for the spring stabilization, without exception!

That being said, you have a couple of options. This is a route off Colorado Mines Peak so if you actually have enough snow, skin or hike the 1,300' to the summit. To locate the lines, drop in due north from the summit for Mines 2 and north northwest for Mines 1.

The trees at the bottom of the line just
above the junction of Mines 1 and 2.

Most of the time there isn't enough snow for a summit ski. In these instances, skin or hike up the old Quicksilver trail, the cut ski trail at viewer's left. As the trees begin to thin, follow the treeline on an ascending, northeasterly heading. This will put you at the top of Mines 1; Mines 2 is higher up and on the other side of the drainage past the stand of trees separating the two lines.

When the base is stable and you get a spring storm on top, this is one of the finest lines around. For Mines 1, drop into the line and ski about 400' of open slopes down to the Christmas trees. They're pretty open at first, then close out on the left. There is a lightly treed gully to skier's right that leads to the junction with Mines 2. Mines 2 lacks the Christmas trees and is narrower. There is a dogleg below the main chute and above the junction; this is a terrain trap. Wait, both lines—in their entirety—are terrain traps. Below the junction, the gully widens and develops steep walls, like a halfpipe. The angle here is pretty mellow. At the bottom of the gully, look for Seven Mile Trail and take it north to the lower switchback.

18b – Colorado Mines Peak	East Cirque	
DIFFICULTY: Expert	DISTANCE: 4.2 Miles Roundtrip	VERTICAL: 1,850' Up/ 3,400' Down
SUNHIT: Sunrise	ASPECT: Southeast	SEASON: Spring
TRAILHEAD: Berthoud Pass Summit	MAP: Page 271	PHOTO: Page 131–132, 250

The East Cirque of Colorado Mines is steep, sweet, and short. The main chutes are steep and tight and usually guarded by cornicing. Those cornices will have to be dealt with if you want to ski these lines. As this peak is lower than most, if you wait for the cornice to fall naturally, most likely the line will be melted out. This line is in the James Peak Wilderness, which seems strange with all the buildings on top of the mountain.

There are multiple options coming off
Colorado Mines Peak's east side.

An early sunhit and late start had us
taking a mellower line due to instability.
athlete: Allison Seymour

Skin or hike up the old Quicksilver trail, the left-most cut ski trail. Use the summit towers as your guide. At the top, approach the edge carefully; if the cornice breaks and you fall here, you may get taken over cliffs. Either cut the cornice over your intended line or accept the risk. Roping up is an option here if you don't want to jump in. The angle is more than 50 degrees and it stays steep through the chokes. The skier's rightmost line is the easiest and still has slopes over 50 degrees, though the choke is less intimidating.

The exit involves climbing back out and skiing Mines 1 or 2, or skiing the ridge and Quicksilver back to Berthoud Pass Summit. The best way to get back to the west side of the divide is to climb to the saddle north of the summit, north of the cornicing, and north of Blue Lake. From the saddle, drop in on a northwesterly heading to hook up with either Mines lines. Going back to the pass summit is a bit weird as you'll need to ski mostly across the hill to get back to the ridge. Once there, ski any of the lines on the ridge that end up at the summit lot.

19 MOUNT FLORA – 13,132'

This is the closest 13er to Berthoud Pass. With an easy trail and a short approach from the highway, this peak can get crowded. When I was here skiing the South Chute, there were close to 30 people on the summit; this was late in the spring, so the trail was clear. Flora is the 528th highest peak in the state. The peak was named by Dr. Charles C. Parry, the botanist who named many other peaks in the zone.

19a – Mount Flora	Flora Creek Bowl	
DIFFICULTY: Expert	**DISTANCE:** 4.6 Miles Roundtrip	**VERTICAL:** 2,000' Up/ 3,500' Down
SUNHIT: Sunrise + 3 Hours	**ASPECT:** West – Northwest	**SEASON:** Spring
TRAILHEAD: Berthoud Pass Summit	**MAP:** Page 271	**PHOTO:** Page 133–135

West-facing lines are difficult to get in good condition, due to the fact that they are usually windward and get stripped of snow by the prevailing winds. Most drainages aren't just west facing; they have different aspects that work their way around the drainage. Flora Creek has just such a scenario. The northwest-facing element of this drainage is actually a lee slope and sees lots of loading. The direct fall-line off the summit is more windward. The chute to skier's right (north) of the summit is windward, but its topography means that it does hold snow. It's all about the nuances. Angles reach to the high 40s in places. There is a serious issue to deal with on the exit to this line. The lower creek is a giant terrain trap. It

Check out conditions from the north side of Berthoud Pass on Highway 40.

gets very narrow and the walls are very steep, in the 50s. It's tough to traverse above these slopes, so you have to deal with the threat. Go one at a time and only attempt this line when the snowpack is stable. Triggered slides from below are the most dangerous slides. Doing so in a terrain trap makes it even more dangerous; hence the expert difficulty rating. Your assessment can't be wrong here.

Hike or skin up the old Quicksilver trail, initially heading for Colorado Mines Peak and then doing an ascending traverse to avoid the extra vertical gain. Aim for the saddle to the north of Colorado Mines Peak. There is a false summit and then the actual summit. The ridge is rolling terrain and the trail is very good and easy to follow.

At the summit, ski to the west and assess your options. You will see the ridge that forms the southern boundary of the Flora Creek drainage. This is where the powder will be if there is any. Fall-line west is the mellowest entrance. To skier's right there is a chute that is often filled in. You can check conditions from near the First Creek Trailhead and at other points along US 40.

The viewer's right line in Flora Creek Bowl is in the high-30 to low-40 degree range.

Things mellow out for the base of the zone above treeline. Initially the trees are pretty mellow; when they get steeper, think about which side of the creek you want to be on. The north-facing side is the place to be if it's sunny. If it's not too hot, the south-facing slope can be the way to go. Either side will eventually put you down into the creek. Ski one at a time, and ski fast through this very dangerous section. It helps to have radios to assist with communication. Be sure to have skins on this line if you have to go back uphill to perform a rescue. Flora Creek meets up with Seven Mile Trail. Take a right at that trail to ski to the northernmost switchback on Berthoud Pass.

The upper part of Flora Creek Bowl is super fun; the lower section is a scary terrain trap.

19b – Mount Flora	Northeast Bowls	
DIFFICULTY: Expert	DISTANCE: 7.3 Miles Roundtrip	VERTICAL: 3,800' Up, 5,300' Down
SUNHIT: Sunrise	ASPECT: Northeast	SEASON: Spring
TRAILHEAD: Berthoud Pass Summit	MAP: Page 271	PHOTO: Page 135–136

The Northeast Bowls are short, steep and sweet; at least the upper bowls are, directly off the divide. You can extend the fun by skiing down to near Bill Moore Lake. Berthoud Pass is the only real option to approach this peak. You could get to the Northeast Bowls via the 4x4 road to Bill Moore Lake, but by the time this road is clear, there usually isn't very much skiing left. So if you want this line you will need to climb back out and return to US 40 via either Flora Creek, the approach trail or the Mines lines. This line is in the James Peak Wilderness.

Hike or skin up the old Quicksilver trail, initially heading for Colorado Mines Peak and then doing an ascending traverse to avoid the extra vertical gain. Aim for the saddle to the north of Colorado Mines Peak. There is a false summit and then the actual summit. The ridge is rolling terrain and the trail is very good and easy to follow.

Summit

The next bowl to the north has some nice options.

From the summit, head northeast to access the bowls. If you go along the ridge you can access other entrances. The next bowl to the north, after a short ascent, is also a fun ski. Most years, all these lines are guarded by overhanging cornices. Unlike the lines on Colorado Mines most of the cornices don't threaten choked out, cliffy terrain. Not that getting taken out by a cornice fall in open terrain is any less painful; at least you're not dealing with getting taken off a cliff. Cut the cornice, wait for it to fall naturally, or accept the substantial risk of skiing under the cornice. The upper bowl of the main line skis down to Edith Lake and offers 600' of vertical. Stay to skier's right of Edith Lake to get the next section down to Byron Lake. Below Byron there is a nice steep, rocky section.

Once you get down to the valley, return to Flora via the path of least resistance. Ascend back to Byron Lake and then ascend the East Ridge of Flora. From there either combine with Flora Creek or hike back along the trail to the Mines lines or Berthoud Pass Summit. The distance measure in the route stats reflects a ski of Flora Creek as your exit.

Both bowls seen from near the summit of Witter Peak.

Flora
Summit

1,700' of perfect corn skiing right from the summit of Flora.

19c – Mount Flora	South Chute	
DIFFICULTY: Advanced–Expert	**DISTANCE: 5.6 Miles Roundtrip**	**VERTICAL: 3,800' Up, 5,300' Down**
SUNHIT: Sunrise + 2 Hours	**ASPECT: South**	**SEASON: Spring**
TRAILHEAD: Berthoud Pass Summit	**MAP: Page**	**PHOTO: Page**

This is a really sweet corn ski. When I got it done, the timing was perfect and the corn was a few inches deep. At about 1,700' it was a leg burner because it was just too awesome to stop skiing. Once you are done you have to return to the west side of the divide. Access via Mad Creek is possible but I've never done it that way and can't speak to those details. This line is in the James Peak Wilderness, while Flora Creek isn't.

Looking down the line.
Keep an eye on the small cornice.

A look back at one of the finest corn runs in this book.

Hike or skin up the old Quicksilver trail, initially heading for Colorado Mines Peak and then do an ascending traverse to avoid the extra vertical gain. Aim for the saddle to the north of Colorado Mines Peak. There is a false summit and then the actual summit. The ridge is very easy, rolling terrain and the trail is very good and easy to follow.

To locate the line, drop in on a southerly heading. Some years a cornice develops at the top of this line. By early June it's usually rounded off from natural cornice fall and melting. Ski the low-30 to low-40 degree chute as far down as the snow allows. The angle and aspect are perfect for corn snow harvesting.

At the bottom, boot back up the chute, and stay near the margins to reduce your chance of getting slid from above should another group or solar action trigger a slide. Be aware of what's going on above you while you're climbing back up. At the top of Flora again, choose Flora Creek for an expert selection, or ski Mines or return to Berthoud Pass Summit for intermediate selections.

20 WITTER PEAK – 12,884'

I researched the naming history for this one for a while; I didn't find much. There are three places in Colorado named Witter: this peak, Witter Gulch, and the Jake Witter Mine. One can only assume that it's named for Jake Witter; too bad the decision card isn't preserved in the Board of Geographic Names database. The reason I cared so much was because the line I skied and the other line I wanted to ski, which is in the teaser section, are so awesome. The peak doesn't muster enough vertical above its saddle with Mount Eva to have an official rank, but it ranks as awesome in my book.

20a – Witter Peak	Welcome Couloir	
DIFFICULTY: Expert	DISTANCE: 3.1 Miles Roundtrip	VERTICAL: 2,400'
SUNHIT: Sunrise	ASPECT: Northeast	SEASON: Spring
TRAILHEAD: Fall River Reservoir	MAP: Page 273	PHOTO: Page 139–140

Rising over Sherwin Lake, east of the divide, this line is very aesthetic. Being on the east side of the divide is great for this route's snowpack development. You can usually get pretty far up Rainbow Road, close to the Fall River Reservoir trailhead, while the snow is still good in the line. If you can't get all the way, walk or skin the remainder. You can check conditions of the line from the Genesee bridge view on I-70. The Chinns Lake Road is a shorter approach but it holds snow longer in the spring, so the main Fall River Trailhead is actually easier. This line is in the James Peak Wilderness.

Looking down from the entrance to the Welcome Couloir.

The steppe below the line makes for a nice bivy spot.

From the Fall River Reservoir, hike or skin south, uphill to Chinns Lake. Skirt the north side of Chinns Lake to get to Sherwin Lake. Head around Sherwin Lake after you decide which line you want to tackle. Ascend the one that suits you. There are numerous choices; viewer's left is the cleanest. Head up the North Ridge for some fun rocky scrambling. The other lines end at a ledge so they are more serious. At the top of the face, head for the summit, which is the second hump.

Ski the line of your choosing. The angle reaches the low-50s to skier's left and at the very top of all the lines. Return the way you came. This line combines very well with Eva's Southeast Bowl.

oking over at Eva from the
mmit of Witter in the spring..

Mount
Eva

Parry
Peak

Mount
Bancroft

21 MOUNT EVA – 13,130'

"Charles Christopher Parry, 1823-1890, was a highly respected doctor, explorer, and naturalist; a member of the Mexican Boundary Survey (1849-1852); the first botanist in the United States Department of Agriculture (1869-1871); and an acclaimed botanical collector and taxonomist in the mid-west, Colorado, and other western states for forty-eight years… On and off for twenty years, Parry spent his summers in a cabin at the base of Grays and Torrey's peaks. He named not only these two peaks but many others, including Mount Eva (for his wife), Engelmann Peak, James Peak, Mount Guyot, Mount Flora, and Parry's Peak." The info comes from William Weber's book, *King of Colorado Botany, Charles Christopher Parry.*

This zone of the Front Range has been called the "Botany Peaks."

21a – Mount Eva	Southeast Bowl	
DIFFICULTY: Advanced	DISTANCE: 4.2 Miles Roundtrip	VERTICAL: 2,400'
SUNHIT: Sunrise	ASPECT: Southeast	SEASON: Spring
TRAILHEAD: Fall River Reservoir	MAP: Page 273	PHOTO: Page 141–142

This line is in the James Peak Wilderness. From the south side of the Fall River Reservoir dam, head west around the lake to a gully about two-thirds from the west end. Go up the gully or up the trees to the side of the gully. Heading up here is easier than going up around Chinns Lake and then around Sherwin Lake as there are a lot of glacial knobs to deal with. This way you will only need to deal with the zone around Slater Lake. Once past Slater, negotiate the willows, which aren't too awful. The peak is to viewer's right of the saddle, at the head of the valley. Head for this saddle to avoid the cornice if needed. Then head up the ridge on a northerly route to the summit. Near the summit is a cool, shiny metal building.

Early season view from the summit of Mount Eva .

The direct line off the summit is steep—in the high-40s—and is guarded by a cornice, as all the lines east of the divide seem to be. Navigate the cornice or ski the ridge to a more reasonable entrance. Follow your ascent back to the trailhead. Combine with Witter's Welcome Couloir.

22 PARRY PEAK – 13,391'

Though not noted in the USGS information, according to www.swcoloradowildflowers.com, the peak is named for Charles Christopher Parry (1823-1890), a highly respected doctor, explorer, and naturalist; a member of the Mexican Boundary Survey (1849-1852); and the first botanist in the United States Department of Agriculture (1869-1871); He named not only these two peaks but many others, including Mount Eva, Engelmann Peak, James Peak, Mount Guyot, Mount Flora, and Parry's Peak. I must say I have a hard time believing he named a peak after himself. The info comes from William Weber's book, *King of Colorado Botany, Charles Christopher Parry*.

This zone of the Front Range has been called the "Botany Peaks." The other Parry Peak was named after him as well; that peak is in the Sawatch.

Parry's South Face from the summit of Mount Bancroft.

22a – Parry Peak	South Face	
DIFFICULTY: **Advanced**	DISTANCE: **3.8 Miles Roundtrip**	VERTICAL: **3,600'**
SUNHIT: **Sunrise**	ASPECT: **Southeast – South**	SEASON: **Spring**
TRAILHEAD: **Fall River Reservoir**	MAP: **Page 273**	PHOTO: **Page 143–144, 147**

Here's a great way to get the highest point of the James group of four 13ers—five if you include Bancroft, which is unranked. James gets the wilderness area name, the group name, and all the hype. Why? Because James' East Cirque is amazing. This line is in the James Peak Wilderness. Access is easy and the skiing isn't very complicated. Make your way to the north side of Fall River Reservoir's dam and hike or skin around the lake. Before you get to the inlet on the other side, head west up the valley. Once past the initial steep, the angle eases and the

The South Face has steep
and mellow options.

Early season condition
on the South Fac

trees give way, giving you a great view of your options. You have the direct southeast-facing option, the saddle gully, and the rock chutes on the Bancroft side of the saddle; as the latter are closer to Parry, they are here, too. Head up the saddle gully to the summit. Ski the line of your choice and either return to Fall River or combine with Eva's Southeast Face and return to Fall River Reservoir via the Slater Lake gully.

22b – Parry Peak	The Bear Claw	
DIFFICULTY: Advanced	**DISTANCE:** 6.5 Miles Roundtrip	**VERTICAL:** 4,200'
SUNHIT: Sunrise + 3 Hours	**ASPECT:** West	**SEASON:** Spring
TRAILHEAD: Parry Creek	**MAP:** Page 273	**PHOTO:** Page 145–146

James may have all the names and adulation, but Parry has the big line. There aren't many lines that are over 4,000' in this book; in fact there aren't any others. There are some bigger verticals, but these are mostly approaches. The Bear Claw is a classic and the fact that it isn't in every year makes it that much better. You need a decent snow year or at least a decent spring with plenty of upslope storms to load this face up.

From the pull-off at the trailhead, go around the gate and up the road 50 feet. Turn right onto a path, and follow this to a good spot to cross the Fraser River. Get on the Denver Water Road and head south. Go east around the water diversion project. Come to a clearing and enter the woods on the southeast side of it. The first creek you come to in the woods is Parry Creek. Follow the creek up to a small meadow. From here take the climber's left fork and make your way up to the North Ridge of Parry. Follow the ridge to the summit.

Ascending the North Ridge
is the way to go.

The Bear Claw is one of the finest and
biggest vertical lines in the book.

There are a few chutes or claws that cut their way through the face. I hope you picked yours on the way up the ridge. If you ski the summit line, you'll get a nice upper section in the low 40s followed by an occasional rock choke, which in the low 50s. There is a good step around if you don't want to go air it; it's about 15' but the landing is steep. The chute opens up below here and then the apron is nice and long. Whatever line you ski, head to skier's left at the bottom to get a little more open skiing before entering the trees. On aerial photos this section looks really tight, but there is plenty of room for turns. You can ski all the way down to the water diversion project at the Fraser River. Cross it and make for the highway or follow your track from the ascent.

The direct summit "Claw" has a choke that's in the mid-50 degree range and is often rocky.

Bancroft viewed from the Genesee Bridge on
terstate 70. A great place to check conditions.

Parry Peak

Mount Bancroft

23 MOUNT BANCROFT – 13,250'

This peak was named in 1906 for local miner George J. Bancroft at the suggestion of acting governor Jesse Fuller McDonald. The peak was previously known as Lomands Mountain, Millars Mountain, and Perry Peak. It's interesting that Perry Peak was one of the previous local names even though the decision card was from before Parry Peak was named. To me this is the fifth 13er of the James group; it's the unranked peak but it's also not that interesting from a skier's point of view.

23a – Mount Bancroft	Caroline Bowl	
DIFFICULTY: Intermediate	DISTANCE: 6.4 Miles Roundtrip	VERTICAL: 3,000'
SUNHIT: Sunrise	ASPECT: Southeast	SEASON: Spring
TRAILHEAD: Steuart Road	MAP: Page 273	PHOTO: Page 147–148

You can get a great look at the condition on this line from the Genesee bridge view on Interstate 70. From the trailhead, skin or hike up Steuart Road; you can follow the road all the way to Loch Lomond. Avoid the temptation to make for the ridge directly instead of going all the way to the lake; the lower section of the ridge is a start zone with some terrain traps. There is an old road that goes up the ridge from the Loch, which is much easier and safer. Follow the East Ridge to the summit.

Be sure to look at Caroline Bowl on your way up the ridge to plan your descent. Straight down to the lake is easiest. If you head north along the ridge, there is some spicier skiing. Ski around Lake Caroline and enjoy another fun steep shot on your way down to Loch Lomond. From there, follow the road back to the car. Don't forget to wax to make the exit skating a little faster.

Early season snow on a very windy epic.
athlete: Brian Lindahl

24 JAMES PEAK – 13,294'

The following is a quote taken from *King of Colorado Botany: Charles Christopher Parry, 1823-1890* by William A. Weber: "Thanks to Parry, the region of Upper Clear Creek commemorates several great botanical personalities of his time. The ridge of the Continental Divide north from Empire has as one anchor James Peak—for Edwin James, botanist with the Long Expedition, named by Dr. Charles Christopher Parry." Though the rank is only the 405th highest, James is a magnificent peak with a stunning East Cirque and an equally impressive West Face. This peak isn't just about gnarly faces; there are moderate lines and easy access so everyone can enjoy this beautiful summit. The James Peak Wilderness is a special place. Treat it with love for our future generations.

24a – James Peak	Southeast Slopes and St. Mary's Glacier	
DIFFICULTY: Intermediate	DISTANCE: 2.3–7.5 Miles Roundtrip	VERTICAL: 1,100'–2,900'
SUNHIT: Sunrise	ASPECT: Southeast – East	SEASON: Winter – Spring
TRAILHEAD: St. Mary's Glacier	MAP: Page 273	PHOTO: Page 149–150

This zone has a long history of skiing. Above the lower parking lot are the remnants of the St. Mary's Ski Area. This isn't the zone covered in this section, but it is covered nicely in *Powder Ghost Towns* by Peter Bronski. The treed lines offer about 700' of vertical. The ski area closed in 1986 but the bull wheel of the lift still remains, just south of the parking lot. The actual glacier is what I'm covering as well as using that access for a moderate descent of James Peak. Whether St. Mary's Glacier is actually a glacier has been the source of some debate. There's no doubt that it was a glacier; a river of ice moving forward. Then it became a remnant glacier, with ice in retreat. At this point, with all of the melting and having looked at recent satellite photos, I'd say it has reached the permanent snowfield stage: the stage of no movement.

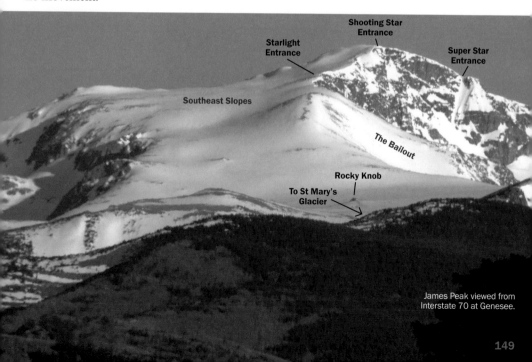

Shooting Star Entrance

Starlight Entrance

Super Star Entrance

Southeast Slopes

The Bailout

Rocky Knob

To St Mary's Glacier

James Peak viewed from Interstate 70 at Genesee.

Starting at either parking lot, walk to the old 4x4 road that is the St. Mary's Glacier Trail. Head up the trail a little more than 0.1 mile and take the left trail at the junction. A few hundred feet past this there is another junction; take this left too. A little over 0.3 mile up there is a maze of trails as you approach St. Mary's Lake; at this point just head north and you will reach the lake. At the lake, hike around the east side; there is a bridge to cross the outlet. Follow the trail past the bridge and hike up to the base of the glacier. Either climb up the snow or follow the trail to the north side flank. About 1.1 miles from the road you will reach the top of the snow of the glacier. Ski here or continue upward for the summit of James Peak. If you are continuing onward, hike along the trail that ascends from the top of the glacier. This trail comes to a road. Cross it, leaving the trail momentarily. You will regain the trail and make your way up the Southeast Slopes. Follow the trail to the summit.

If you summited, then ski your ascent route back to the glacier. Use care if you venture near the East Cirque, as the drop-off is pretty huge. The Southeast Slopes offer mid-20 degree slopes with a few rollovers that are steeper. You could ski this line in the winter and not have much avalanche hazard to deal with, except for getting up the initial steeps of the glacier. From the summit, ski down to the glacier and then down to the lake. If you lose the trail, use the rocky knob to the north of the glacier as a reference. Initially the glacier is pretty flat. To skier's left it stays mellow to the lake. The farther to skier's right you go, the steeper it gets, all the way to the chutes above the lake. Fatalities have occurred here in the past, most recently just this past season. The lake is a terrain trap that will see deeper debris. I'd save the lines above the lake for the spring. On the trail back to the road, if you are skiing, take it easy. This is one of the busiest trails in the Front Range—it's got an exit sign on the interstate.

The trail goes around the right side of the photo.

24b – James Peak	East Cirque	
DIFFICULTY: Advanced to Expert	DISTANCE: 7.6 Miles Roundtrip	VERTICAL: 4,000'
SUNHIT: Sunrise	ASPECT: Northeast – Southeast	SEASON: Spring
TRAILHEAD: St. Mary's Glacier	MAP: Page 273	PHOTO: Page 149, 151–153

When people think of James Peak, this is the zone they are referring to. There are some very tough lines in the East Cirque of James. There are also a lot of them: **Shooting Star, Super Star, Starlight, Starbright, Sky Pilot, One Star, Bailout, Lake Chutes,** and **Lake Bowl**. I've skied a few of them and had a super close call in Shooting Star. I discuss that incident in the Cornices section of the introduction. I was going to put each of the routes that I haven't skied in the teaser section, but will add them here to complete the topo photo for beta.

All these lines are spring lines. With an east-facing exposure, starts need to be early to avoid avalanche hazard. This peak sees more visitors than most, so expect people to be above you when you're in your line. Many of the lines have cornices that threaten them. This is a recipe for potential disaster, so minimizing your time spent in harm's way is a key to success. That being said, it's best to approach these lines from above, provided you have beta on conditions. Access the mountain from the St. Mary's Trailhead. Above the glacier, hit the road and make for the East Ridge's edge. The first hump you encounter on the ridge is the entrance for **Bailout**. This can be used to ski down to James Peak Lake. The angle is in the low-40s on average and it's pretty long at 1,300' of vertical to the lake.

Above this hump, the next line you will come to is **Starlight**. This line is steeper for longer and is much narrower; it's about 10' wide at its narrowest. The angle is in the mid-40s to the apron and there is a steep entrance in the low-50s.

The next line up the ridge is **One Star**. This is an exception to the climbing rule as the entrance is in the 60 degree range, so you should climb it from the bottom, or just rappel into it. The entrance to the bottom is at the base of Starlight. The couloir snakes its way up and gets steeper as you go. Go as high as you like.

Back on the ridge the next line is **Sky Pilot**. You can check conditions of this dangerous line from Genesee on I-70. It is the band of snow that cuts across almost the entire East Face. Many people ski this mistaking it for Shooting Star. The line has multiple 50 degree pitches, all of which are off fall-line. The fall-line leads to the cliffs below. This is an extreme line; if you fall, you will most likely die.

Just below the summit you'll come to **Shooting Star**. This line is threatened by multiple cornices, both above the main couloir and from Super Star. The entrance is steep and tight, around 50 degrees. The rest of the chute is in the high-40s with a few steeper sections along the way. The narrowest section is about 10' wide. This opens up past the choke. All of this upper section is over a cliff. It's only the bottom third that is clear of this hazard. The line has a mild dogleg over the cliff, and then ends at the junction with Super Star Couloir. Below this is the apron for some more steep vertical, but at least it is wide open. Combined vertical for the line, the couloir, and the apron is 1,300'. You can gain 700' more vertical by skiing down to James Peak Lake; a little more if you ski the Lake Chutes option.

Northeast from the summit is the entrance to **Super Star**, the cirque's test piece. The entrance is usually guarded by a massive cornice. Most people rappel into this line. The slopes below the cornice are in the high 50s and the line is 50 degrees average to the junction with Shooting Star. Below that is a fun apron that stays pretty steep.

The spine that creates the skier's left side of Super Star is also the skier's right side of **Starbright**. This is a much easier line than Super Star. It's the northern-most line on the East Face proper. It still has an entrance that is in the 50s and high to mid-40 degree skiing the rest of the way. It's a 1,000' shot of mostly moderate goodness.

Shooting Star's entrance from just below the summit.
This route is threatened by cornice for almost it's entire length.

Gary Fondl's POV
in Starlight Couloi.r

Off the main east lines are the **Lake Chutes** and **Lake Bowl**. The Lake Chutes descend off the rib separating the Bailout from Starlight, above James Peak Lake. Since these routes aren't usually corniced and most likely won't have people above them, they are best ascended from the lake. Some of them are very twisty and benefit from route finding by boot-pack. Some of these lines are in the mid-50s and over cliffs. They offer about 750' of vertical.

Lake Bowl is the 1,200' line coming off of the north ridge of the drainage. The angle here is pretty moderate, in the low 40 degree range. This bowl makes for a fun evening option if staying overnight at James Peak Lake.

For the exit, ski down to James Peak Lake and ascend the Bailout. Aim for the climber's left top out. Alternatively you can climb up Starlight. From there, locate the rocky knob to the north of the glacier trail and then on down to the St. Mary's Glacier. Check the route description for descent options around St. Mary's Lake.

24c – James Peak	West Couloir	
DIFFICULTY: Advanced	DISTANCE: 8 Miles Roundtrip	VERTICAL: 4,300'
SUNHIT: Sunrise + 4 Hours	ASPECT: West	SEASON: Spring
TRAILHEAD: Jim Creek	MAP: Page 273	PHOTO: Page 154–156

Of all the lines this spring, this was one of the coolest. We had no information, not even from the internet, and it took three trips to get it done. The first was a recon trip, but we got snowed out and only saw the bottom few hundred feet of the line. For the second attempt, the sun was blocked by a lenticular and we didn't want to ski it in icy conditions. The third time was the charm and we got perfect corn. If Parry's Bear Claw is in, then this line should be too. You can see the upper portion from Fraser, but the high walls of the couloir block a view of the lower section. Though the day is over 4,300', the west face is only 2,500' of it. There is plenty of skiing below that; but Parry's Bear Claw keeps its title as the longest ski in the book.

Follow the Jim Creek trail up through the drainage. At about the 1.5 mile mark you will reach the base of the Y Gully of "Heartbeat Peak"; this line is in the teaser section. The skinning is easier on the east side of the creek, so cross here. Be aware of the slopes above you as you work

The West Face of James Peak seen from Fraser.

The West Face of James Peak seen from Parry Peak.

Above the West Couloir and approaching the Northwest Ridge.

The West Couloir of James Peak.

your way up to the base of the line. There is a mining claim at the base of the couloir and "no trespassing" signs. To avoid this, do an ascending contour to the base across the top of treeline; this track and lot are marked on the topo map. Switch to boots and climb the couloir. It snakes its way up the face and you can't really see all of it from this side of the creek. The couloir is moderate in steepness with a 40 degree average angle and a couple chokes in the high-40s. At the top of the couloir, things open up a bit. You'll then get to a snowfield that leads around, to climber's right, to the summit pitch. This section has a choke in the 50s and isn't always in. Alternately you can ascend to the summit via the North Slopes.

For your descent, follow your ascent route. When you pop out at the bottom stay high, to skier's right, to milk the open slopes and hopefully ski-walk less. Be mindful of those slopes above you, especially if the temps are rising. Below the Y Gully of "Heartbeat Peak," expect to do a lot of skating.

Just above the choke of the West Couloir.
athlete: Scott Edlin

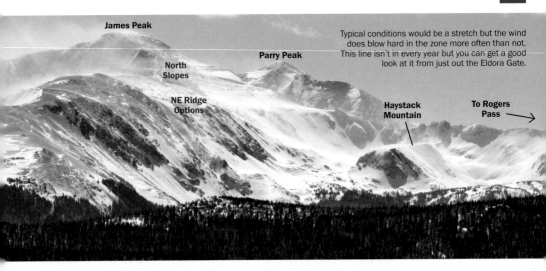

James Peak

North Slopes

Parry Peak

NE Ridge Options

Haystack Mountain

To Rogers Pass →

Typical conditions would be a stretch but the wind does blow hard in the zone more often than not. This line isn't in every year but you can get a good look at it from just out the Eldora Gate.

24d – James Peak	North Slopes	
DIFFICULTY: Intermediate	**DISTANCE:** 10 Miles Roundtrip	**VERTICAL:** 4,500'
SUNHIT: Sunrise + 1 Hour	**ASPECT:** North	**SEASON:** Winter – Spring
TRAILHEAD: Moffat Tunnel	**MAP:** Page 273	**PHOTO:** Page 157–158

This is a great route for a winter ascent of a 13er. At 4,500' this is one of the biggest days, vertically speaking. However, the actual North Slopes of James are only 1,900' of vertical. The approach is skiable, but it's a beginner run to the confluence with the creek coming down from Clayton Lake. Below that, it's mostly ski walking. At the Moffat Tunnel, if you hear a high-pitched whine, it is the exhaust fan for the tunnel and that means a train is coming through soon. Stick around and watch—it's kind of cool.

Great chutes on the Continental Divide between James Peak and Rogers Pass.

From the Moffat Tunnel, hike or skin up the South Boulder Creek Trail. You'll want to stay on this trail at all of the trail junctions. If you lose the trail, just follow South Boulder Creek. As you near treeline at about 3.5 miles, just below Rogers Lake, head southwest; keep the Northeast Ridge of James close at hand and keep Haystack on your right. Take this drainage up to the lake. From here you are right on the edge of avalanche terrain, with the lower section having a few start zones. Choose your line carefully and ascend the North Slopes to the summit.

You can either ski the North Slopes directly or find more challenging angles to skier's left, down the ridge toward the saddle. This zone is high-40 degree terrain. Another option lies off the north side of the Northeast Ridge. This 1,100' 40 degree gully can be reached by traversing the Northeast Ridge after you ski the upper North Slopes. From here, ski back down the trail. In spring, you can combine with Haystack by ascending from the lake. Go up the south side of the peak, the saddle to the west of Haystack is the easiest approach. You can also combine with the Iceberg and Crater Couloirs; going across the divide is the easiest way to combine these, via Rogers Pass.

A couloir wonderland as viewed from Byers Peak.

UN12393
Summit

25 UN12393 – 12,393'

This ridge summit has been in my sights for years; this year I got it, and I'm glad I did. Located just south of Byers Peak, the condition of it can be seen from Fraser. The north-facing lines look so good from here. They look even better from the top or from Byers Peak. There are multiple options cascading off the ridge. The summit line is the most serious, and the line it meets up with is nearly as steep.

25a – UN12393	Iron Creek Couloirs	
DIFFICULTY: **Advanced to Expert**	DISTANCE: **5 Miles Roundtrip**	VERTICAL: **2,900'**
SUNHIT: **Sunrise**	ASPECT: **North – Northeast**	SEASON: **Spring**
TRAILHEAD: **Iron Creek**	MAP: **Page 272**	PHOTO: **Page 159–160, 162**

The north-facing lines that come off this ridge are sweet, steep, and plentiful. Averaging about 1,600' and in the high 40s, they are worth a visit. If you like steep lines and spend any time in Fraser, you know these lines exist because you always look at them instead of Byers Peak.

Make your way to the Iron Creek Trailhead, either by driving or by riding your bike or hiking if the road is still closed. It will be easier to get this line if the trees down low still have snow and are skinable. There is a

The access to the East Ridge of UN12393.

One of many fine lines a couple miles from the road.

lot of deadfall to deal with for this bushwhack. From the water diversion project, hike or skin up the north side of Iron Creek. There is an old trail here; it is worth finding as it's so much easier than bushwhacking. The trail eventually peters out. Make your way up valley to the base of the East Ridge of UN12393. Either ascend the ridge here or work the margins of treeline to get to the base of the line you want to ascend. As there are multiple options going across, the bottom is a good way to see what your options are. Climb it to the summit.

The skiing reminds me a bit of "Big Eyes" on Red Peak in the Gore, only this zone is a little shorter and has almost no approach. It also sees almost no activity, so crossing tracks isn't likely. Combine this line with Byers Southeast Gully. Return the way you came. Hopefully there is enough snow through the trees that you don't have to deal with all the deadfall.

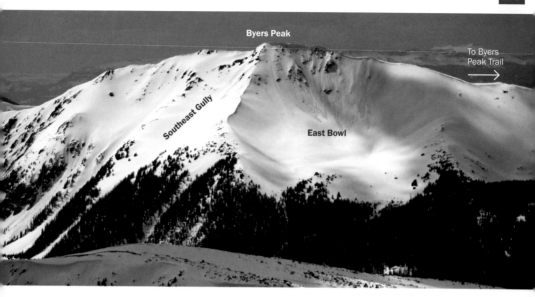

Byers Peak

Southeast Gully

East Bowl

To Byers
Peak Trail

26 BYERS PEAK – 12,804'

The peak was named for Rocky Mountain News founder William N. Byers in 1959 to honor the 100th anniversary of the paper. Byers for many years owned a homestead ranch near Hot Sulphur Springs, north of his peak in Middle Park. Byers was an active mountaineer. He climbed the peak named for him during the last few years of his life, and was in the first ascent party of Longs Peak. The monarch of Middle Park with a prominence of 226 largest can be seen from Fraser to Granby. It ranks as the 778th highest in the state.

26a – Byers Peak	East Bowl	
DIFFICULTY: Advanced	DISTANCE: 11.8 Miles Roundtrip	VERTICAL: 4,900'
SUNHIT: Sunrise	ASPECT: East	SEASON: Spring
TRAILHEAD: Deadhorse or Byers Peak	MAP: Page 272	PHOTO: Page 161–162

This is the classic line on Byers, not so much because it's the best line but because you can see it from Fraser. Ski what you see, the old adage goes. Many locals see this line as a rite of spring. Because the road opens later, some people resort to riding their bikes to the Byers Peak Trailhead via St. Louis Creek Road. This is actually more work than going up from Deadhorse Creek. Either way you do it, reach the upper Byers Peak Trailhead and head up to the North Ridge via the Byers Peak Trail. If there is snow, just take a southwest heading to gain the ridge at treeline. If the snow has melted, take the trail. The East Bowl is actually a couple of

The Northeast Ridge at treeline. East Bowl is to the left of the ridge. Beware of cornices.

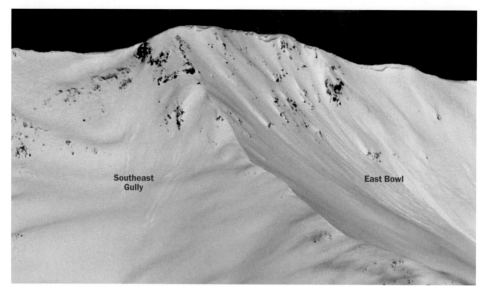

bowls. The first one you will see at treeline. This bowl drains into Byers Creek and has slopes in the mid-30s with a short, steeper entrance in the 40s. The second bowl is the summit bowl. This drains into Iron Creek and is guarded by a massive cornice. Skin and hike along the ridge to the summit unless your plan is to ski the first bowl. Stay clear of the edge as the cornice is usually overhanging and is over 60+ degree slopes.

For the summit line, you can find a steep entrance that is cornice-free at the rib separating the Southeast Gully and the East Bowl. Drop in here and ski mid-40 degrees slopes for the upper portion of the 1,400' bowl. At the bottom, skin north over the ridge separating the two East Bowls. Cross the bottom of the bowl and make your way back up to the trail at the ridge. Due to snowmobile compaction, you can often ski the Byers Peak trail all the way back to the Deadhorse Creek Trailhead; this is why it's easier to go for this summit from here. This line can also be combined with the Southeast Gully and an exit out Iron Creek.

Southeast
Gully

26b – Byers Peak	Southeast Gully	
DIFFICULTY: Advanced	DISTANCE: 5.4 Miles Roundtrip	VERTICAL: 3,400'
SUNHIT: Sunrise	ASPECT: Southeast	SEASON: Spring
TRAILHEAD: Iron Creek	MAP: Page 272	PHOTO: Page 161–163

This is one of the Front Range's rare 2,000'+ lines, though it isn't my favorite for the peak. It can get hot fast on this line as it did for my descent. At 2,300' of quality vertical before entering the trees, the consequences for having this line slide are huge; the Christmas trees at the bottom will punish those who err here. I approached this line from the Byers Peak Trail but have to say that the Iron Creek approach is easier. This line can be combined with the East Bowl route as the second line and the exit.

From the water diversion project, skin or hike up the north side of Iron Creek. There is an old trail here; find it to avoid some of the headaches of all the deadfall. Follow the creek to the base of the Southeast Gully. Skin up the trees to climber's right of the gully. This will lead to the East Ridge of Byers and a clean entrance to the summit.

Summit Crux

Drop into the upper Southeast Gully. You do not want to fall here as you will go over a cliff. To skier's right there is a break in the summit cliff. This is a very short 50 degree section and the choke is very narrow at about 7 feet. Once below the choke, things open up. The snow to skier's right will be softer as it is more east facing. Stay left for firmer snow. There is the main gully below you or you can find a couple more gullies to skier's right; you'll need to do some serious traversing to get them, though. The lower section of the mainline offers the classic: gully Christmas trees or meat grinder. Do not get slid on this line. Once you make it to treeline, deal with the trees back to the road. This line combines very well with the Iron Creek Couloirs.

26c – Byers Peak	West Gully	
DIFFICULTY: Advanced	DISTANCE: 6.8 Miles Roundtrip	VERTICAL: 5,200'
SUNHIT: Sunrise	ASPECT: Southeast & West	SEASON: Spring
TRAILHEAD: Iron Creek, Byers Peak or Deadhorse	MAP: Page 272	PHOTO: Page 164–164

This is my favorite line on Byers Peak. I did this route as a part of an overnight to ski Bill's North Face. I got it with a foot of well-bonded powder. It was awesome to ski it and then bivy under the stars in the beautiful Keyser Creek Drainage. There is a feeling of isolation when you get back into this zone; crossing into the next drainage over is always a commitment. You need a good set of spring storms to fill this line in. Upslope storms don't benefit this line zone as favorably as the lines on the Continental Divide. This line can also be approached via the Keyser Creek Road, though you will need a snowmobile for this; access from the Upper Tipperary Trailhead and ride around Ptarmigan. I've never done this so I can't speak of the details on this. You can check out conditions while driving south off of Willow Creek Pass; the bottom is hidden, though. Generally if Parry Peak's Bear Claw line is in, this one is too.

Looking back at the two summit lines of the West Face.

Byers Peak

Byers and Bills seen
from Bottle Peak.

Bills Peak

A good look at the angle of the West Face
from the North Ridge near treeline.

Bills Peak

Looking down on one of the summit lines of the West Face.

Get to the top of Byers however you like; either via the Byers Peak Trail or the Southeast Gully Route. Once on the summit, drop in due west, linking snow as needed to make it clean. There are two gullies that are both skiable from this drop-in aspect. Both have cliffs near the bottom, but both have nice lines through those cliffs—you just can't see them from the top. The face offers about 1,800' of skiing. The slope is moderately steep in the high-30s with a steeper mid-40 degree section through the cliff at the bottom.

You have a couple options to return to the St. Louis Creek drainage. You can ascend the West Gully to the summit of Byers and descend via the East Bowls or Southeast Gully routes. If the weather is bad, you can stay low by heading down valley and then ascend to near the saddle of Bottle and Byers. This is a nice option to have with spring thunderstorms; this option also lets you combine the route with Bottle Peak's Deadhorse Bowl, or just return to Byers Peak Trail.

The North Face of Bills offers lots of choices. The cornice on the right side of the peak gets very large.

To Iron Creek

27 BILLS PEAK – 12,703'

After some research, I could only find that this peak was named for a local prospector. Unfortunately his last name has been lost to history. I would love to update this for the second edition with his last name, if anyone has information. This is one of my favorite mountains in the Front Range, mainly due to how amazing my descent of the North Face was; I got it with about a foot of powder. Rank is 857th highest in the state, but the North Face ranks in the top 10 in my book.

27a – Bills Peak	North Face	
DIFFICULTY: Expert	**DISTANCE: 6.8 Miles Roundtrip**	**VERTICAL: 4,000'**
SUNHIT: Sunrise + 2 Hours	**ASPECT: North**	**SEASON: Spring**
TRAILHEAD: Iron Creek	**MAP: Page 272**	**PHOTO: Page 165, 167–168**

This is one of the finest expert lines in the Front Range. The slopes are steep with average angles in the high 40s and 50+ degree cruxes, all over cliffs, and many of the lines are threatened by overhanging cornices. Given the cornice situation, I advise ascending from the saddle along the East Ridge instead of ascending the lines.

From the water diversion project, skin or hike up the north side of Iron Creek. There is an old trail here; find it to avoid some of the headaches of all the deadfall. Follow the creek to the base of the Southeast Gully and pass it, continuing to follow the creek. Head to the unnamed lakes below the Bills/Byers saddle; then up to the saddle. Or combine this line with Byers West Face and make your way up to the saddle on the East Ridge via Keyser Creek. From here you get a decent view of the lines. The ridge gets spicy to the summit. Usually the cornice ends at the ridge and you can make your way to the summit.

Looking up at the central line.

There are four lines that cut through the face. The viewer's left is the tightest and is the only one that isn't threatened by the cornice. If attempting the lines threatened by the cornice, do so with a spotter who can let you know if there is danger/movement from above. Choose your line and risk level and ski the 1,300' face. From there return to the saddle and either ski from there the way you came up or combine with either Byers Southeast Gully or UN12393's Iron Creek Couloirs. If the weather is bad you can stay low by heading down valley and then ascend to near the saddle of Bottle and Byers. This is a nice option to have with spring thunderstorms; this option also lets you combine the route with Bottle Peak's Deadhorse Bowl.

Skiing the looker's left slot couloir.

Winter ski of the Bottle Peak trees.
athlete: Yuki Tsuji

28 BOTTLE PEAK – 11,584'

This short peak offers some surprisingly good skiing in Deadhorse Bowl. The chutes in the bowl, however, should be a spring objective. The trees at the southern margin of the bowl make for very good winter skiing. They are tight enough to hold good powder for days after the storm. There are tight tree chutes that are super fun in the high 30 degree range. Farther south along the ridge there are more moderate, well-spaced trees.

28a – Bottle Peak	Deadhorse Bowl	
DIFFICULTY: Intermediate to Advanced	DISTANCE: 6.3 Miles Roundtrip	VERTICAL: 3,000'
SUNHIT: Sunrise	ASPECT: East	SEASON: Winter or Spring
TRAILHEAD: Deadhorse Creek	MAP: Page 272	PHOTO: Page 169–170

Crossing the water project on lower Deadhorse Creek.

There are plenty of options in this zone of Bottle Peak. You can find moderate trees, steep tight tree chutes, and steep open bowl skiing. Half of the bowl proper is threatened by an overhanging cornice. Angles in the bowl are in the low 40s with steeper entrances. The bowl offers about 1,000' of vertical before the trees close things out. You can still ski most of the lower trees back to the trailhead.

The main bowl from just below the summit is guarded by a large cornice

To skier's right of the summit there is a cornice free line.

The tree lines are awesome. athlete: Jon Bloomfield

From the trailhead, start up the Byers Peak Trail. After about 0.1 mile look for a trail that follows closer to Deadhorse Creek. Follow this trail to avoid the road, which can be a rutted mess from Forest Service snowmobiles; the trail also shortcuts the road's switchbacks. Keep following the creek to the base of the Deadhorse Bowl. To climber's left is the best route for your ascent. The trees are well spaced and the angle is manageable. Remember that your skin track is supposed to be the safe option for your exit should your objective be unsafe. Ascend the trees to the ridge at treeline and then on to the summit.

If it's spring, go for the Deadhorse Bowl and ski steep snow for the upper section. Choose your line carefully as the skier's left side of the bowl usually has a large overhanging cornice. Lower down the line is mellower but is still fun until the trees close up. Another option involves skiing the trees of your ascent. Basically return the way you came, varying the line to take advantage of openings in the trees. The angles range from the high-30s to the mid–20s. The lower trees are fairly skiable but be sure to wax your skis to make the exit easier.

A look at Ptarmigan Peak
from Green Ridge.

29 PTARMIGAN PEAK – 11,772'

This is the lowest of Colorado's three Ptarmigan Peaks. It is named for the ubiquitous alpine bird that possesses some of the best camo in the animal kingdom. The other Ptarmigan Peaks are next to Horseshoe Mountain, in the Mosquito Range, and above Silverthorne. The one near Silverthorne is in the Williams Fork Mountains of the Front Range and doesn't really merit inclusion in this book because it doesn't have much good skiing. It does, however, merit a small wilderness area that was named after it.

29a – Ptarmigan Peak	Crystal Bowl	
DIFFICULTY: **Advanced**	DISTANCE: **9.5 Miles Roundtrip**	VERTICAL: **3,400'**
SUNHIT: **Sunrise + 3 Hours**	ASPECT: **North**	SEASON: **Spring**
TRAILHEAD: **Upper Tipperary**	MAP: **Page 272**	PHOTO: **Page 171–172**

This is another line that offers winter and spring options. The Crystal Bowl isn't quite as steep as Deadhorse Bowl but offers a longer ski before heading into the woods. The winter lines are steeper, hence the higher difficulty rating. Access can be drastically shortened with a snowmobile assist.

Like Bottle Peak, this one had
a giant cornice to skier's left.

With the consequences of getting taken into the trees, be sure the route is stable before committing.

Skin or get a snowmobile lift 2.5 miles up the road. At this point, turn south and follow Crystal Creek through the woods and up to the base of the bowl. Take a moment to choose your descent route. Note which lines have cornices; there are some massive ones in Crystal Bowl. The safest option for the ascent is through the trees on the margin of the looker's left chute. Switchback up the steep trees to the East Ridge of Ptarmigan and then on to the summit.

The meat of Crystal Bowl is in the mid-40s with some steeper options. There are terrain features for jumps as well as terrain traps down low should you get the bowl to slide. The trees you ascended can be navigated in winter even though they are in the prime time slide zone of the high-30's; they are generally tight enough to dither the wind's formation of slabs. Return to the road for the long slog out. It feels kind of like the road is uphill both ways for this one. Wax helps, but not as much as getting a snowmobile tow. Leave a case of Upslope beer in the vehicle to trade for that ride.

Haystack Mountain

North Face

30 HAYSTACK MOUNTAIN – 11,762'

Eleven summits in the state are called Haystack; this is the second highest. The highest is a sub-peak of Mount Daly in the Elk Mountains, near Capitol Peak and the town of Snowmass Village. Our peak resembles a haystack from Rogers Pass Lake, with its rounded summit and steep lower slopes—obviously the product of glacial sculpting. It doesn't garner a ranking due to the short rise from its saddle with the Continental Divide.

30a – Haystack	North Face	
DIFFICULTY: Advanced	DISTANCE: 8.3 Miles Roundtrip	VERTICAL: 3,100'
SUNHIT: Sunrise + 2 Hours	ASPECT: North	SEASON: Spring
TRAILHEAD: Moffat Tunnel	MAP: Page 273	PHOTO: Page 173–174

This is a great little line with surprisingly steep slopes. From the Moffat Tunnel, hike or skin up the South Boulder Creek Trail. You'll want to stay on the trail at all of the trail junctions. If you lose the trail, just follow South Boulder Creek. Follow the trail all the way to Rogers Lake at about 4 miles. At the lake, take a look to the southwest to plan your line up and down. The easiest ascent is to use the saddle between Haystack and the Continental Divide. The North Face is short at about 600' of vertical, so try to take advantage of some of the other lines in the area. Combine with James' North Face, Iceberg Couloirs, and Crater Couloirs.

Summit

Just after making a hasty descent
due to incoming weather.

The lines hold snow late into the summer.
Seen from the point south of "Sprint Peak"

31 ICEBERG COULOIRS – 12,160'

These chutes benefit from some of the heaviest loading in the Front Range. This is true of most of the peaks from here, north to Neva. The entire zone holds snow year-round. This is a great place for summer skiing when Rollins Pass Road makes access easy; just make sure the weather is stable enough to drop into the other side of the divide and still make it home.

31a – Iceberg Couloirs		
DIFFICULTY: Advanced	DISTANCE: 2–7.2 Miles Roundtrip	VERTICAL: 1,500–3,500'
SUNHIT: Sunrise	ASPECT: East	SEASON: Spring
TRAILHEAD: Rollins Pass West or Moffat Tunnel	MAP: Page 273	PHOTO: Page 175–176

The best way to get this line is from the west. Unless you are combining this route with other routes in the area, going at it from the east is a lot of work for a little line. From the west, it's less than a mile to the drop-in spot. From the Rollins Pass West trailhead corner, at the old railroad trestle, ascend on an east-southeasterly heading to get to the top of the line. It's only 900' of vertical gain to the divide. Ski, then climb back up to the divide to return to your vehicle, or you can repeat as needed; there are multiple options so you don't need to ski the same line over and over. Be sure of

Cory Reppenhagen gets into position to shoot video.

Looking down the line. This is more mellow than other summer ski routes.

weather before you drop in as you'll need time to climb back over the Divide.

From the east, if you must, hike or skin up the South Boulder Creek Trail. After about 2 miles, look for the creek leading to Clayton Lake. Skin up the south side of the creek to Clayton Lake and beyond to Iceberg Lakes. Pick your couloir, climb it, and ski it. If you are coming from the east side, you can combine nicely with "Sprint Peak," Crater Couloirs, "Frosty Mountain," and even Radiobeacon. All of these drain to the Moffat Tunnel Trailhead.

Be sure of the weather if you are accessing this line from the west side.

The entrance to this line is the crux.

32 "SPRINT PEAK" – 12,110'

This point between Radiobeacon and James Peak was named by Gerry Roach in *Colorado's Indian Peaks: Classic Hikes and Climbs,* after his race against a lightning storm. Though it doesn't have enough rise to qualify for a ranking, this peak has an impressive eastern scarp and offers the quality ski mountaineering lines known as the Crater Couloirs. Like the previous line just down the ridge, these couloirs hold snow late into the summer and are easiest to get from the west.

32a – "Sprint Peak"	Crater Couloirs	
DIFFICULTY: **Advanced**	DISTANCE: **2.1–6.2 Miles Roundtrip**	VERTICAL: **1,600'–3,400'**
SUNHIT: **Sunrise**	ASPECT: **East**	SEASON: **Spring**
TRAILHEAD: **Rollins Pass West or Moffat Tunnel**	MAP: **Page 273**	PHOTO: **Page 177–178**

The Crater Couloirs aren't summit skis; they start south of the peak but empty into the same drainage as "Sprint's" South Face. These couloirs are steeper than their southern neighbors, the Iceberg Couloirs. Like their neighbors, they are beyond easy to access once the west side of Rollins Pass is open. From the east, they are best combined with the Iceberg Couloirs, "Frosty Mountain," and even Radiobeacon to make all that effort of the approach worthwhile.

From the Rollins West Trailhead, hike southeast to the top of the couloir. There are

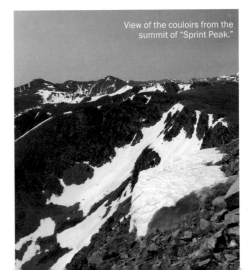
View of the couloirs from the summit of "Sprint Peak."

The entrance is steep but not as serious as Challenger Glacier.

a couple of options; ski your choice to Crater Lake below. Ascend the couloir to return to the trailhead. Crampons and an ice axe are helpful for the return as the top reaches the low 50s; it's even steeper if the cornice is still in place. This is another reason to wait for summer.

From the east, hike or skin up the South Boulder Creek Trail to the Crater Lakes Trail junction at about 2.2 miles. Take the Crater Lake Trail up past all the Crater Lakes. At the top lake, pick your line and giterdun. Combine with the lines mentioned above.

A wind rib usually develops to skier's right in the line.

A look at the options from "Sprint Peak."

"Frosty Mountain" Radiobeacon BM

Arapaho Lakes

33 "FROSTY MOUNTAIN" – 12,110'

This mountain doesn't have enough rise for an official ranking. It's between Radiobeacon and "Sprint Peak" on the Continental Divide, and rises to the west of Arapaho Lakes. The peak has a very favorable position to benefit from orographic lift and receives copious amounts of snow and wind.

33a – "Frosty Mountain"	East Side	
DIFFICULTY: Intermediate to Advanced	DISTANCE: 2.4–6.3 Miles Roundtrip	VERTICAL: 1,500'–3,000'
SUNHIT: Sunrise	ASPECT: Southeast through East	SEASON: Spring
TRAILHEAD: Rollins Pass East, West or Moffat Tunnel	MAP: Page 273	PHOTO: Page 179–180

Like the other lines in this zone, it's best to wait for summer and the opening of Rollins Pass' west access to make this trip easy. From the east it's a haul for not much vertical, unless you're planning on hitting multiple lines. The route combines well with "Sprint's" Crater Couloirs and Radiobeacon.

From the Radiobeacon BM parking on Rollins Pass' west side, take a northeasterly heading to get to the summit of Frosty. The peak is only 0.8 mile and 800' of vertical. Drop into your line and return to the divide. Be sure the weather is stable enough to make it back.

There are some steeper options between Frosty and Radiobeacon.

Radiobeacon BM

From the summit, the lines to skier's right are fairly mellow, in the low to mid-30s. To skier's left there are steeper lines in the high-40s. These lines get cornices and can be very steep at their entrances.

If you go in from the east side, start at the Moffat Tunnel Trailhead and go about 0.7 mile up the South Arapaho Trail to the junction for Forest Lakes. Take the Forest Lakes trail about a mile to where the creek draining Forest Lakes and Arapaho Creek merge. Take the creek on the left here and hike or skin up to Arapaho Lakes. At the lakes, choose your line and have fun.

"Sprint Peak"   "Frosty Mountain"   Radiobeacon

Skiing Radiobeacon's East Face you get a nice view of some of the other options.
photo: Allison Seymour

Double Fall-Line Couloir

Forest Lakes Bowl

34 RADIOBEACON BM – 12,072'

This peak isn't named Radiobeacon on the USGS map; however, the old radio beacon that used to reside on the summit is marked on the map. Some other guidebooks refer to the peak as "Beacon Peak." Since the map is marked Radiobeacon, I think this is the name we should use. It is a very popular ski as it offers the steepest, most technical lines accessed via Rollins Pass Road.

An important note: the 1:24,000 series USGS topo for this peak is not correct. This is reflected in the appearance of the peak on Google Earth. The more recent U.S. Forest Service topo map is more accurate.

34a – Radiobeacon BM	Northeast Cirque	
DIFFICULTY: Expert	**DISTANCE: 1.8–3.8 Miles Roundtrip**	**VERTICAL: 1,500'– 2,000'**
SUNHIT: Sunrise	**ASPECT: Northeast**	**SEASON:** Spring
TRAILHEAD: Rollins Pass West or Forest Lakes Upper or Lower	**MAP: Page**	**PHOTO: Page**

There are multiple lines in the Northeast Cirque of Radiobeacon. Directly off the summit you have the North Couloir and its two choices of entrance. The entrance is in the 50s and then mellows to the high-40s. The choke is in the 50s. These chutes lead down to a cliff band. In the cliff band, the direct line sometimes doesn't fill in all the way. You may need to jump the gap or rappel for this option. Farther to the north is the Northeast Couloir. This line is also in the 50s but has clean snow to the Upper Forest Lake. The next line to the north is the Forest

Forest Lake Couloir

A look at the entrance from the top of the line closest to the summit. Exposed.

Northeast Couloir

If you drop in for the summit line and the cliff isn't filled i
traverse above the cliffs to hook up with the East Fac

Double Fall-Line Couloir

Forest
Bo

Lake Couloir, which is the steepest option in the high 50s. It leads to upper Forest Lake as well. North of this is the Double Fall-line Couloir; the angle is in the high 40s for this route. North of that is Forest Lakes Bowl; this bowl is the mellowest option in the low-40s with a steeper entrance.

Access is easiest from the Rollins Pass Radiobeacon trailhead on the west side of the divide. Access from the east side is either from the upper or lower Forest Lakes Trailhead on Rollins Pass Road. If going from the lower because the road is closed up high, make sure there is decent snow cover as the zone is filled with deadfall.

34b – Radiobeacon BM	East Face	
DIFFICULTY: Advanced	**DISTANCE: 1.8–3.8 Miles Roundtrip**	**VERTICAL: 1,500'–2,000'**
SUNHIT: Sunrise	**ASPECT: Northeast**	**SEASON: Spring**
TRAILHEAD: Rollins Pass West or Forest Lakes Upper or Lower	**MAP: Page 273**	**PHOTO: Page 183–184**

This is a milder option to summit Radiobeacon. It flirts with the Northeast Cirque and even ventures into it as a lower option, but the angle and the consequences are generally lower on this aspect. Access from either Rollins Pass Radiobeacon Trailhead on the west side of the

At treeline above Lower Forest Lake. This is the way to the Southeast Ridge/East Face of Radiobeacon.

The upper section melts out first and the snow can get pretty punchy.

The upper East Face is fairly
mellow–in the 30 degree range.
athlete: Allison Seymour

divide or the upper or lower Forest Lakes Trailhead on Rollins Pass Road. Take a northeast heading from the west access to summit Radiobeacon. Access from the east side is more complicated if going in from the lower trailhead. The trees here aren't depicted accurately on the map and are steeper than drawn. Get to Forest Lake and ascend the couloir to the south of the upper lake to the upper East Face.

Drop in over some exposure that still has plenty of room to correct for any mistakes. Ski the upper face and then choose a lower section. Either ski the lower couloir down to the upper Forest Lake or turn southeast to mellower slopes.

The exit gully is steeper, in
the mid-40 degree range.
photo: Allison Seymour

35 ROLLINS PASS – 11,671'

There is a sign at the top of the pass sponsored by the Grand County Historical Society, the Rollins Pass Restoration Association and the Forest Service. It reads, "John Quincy Adams Rollins established a toll wagon road through this pass in the mid-1860s. Davis H Moffat's Denver, Northwestern and Pacific Railway crossed the Continental Divide at this point in 1903. First known as Boulder Pass, then Rollins Pass, the railroad workers dubbed it 'Corona,' the crown of 'Top of the world.' A railroad station, hotel, restaurant, and workers quarters existed here until 1928 when the railroad was abandoned due to the building of the Moffat Tunnel." On the map, the pass is named Rollins Pass, but the town is named Corona. This is confusing because the road is called Corona Pass on the sign at the bottom of the west side access from US Highway 40 in Winter Park. I refer to the road as Rollins Pass at all times. There are numerous trailheads along the road on both sides of the divide. This section covers routes accessed from the summit. Radiobeacon, "Sprint Peak," "Frosty," and the Iceberg Couloirs can all be accessed from Rollins Pass Road's west side, but since they are peaks, they have their own sections in the book.

s seen from Rollins Pass Road
om above Jenny Lake.

To Rollins Pass →

Jenny Lake Bowl

35a – Rollins Pass	Jenny Lake Bowl	
DIFFICULTY: **Advanced**	DISTANCE: **1.6 Miles Roundtrip**	VERTICAL: **1,300'**
SUNHIT: **Sunrise**	ASPECT: **East**	SEASON: **Spring**
TRAILHEAD: **Rollins Pass East or West**	MAP: **Page 273**	PHOTO: **Page 185–186**

Access is about the same from both sides, but snow can keep you from getting all the way up to the Jenny Lake turn on the east side. It can be a lot longer from the east side if this is the case. The access from the summit is usually the easiest. From the summit, hike southwest along the divide directly to the drop-in. This is only 0.4 mile and 400' of vertical. This option doesn't allow you to feel the snow on the way up. It also doesn't allow you to see if the couloir goes through without a rock choke. Hike down the ridge to get a better view of the line, but use care at the edge due to potential cornicing. From the east and the Jenny Lake turnoff, aim for the line you want and head into the trees. Don't go up to the lake as the willows above the lake are tough to deal with. Cross the upper road and then ascend the couloir you want to ski.

The entrance is steep and over a dogleg so a fall has consquences.

The entrance is steep in the low 50s. It mellows for a short section, then gets steep again as it approaches the choke. From there, it opens up and continues down to the upper portion of the Rollins Pass Road eastside. It's a 900' vertical drop to the road. From there, either ski the trees to the Jenny Lake turnoff or ascend the southeast ridge of the line to get back to the divide and then hike back to the summit.

Forest Lake

I like skiing in shorts.

The choke is about 50 degrees.

35b – Rollins Pass	Skyscraper Glacier	
DIFFICULTY: **Advanced**	DISTANCE: **3.9 Miles Roundtrip**	VERTICAL: **1,200'**
SUNHIT: **Sunrise**	ASPECT: **East**	SEASON: **Spring**
TRAILHEAD: **Rollins Pass Summit**	MAP: **Page 273**	PHOTO: **Page 187**

This route is the site of the streaks. Most of the people I know who are pursuing "turns all year" streaks get their summer turns done here. If you're skiing every month throughout the year, you need reliable snow in August and September. Sure, you could go to Mt. Hood or South America but why would you do so when Skyscraper Glacier offers more than 800' of vertical for such little effort. Lap it to make the effort worth it.

The looker's left entrance on Skyscraper Glacier is in almost every year.

The looker's right entrance is in only occasionally and is much mellower.

From the summit lot, hike north along the Continental Divide for about 1.8 miles. The trail is very nice. At this mark, head due east to get the top of Skyscraper Glacier. The snow sets up differently each year. The entrance is steep but the angle eases quickly. There is 800' of vertical drop to Bob Lake.

From Bob Lake, take a southerly course overland toward King Lake. You will need to weave through willows to get there. Along the way, you will hook up with a good trail that ascends back to the pass summit via the south side of King Lake.

In late August this is one of the few places to make some turns.

Bob Lake

35c – Rollins Pass	Challenger Glacier	
DIFFICULTY: Expert	DISTANCE: 4.9–5.2 Miles Roundtrip	VERTICAL: 1,500'–1,900'
SUNHIT: Sunrise	ASPECT: Northeast	SEASON: Spring
TRAILHEAD: Rollins Pass Summit	MAP: Page 273	PHOTO: Page 188

This line is steeper than Skyscraper Glacier, especially at the entrance. It's about the same length; at least the snow that survives through the summer is. To access this line, hike north along the Continental Divide Trail from the summit for about 2 miles. At this point, hike northeast to the entrance of the Challenger Glacier. The entrance is corniced until late in the spring, which is one of the reasons to get this one in summer. Even without the cornice, the entrance is in the upper 50s some years. It stays steep longer than Skyscraper Glacier. The line ends at the talus after about 800' of vertical.

For the return to the trailhead, climb back to the divide via the glacier. At this point you have a choice: ski Skyscraper or hike back the trail. It's actually shorter to ski Skyscraper, but you will climb more vertical. This is a good thing; it's two for almost the price of one.

The exit/entrance is very steep.
athlete: Jeremy Dobish

The entrance can also be complex.
athlete: Jeremy Dobish

Challenger Glacier is really close to the top of Skyscraper Glacier.

Skyscraper Glac
Entrance

Challenger
Glacier

To Eldora
BC Access Gate

Lost Lake Bowl

Lost Lake Bowl viewed from Lost Lake.

36 ELDORA BACKCOUNTRY

Eldora Mountain Resort opened in 1962 and is one of four ski areas in the zone covered by this volume; the others are Loveland, Winter Park and Ski Granby Ranch. The fact that the ski area abuts the Indian Peaks and there is a gate at the top makes for a perfect fit with this book. I love ski area backcountry. Call me lazy, but riding lifts for less trammeled snow is right up my alley. For many years, Eldora didn't allow uphill access, they now do, though it isn't for free. You can also use this gate to access the Arestua Hut on Guinn Mountain, 2 miles from the backcountry access gate, west along the ridge. Going to a hut from a ski area is very common in Europe and not so common in the United States.

36a – Eldora Backcountry	Lost Lake Bowl	
DIFFICULTY: **Intermediate to Advanced**	DISTANCE: **2–5.5 Miles Point to Point**	VERTICAL: **150'–2,000 Up, 1,500'–2,000 Down**
SUNHIT: **Sunrise**	ASPECT: **Northeast**	SEASON: **Winter–Spring**
TRAILHEAD: **Eldora BC Gate or Hessie**	MAP: **Page 273**	PHOTO: **Page 189–190**

You don't need to buy a lift ticket to ski this zone if you are cheap like me. You can access the terrain by ascending from the Hessie Trailhead. From the winter trailhead, it's a bit of a haul to get back here. Skin up the snowy Fourth of July Road for 0.8 mile to the Hessie junction and take a left. Continue along the road to the summer trailhead at the 1.3 mile mark. Follow the trail from here, taking the left option at all the junctions. The goal is to get up to the east

Eldora Backcountry trees viewed from Lost Lake.

To Eldora Backcountry Access Gate

To Lost Lake Bowl

Return to Eldora or Hessie Trailhead

Eldora Backcountry
Access Gate

Looking over from Guinn Mountain.

Top of
Lost Lake Bowl

Lost Lake
behind the tree.

Typical terrain for the trees of Eldora Backcountry.

shore of Lost Lake. Ascend the gully that rises to the south of Lost Lake around to the back of the Lost Lake Bowl.

From the top of the Corona Quad lift, skate west along the ski area's ridge to the backcountry access gate. Check the BCA beacon tester to make sure your beacon is broadcasting and head up the trail past the antenna array. Get to the top of the hill and drop in to the north to ski intermediate trees. Take the trees down to just below Lost Lake to catch the trail back to the ski area.

If your objective is the Lost Lake Bowl, continue west along the ridge from the gate a little ways to get to the gully that drains into Lost Lake. The snow getting into this gully can be a bit funky. Ski to the other side of the gully and ascend to the back side of Lost Lake Bowl.

The bowl offers 600' of steep vert with most of the line in the low-40s and chokes in the high-40s. At the bottom, stay to skier's right to hook up with the catch trail back to the area. Or if you came from Hessie, follow your ascent route. There are a couple other short, fun sections if you came from Hessie.

Devil's Thumb Pass

Jasper Peak

Woodland Mountain

37 WOODLAND MOUNTAIN – 11,205'

This wooded ridge provides a rarity in the Indian Peaks: a quality winter zone with decent vertical. But it's also short enough vertically to get in multiple laps and offers enough acreage to handle multiple groups. Access is either from the Hessie Winter Trailhead or from Lost Lake and the Eldora Backcountry Gate.

37a – Woodland Mountain	South Slopes	
DIFFICULTY: Advanced	**DISTANCE: 7–8 Miles Roundtrip**	**VERTICAL: 1,900'–2,800' Up, 3,800' Down**
SUNHIT: Sunrise + 2 Hours	**ASPECT: South–Southeast**	**SEASON: Winter–Spring**
TRAILHEAD: Eldora Gate or Hessie Winter	**MAP: Page 273**	**PHOTO: Page 191–192**

Accessing this line from Eldora is the easiest way to go. You have to put 900' of less effort in via this route. That leaves more energy for skiing laps on Woodland and you also get to ski Lost Lake Bowl. From the lake, find the Lost Lake trail on the west side of the lake. Take it a

The South Slopes of Woodland Mountain offer short, steep sections mixed with more mellow terrain. athlete: Matt Hart

There are cliff zones, trees and mellow meadows for your enjoyment.

few hundred feet and then keep going west into the trees. Hook up with the King Lake Trail on the other side of the meadow and take it west, up valley to the base of the south slopes of Woodland. Try to pick your line from Eldora or the top of the Lost Lake Bowl, as you'll have a really good view of the options from the ridge.

Alternatively, you could approach this route from Hessie. Skin up the road 0.8 mile to the Hessie Junction and take the left. At about 1.3 miles you will get to the summer trailhead and the King Lake Trail. Take the trail up into the basin for King Lake and the drainage for the South Slopes. At about the 2.1 mile mark you will come to the junction for that drainage.

Once at the base pick your line. This route is advanced because there are slide zones here. You need to be aware of the slopes above you and choose the line of least resistance. I like to set a skin track and reuse it. The zone has cliff sections, open trees, tight trees and short chutes. It is south facing, though, so the snow can get cooked by the sun. You can also find sun crusts that get buried. The snowpack also tends to be thinner on this aspect, so earlier is better.

On the way out, do yourself a favor and skin up to Lost Lake and finish with that route's exits.

For snow like this get on it during or right after a storm. The south aspect can lead to cooked snow after the sun comes out.
athlete: Matt Hart

Checking out the Snow Lion and Jasper's main summit from "Northeast Jasper."

38 MOUNT JASPER – 12,923'

This peak is the highest point between South Arapaho and James Peak, just short of the 13er realm. The western summit is the high point. It is harder to access than its 13er neighbors. Mount Jasper is the 700th highest point in Colorado, and was named by Gerry Roach, author of *Colorado's Indian Peaks: Hikes and Climbs*; this is referenced by the BGN on the official decision card. The peak benefits immensely from being the highest in the zone and its east side is usually chock full of snow late into the summer. There are more than a few viewpoints of this aspect of the mountain from along the Peak to Peak Highway south of Rollinsville, as well as on Colorado 72 near Wondervu. The western route of the peak can be seen from Fraser.

38a – Mount Jasper	Snow Lion	
DIFFICULTY: Advanced–Expert	DISTANCE: 7.5 Miles Roundtrip	VERTICAL: 3,500'
SUNHIT: Sunrise	ASPECT: Southeast	SEASON: Spring
TRAILHEAD: Fourth of July	MAP: Page 274–275	PHOTO: Page 193–194, 196

This is one of the finer lines in the Front Range. It offers a nice, steep descent and even steeper options for those who want the thrill. Access is easy once the Fourth of July Trailhead is clear. It holds snow late into the spring, so you can be sure that the route has snow. There are plenty of places to check the conditions along the Peak to Peak Highway.

Dropping-in on Snow Lion.

From the Fourth of July Trailhead, hike up the Arapaho Pass Trail for about 1 mile to the Diamond Lake Trail. Follow this trail to the bridge, crossing the creek. Once past the creek, hike southeast a few hundred feet and bushwhack up the hill in a southwesterly direction. The goal is to reach the chute below the East Ridge Flank and ascend it. This is a quicker option than going all the way to Diamond Lake, but that's another alternative if you don't want to deal with bushwhacking. From either of these routes, make your way into Upper Diamond Lake Basin and to the East Bowl to the west of the upper lake.

Ascend the line you want to ski. Every time I've been on Jasper, I've seen tracks on this line but I've never seen any people. The main Snow Lion route is a steep 40 degree line with a slight rollover that is about 50 degrees. There are steeper lines to skier's right of the summit. Lower down the Southeast East Ridge, and not a summit ski, is Snow Leopard. The entrance, which is usually corniced, is very steep, near 60 degrees. The bulk of the couloir is over 50 degrees; this is the expert line.

This route combines with the East Ridge Flank line. Exit via the Diamond Lake trail so you can utilize the bridge to cross what is usually a raging North Fork Middle Boulder Creek.

38b – Mount Jasper	Northeast Face	
DIFFICULTY: Advanced	DISTANCE: 6.5 Miles Roundtrip	VERTICAL: 3,600'
SUNHIT: Sunrise	ASPECT: Northeast	SEASON: Spring
TRAILHEAD: Fourth of July	MAP: Page 274–275	PHOTO: Page 195, 200

This is a milder option for getting Mount Jasper done. The line descends from the lower "Northeast Mount Jasper" summit. Access is easy via the Fourth of July Road. Loading is great and the route holds snow late into the spring. The skiing is less difficult than the Y Couloirs on the west side or Snow Lion on the east side. As you leave the trail and have an extended bushwhack, getting to and from this line is a little tough.

From the Fourth of July Trailhead, hike up the Arapaho Pass trail for about 1 mile to the

East Ridge Flank

"Northeast
Jasper"

Diamond Lake Trail. Follow this trail to the bridge crossing the creek. The North Fork of Middle Boulder Creek is usually pretty full at the time of year that people ski this route, and the bridge makes getting across it easy. On the other side, make your way up on a southwesterly course into the basin of the Northwest Face. You'll reach an unnamed lake below the face. There is airplane wreckage at this lake, the gravity of which sank in for me halfway up the face. Pick your line, either taking the face or going to the saddle and then up the ridge. If you want, scramble the ridge over to the western, true summit of Mount Jasper.

Descend the 1,200' face to the unnamed lake. From there, either retrace your steps or combine with the East Ridge Flank route via ascending back up to the East Ridge.

Northeast Face

Upper section of East Ridge Flank.

Lower section of East Ridge Flank.

38c – Mount Jasper	East Ridge Flank	
DIFFICULTY: Advanced	DISTANCE: 5 Miles Roundtrip	VERTICAL: 2,700'
SUNHIT: Sunrise	ASPECT: East	SEASON: Spring
TRAILHEAD: Fourth of July	MAP: Page 274–275	PHOTO: Page 195–196

Once the road is open all the way to the Fourth of July Trailhead, you can get this route done in a hurry. The line is east facing and heats up quickly since it's lower than most of the other lines in the zone, so get an early start. Another option is to get this line "after work," waiting for it to refreeze a little once the sun is on the other side of the mountain.

From the Fourth of July Trailhead, hike up the Arapaho Pass trail for about 1 mile to the Diamond Lake Trail. Follow this trail to the bridge, crossing the creek. Once past the creek, hike southeast a few hundred feet and bushwhack up the hill in a southwesterly direction. The goal is to reach the chute below the East Ridge Flank and ascend it. Ascend the steep lower couloir to the bench below the upper, east-facing portion of the East Ridge Flank; be sure to pick a clean line through the lower couloir zone, as some of the options cliff out. Above the bench, ascend to the "summit" of the East Ridge Flank.

The upper section of the route offers slope in the high 30s with a few chokes that develop as the talus slopes melt through. You then get to a mellow bench and have multiple options for the lower section. Many of these options cliff out, so it's best to figure out the correct option and ascend it, then descend, following your boot prints.

38d – Mount Jasper	Y Couloirs aka Cabin Creek Couloirs	
DIFFICULTY: Advanced	DISTANCE: 7.3 Miles Roundtrip	VERTICAL: 3,500'
SUNHIT: Sunrise + 3 Hours	ASPECT: West	SEASON: Spring
TRAILHEAD: Devil's Thumb	MAP: Page 274	PHOTO: Page 197–198

Finding lines that face west can be a bit of a challenge due to the prevailing westerlies that strip these windward routes of their snow. Finding a classic west-facing route could be called priceless. The key lies in the wet, spring, upslope storms that load from the east and northeast. When other west faces like Parry's Bear Claw and the West Couloir of James are in, this line is usually in. You can get a great look at this route from Main Street (Xerex Drive/US-40) in Fraser (it is northeast of town) to make sure it's good to go. Given the aspect, be sure to start later than you would for east-facing routes to avoid skiing this steep line in firm conditions.

Follow the Devil's Thumb Pass Trail as it hugs the north side of Cabin Creek. At about the 0.6 mile mark you will get to Devil's Thumb Park, a large meadow; cross it, staying on the north side of the creek as the trail joins the High Lonesome Trail. At the 1.3 mile mark, you will come to another meadow. You get a great look at the Y Couloir here. Stay left here to stay with Cabin Creek. Make your way to the entrance of the West Slopes of Mount Jasper and follow these 30 degree slopes on to the summit.

This line descends from the first saddle on the ridge, connecting Jasper with Neva. You can connect the Y Couloir to the summit via a ski of the Northwest Ridge. To locate the couloir, ski down the ridge to the first rib that defines the skier's right side of the West Slopes. The Y

Mount Jasper

Y Couloir

Cabin Creek

The looker's left branch is a cleaner ski and holds more snow.

Y Couloir

The ice bulge crux.

Couloir is located on the other side of this rib. The line is steep, in the mid-40s for most of it. After getting out of the walled couloir, there is a wind lip that develops at the apron. The slopes stay steep down to the Christmas trees where you get to an ice bulge. This is the crux of the route and is in the high-50s. You can usually get around this feature but use care above the bulge as the snow will be icy and a fall off the bulge would be painful. Below the crux, you get more lightly treed vertical down to the creek. From the entrance at the ridge to the creek, the line offers 2,100' of steep vertical. For the exit, ski along the creek to meet up with your skin track.

The Y Couloir isn't super steep but it does have some fun steep sections. I'm always stoked to ski fun, west facing lines when they fill in.

Mount Neva and Caribou Lake Bowl seen from the summit of "Hopi Peak."

39 MOUNT NEVA – 12,814'

James Dziezynski's book, *Best Summit Hikes in Colorado: An Opinionated Guide to 50+ Ascents of Classic and Little-Known Peaks from 8,144 to 14,433 Feet*, says the peak was named for Chief Niwot's brother Neva. "According to CU Boulder professor Dr. Andrew Cowell, "'I have never seen an official explanation of the word, but it has to be either niibei(t) or niiboo(t) I would imagine. Niibei would be most likely—it means 'singer' or 'singing.'" Neva and Niwot are believed to have been killed at the Sand Creek Massacre. The peak is very popular with skiers once the Fourth of July Trailhead is open and even before that. It is the 773rd highest peak in the state.

39a – Mount Neva	Northeast Face	
DIFFICULTY: **Advanced to Expert**	DISTANCE: **7.5 Miles Roundtrip**	VERTICAL: **3,100'**
SUNHIT: **Sunrise**	ASPECT: **Northeast**	SEASON: **Spring**
TRAILHEAD: **Fourth of July**	MAP: **Page 274–275**	PHOTO: **Page 199–200**

Neva's 500' Northeast Face is one of the classic spring ski descents of the Front Range and the Indian Peaks. This is due mainly to the deep access provided by the Fourth of July Trailhead and the deep snowpack that the westerly driven loading delivers.

Mount Neva seen from the Arapaho Pass Trail. Head for Lake Dorothy and then up the line of your choice.

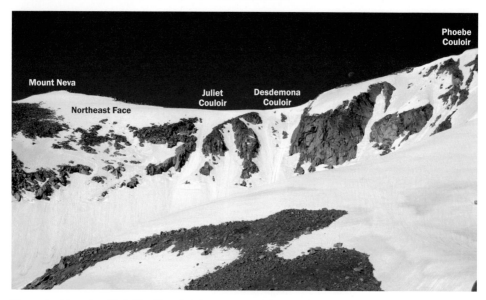

From the Fourth of July Trailhead, hike west on the Arapaho Pass Trail about 3 miles to the Arapaho Pass/Lake Dorothy junction and take the trail south to Lake Dorothy. Skirt the lake on the east side and make your way over a hump to the base of the Northeast Face; there is often a cornice on this hump. Pick your line up the face and climb it, taking the upper West Ridge to the summit if climbing the climber's right lines. There are multiple named couloirs on this face; they are from viewer's left to right, **Northeast Face, Juliet, Desdemona, and Phoebe**. The Northeast Face is the most direct, dropping in right from the summit, as it doesn't have a cornice. The line is usually a bit meandering as there are rock bands that need to be negotiated. The couloirs usually have cornices guarding their entrances. They are steep, averaging in the high-40s with cruxes in the mid-50s; the entry from the ridge is a crux on most. Ski your ascent.

For the exit, continue skiing down the drainage of the face, instead of returning to Lake Dorothy. Squeeze some extra vertical in before heading overland back to the Arapaho Pass Trail leading back to the trailhead.

Caribou Lake Bowl seen from the shores of Caribou Lake. Lots of fun options for those willing to put in the work.

39b – Mount Neva	**Caribou Lake Bowl**	
DIFFICULTY: **Advanced**	DISTANCE: **7.3 Miles Roundtrip**	VERTICAL: **3,200'**
SUNHIT: **Sunrise + 2 Hours**	ASPECT: **North**	SEASON: **Spring**
TRAILHEAD: **Fourth of July**	MAP: **Page 274–275**	PHOTO: **Page 199, 201–202**

The Indian Peaks are a beautiful place; this is known by all who visit. Caribou Lake is one of the most popular backcountry camping zones in the Indian Peaks, mainly due to its amazing views of the Arapahos, Apache, Navajo, Mt. George, "Iroquois," and "Hopi"—when the peaks are reflected in the still lake, it takes your breath away. Caribou Lake Bowl offers great skiing for those who want to combine backpacking and skiing and soak in those views. Access is easy, and if you get this route in before the camping restrictions go into effect on June 1 each year, it is free.

From the Fourth of July Trailhead, hike west on the Arapaho Pass Trail about 3 miles to the Arapaho Pass/Caribou Pass junction, leave the trail here, and hike northwest up to the first

Caribou Lake Bowl can have a funky cornice guarding its entrance.

Caribou Lake Bowl has some short steep lines guarded by large cornices near the saddle to the east of Satanta Peak.

hump on the North Ridge of Neva. From here, the entrance of the Caribou Bowl is on a northwesterly heading.

The 1,300' bowl is a ski-it-from-the-top kind of line. There is a cornice that guards most of the entrances. The longest line is fairly mellow, in the mid-30s. To the west or skier's left, down the ridge toward Satanta, there are steeper, shorter lines.

Camp at the lake and if it's after June 1, make sure you have a permit as USFS rangers patrol this area and will ticket you. Around the lake, camping is only allowed in designated campsites. Return to the east side of the Continental Divide by ascending to Arapaho Pass. This route combines well with an overnight and a ski of North Arapaho's North Star Couloir.

Caribou Lake

Caribou Lake Bowl's main and longest line offers up 1,200' of fun gully turns to the lake.

Skywalker
Couloir

North Star Couloir
Access

40 SOUTH ARAPAHO PEAK

The peak is named in honor of the local tribe, the Arapaho. Their leader, Chief Niwot, aka Left Hand, lived in the Boulder Valley. Chief Niwot was welcoming to the settlers prospecting for gold even though they were in violation of a peace treaty. It is believed that he was killed at the Sand Creek Massacre by John Chivington's troops on the orders of Governor Evans. The Arapaho tribe originated in Manitoba and expanded through the west, forming alliances with the Cheyenne, Lakota, Dakota, and later the Comanche and Kiowa. South Arapaho is unranked, as it only rises 97' from its saddle with North Arapaho. The Arapaho Glacier resides on the north and east flanks of South and North Arapaho Peaks, respectively. This could be a great resource for us skiers; unfortunately Boulder Water owns the Arapaho Glacier and doesn't let anyone visit it, for fear of contaminating the drinking water supply for the city. The entire north side of the mountain is closed because of this. However, the ridge connecting the peak with its northern neighbor is considered open. Do not test the resolve of the Boulder County rangers; they will catch you if you try to visit Arapaho Glacier or anywhere else within the closure. Check the map on pages 274–275 for a clearer picture of how large the closure is and its exact boarders.

40a – South Arapaho Peak	Skywalker Couloir	
DIFFICULTY: Advanced	DISTANCE: 5.1 Miles Roundtrip	VERTICAL: 3,400'
SUNHIT: Sunrise + 2 Hours	ASPECT: South	SEASON: Spring
TRAILHEAD: Fourth of July	MAP: Page 274–275	PHOTO: Page 203–204

This is one of the classic ski lines of the Front Range. This deeply inset, 1,500' couloir, which breaks the South Face of South Arapaho, is long, steep, and super easy to access. The angle is in the mid-40s with low-50s at the top of the main couloir. Above that you have an even steeper branch couloir known as Leia. This narrow finger is in the mid-50s. From the top of

Ice axe, crampons and helmet are mandatory gear on Skywalker.

Leia, it's only a 300' vertical scramble to the summit of South Arapaho; this section usually isn't skiable.

To access the line, hike 1.7 miles to near treeline and the first flat, open terrain on the Arapaho Pass Trail; if you reach the Fourth of July Mine, you have gone too far. At the 1.7 mile mark, head northwest toward the U-shaped saddle at the base of South Arapaho's Southwest Face. As you get around the corner of South Arapaho's South Rib, Skywalker Couloir will come into view. Ascend the couloir and then the peak if you wish.

This route combines well with Neva, though Skywalker would be the second line. Skiing this line later in the day is advised as it's deeply inset nature keeps the snow cool later than most lines.

Skiing the lower choke.
photo: Rob Dickinson

th Star
ouloir

This is a long and fun moderately steep line.
athlete: Allison Seymour

41 NORTH ARAPAHO PEAK – 13,502'

Like South Arapaho, this peak is named for the local Arapaho tribe. It's one of many salutes to the original locals. Chief Niwot is honored as such all over Boulder County and one of the main thoroughfares in Boulder is Arapahoe Avenue. North Arapaho and the Arapaho Glacier are visible from the avenue. Unfortunately, Boulder Water owns the glacier and doesn't let anyone visit it, for fear of contaminating the drinking water supply of the city. The entire east side of the mountain is closed because of this. However, the ridge connecting the peak with its southern counterpart is considered open. Do not test the resolve of the Boulder County rangers; they will catch you if you try to visit Arapaho Glacier and anywhere else within the closure. Check the map on pages 274–275 for a clearer picture of how large the closure is. Arikaree, Kiowa, Albion, and Niwot Ridge are omitted from the book because of this closure. The peak is the 253rd highest in the state.

41a – North Arapaho Peak	North Star Couloir	
DIFFICULTY: **Advanced**	DISTANCE: **8 Miles Roundtrip**	VERTICAL: **5,300'**
SUNHIT: **Sunrise + 3 Hours**	ASPECT: **West**	SEASON: **Spring**
TRAILHEAD: **Fourth of July**	MAP: **Page 274–275**	PHOTO: **Page 203, 205–206**

This 2,300' couloir is a moderately steep gem. It is hard to call this a true classic as the access is so involved, but perhaps this fact pushes it to that classic status because it keeps the riff-raff away. This is a big day and is better as an overnight. Combine with Caribou Bowl to get some really good route beta as well as a fun ski into the west side of the Continental Divide. Another issue with getting this done in a day is that by the time you're ready to return from the other side of the divide, the afternoon thunderstorms are starting to ramp up.

If going for the route in a day or not combining, hike from the trailhead to the Fourth of July Mine. From the mine, at about 1.9 miles up the trail, aim north for the saddle below the Southwest Face of South Arapaho. From the saddle, ski down into the upper reaches of Coyote Park to the unnamed lake; head north from the lake to the base of North Star. There are great campsites around this little lake. There are two lines to choose from here: the North Star Couloir and the Near North Couloir. See the topo photo for the locations. The Near North option has no-fall skiing over a cliff to an exit ramp. Ascend the couloir of your choice to the West Ridge of North Arapaho and on to the summit. The ridge to the summit is only in during big years and early in the spring season.

If combining with Caribou Bowl, ski that line first and then contour around the upper reaches of Coyote Park to the base of the North Star line and camp at the little lake. North Star Couloir reaches into the mid-40s at its steepest and the high-30s the rest of the way.

Return via the saddle below the Southwest Face of South Arapaho. Be sure to keep an eye on those thunderstorms, especially if you are attempting to get back in the afternoon.

This is the steepest section of the line.

42 NAVAJO PEAK – 13,409'

The peak was named in honor of the Navajo Indian tribe in 1914 at the suggestion of Ellsworth Bethel; Mount Bethel is named in his honor. He was the director of the CU History Museum in Boulder and worked for the Forest Service. The Navajo people were historical residents of southwestern Colorado, centered mainly around the Cortez area; they now live primarily in Arizona and New Mexico, where their reservation is located. Mountains are integral in Navajo culture with four sacred mountains that delineate their historical territory. Two of these peaks, Blanca Peak in the Sangre de Cristo Range and Hesperus Mountain in the La Plata sub range of the San Juans, are in Colorado. The other two are Taylor Mountain in New Mexico and the San Francisco Mountains in Arizona. The peak is the 314th highest point in Colorado. The peak's summit pyramid is recognizable from many vantage points; however, the best place to check on the snow conditions is from Brainard Lake.

42a – Navajo Peak	Navajo Snowfield	
DIFFICULTY: Advanced	DISTANCE: 10 Miles Roundtrip	VERTICAL: 3,100'/3,400' with summit
SUNHIT: Sunrise	ASPECT: East	SEASON: Spring
TRAILHEAD: Brainard Lake	MAP: Page 274–277	PHOTO: Page 207, 210

The table above *should* read summer instead of spring for the season, as this line holds snow year-round. At 10 miles roundtrip from the Brainard Lake, this line is also best late in the spring or early in the summer when you don't have to start at the winter gate. At only 800' of vertical for quality skiing, it's a pretty far trip and comes up short because of the lack of reward for the effort. You can always go for lines on Apache Peak to make the approach more rewarding; see the Trifecta in the Traverses section.

From the Brainard Lake Trailhead, hike or bike around the lake to the Long Lake Trailhead. Take the trail to Long Lake and then the Lake Isabelle Trail, which is on the north side

Navajo
Peak

Apache
Peak

Apache
Couloir

Navajo
Snowfield

Queen's Way
Couloir

You get good look at Navajo and Apache
from the Brainard Lake parking lot.

of Long Lake. If you lose the trail, just stay on the north side of Lake Isabelle. Take the line of least resistance west, after Lake Isabelle, aiming for Apache Peak. At the base of the Isabelle Glacier, make your way across the bench below the Apache Couloir and Navajo Snowfield. Ascend the snowfield to the saddle, at the base of Dickers Peck. If you want to summit Navajo, have at it—you can't ski it, so I didn't bother. I've heard there are 4th class routes from the saddle.

The skiing is in the high-30s and is usually pretty even. Though the route is short, you can get your money's worth by lapping the snowfield or skiing Apache Couloir or Queens Way. I had awesome weather and managed to ski all three. Return the way you came.

The Snowfield offers the perfect
angle for fast corn skiing.

ajo Peak

Apache Peak

Apache
Couloir

Navajo Snowfield

Queen's Way
Couloir

43 APACHE PEAK – 13,441'

This peak was also named by Ellsworth Bethel, for whom Mount Bethel is named. He was the director of the CU Boulder History Museum. The Apache people had a minimal presence in southeastern Colorado; however, their presence in American history can't be denied or be called minimal. Their battle for freedom against the U.S. Army is one of legend. Geronimo's strategy to use the mountains to increase the power of his force is remarkably similar to what the Spartans accomplished at the Battle of Thermopylae. The peak is ranked the 291st highest in the state. The view of Apache and Navajo together defines the Indian Peaks in my mind, from the east or the west.

43a – Apache Peak	Apache Couloir	
DIFFICULTY: Advanced	DISTANCE: 10 Miles Roundtrip	VERTICAL: 3,200
SUNHIT: Sunrise	ASPECT: East	SEASON: Spring
TRAILHEAD: Brainard Lake	MAP: Page 274–277	PHOTO: Page 207–210

This route is steeper than its neighboring lines, Queens Way and the Navajo Snowfield. At 1,000' of action, it's in the middle of the pack vertically; it's in the middle as well position-wise. The line also features an optional crux section for the middle of the route. This steeper crux offers a low-50 degree choke. This optional route melts out early.

The approach is the same as Navajo and Queens Way. Take the Long Lake trail past Long Lake and Lake Isabelle. Take the line of least resistance up to the Isabelle Glacier's base and

A look up the valley from Lake Isabelle.

Apache Couloir

Looking down valley from the base of the Isabelle Glacier.

Skiing the Apache Couloir.

head to climber's left of the peak, to the base of the Apache Couloir. Climb up the couloir or take the steeper option to climber's left of the main couloir. At the top of the couloir, the angle eases and you get to a thin area. This also melts out early. Above the thin spot, you have an upper snowfield that takes you to the ridge; from there hike to the summit. The ridge from the summit to the line is only in early in the spring.

Ski your ascent route. Watch out for moating on the line. The bulk of the line is in the low-40 degree range. If you want to ski the steeper option, ascend it so you can follow your boot prints for the descent.

The Queen's Way couloir is the longest line in the Isabelle Glacier zone.

43b – Apache Peak	Queen's Way	
DIFFICULTY: **Advanced**	DISTANCE: **10 Miles Roundtrip**	VERTICAL: **3,300'**
SUNHIT: **Northeast**	ASPECT: **Sunrise**	SEASON: **Spring**
TRAILHEAD: **Brainard Lake**	MAP: **Page 274–277**	PHOTO: **Page 208–209, 211–212**

This is the Apache Peak summit ski line; it's also the longest line in the zone though not the steepest. If there were a classic in the zone, this would be the one. Perhaps the three-line combination is the classic.

From the Long Lake Trailhead, take the Long Lake Trail past Long Lake and Lake Isabelle. Follow the easiest way west, up to Isabelle Glacier. The entrance is out of view to climber's right of Apache's East Buttress. Ascend the couloir; maximum angle is around 48 degrees.

Head around the corner to get to the entrance of Queen's Way.

The upper choke in Queen's Way melts out first.

The couloir is not narrow, but the walls are fairly high. The angle eases and you reach a choke; this melts out first. Above the choke you have the summit steeps. The summit ski melts out early but the line stays in well into the summer. Follow your ascent for the descent.

Check out the Traverses section for some thoughts on the Navajo Apache Trifecta. This is a great way to maximize the return on the long approach.

43c – Apache Peak	Fair Glacier	
DIFFICULTY: Advanced	DISTANCE: 16 Miles Roundtrip	VERTICAL: 5,400'
SUNHIT: Sunrise + 3 Hours	ASPECT: North	SEASON: Spring
TRAILHEAD: Monarch Lake	MAP: Page 274, 276	PHOTO: Page 212–215

If distance makes the heart grow fonder, then I have an explanation for why I love this route. It could also be due to the fact that you go by Lone Eagle Peak, or under the amazing West Face of Apache. This line feels like it's as far away as you can get. The angle is steep, in the high 40s. You get the best view of Wheeler Basin and the North Face of North Arapaho. You can also combine this route with other lines around Crater and Mirror Lakes. This zone of

Lone Eagle Peak

Fair Glacier

Mount Achonee

"Hopi Peak"

Mirror Lake is a great place to set up base camps and ski all the great lines in the zone.

Mount George

Fair
Glacier

From the summit of Paiute Peak you get the big
picture of how much terrain there is in this zone.

Mount George　　　Lone Eagle Peak　　　"Hopi Peak"　　　Mount
　　　　　　　　　　　　　　　　　　　　　　　　　　　　　　　Achonee

Fair
Glacier

the Indian Peaks is one of the most beautiful places I've ever seen; you should see it and ski it too. The glacier was named by Junius Henderson, professor of Natural History and curator of the Museum, in the journal *University of Colorado Studies: General Series, Volume 8, Issue 1, 1910*, in honor of Fred A. Fair who in about 1908 discovered the glacier and many other features in the area. Fair served as the engineer for the city of Boulder and helped develop the water resources in the Indian Peaks.

From the Monarch Lake Trailhead, hike around the north side of the lake to the Cascade Creek Trail. This trail leads to Mirror Lake. When you get to the turnoff for Mirror Lake, about 6.5 miles up the trail, leave the trail and continue up the valley, passing underneath Lone Eagle Peak's North Face and then past Triangle Lake. Fair Glacier is at the head of this valley about 8 miles from the trailhead. The top of the glacier is the saddle between Apache Peak and Mount George.

Climb it and ski it. There are some cool-looking lines on Mount George that would make for great combinations with the Fair Glacier. I didn't have time for the Mount George lines as I skied the Fair Glacier as a sunset ski. The angle of the Fair Glacier tops out in the high-40 degree range. Staying at Mirror or Crater Lakes is always a good idea and you can combine this with lines on Hopi, Cherokee, Lone Eagle, or Achonee (see Teasers).

Fair Glacier seen behind the North Face of Lone Eagle Peak.

"Hopi Peak"

Mount Achonee

Hopi Glacier

44 "HOPI PEAK" – 12,780'

This peak was named by guidebook author Gerry Roach. His guidebook *Colorado's Indian Peaks: Classic Hikes and Climbs* is the standard for the zone. He holds true to the spirit of the Indian Peaks by naming significant points throughout the range after Native American tribes, just like Ellsworth Bethel did in 1914. The Hopi people are believed to be descendants of the Anasazi, builders of the Mesa Verde ruins. The Spanish called them the Pueblo people. According to the Hopi Dictionary, their name means "the peaceful people." The peak is the 797th highest in the state. The eastern point is the twin summited peak's highpoint, which is good because that's where the best line descends from.

44a – "Hopi Peak"	Kiva Ramp	
DIFFICULTY: Expert	**DISTANCE: 14 Miles Roundtrip**	**VERTICAL: 5,700'**
SUNHIT: Sunrise + 2 Hours	**ASPECT: North**	**SEASON: Spring**
TRAILHEAD: Monarch Lake	**MAP: Page 274, 276**	**PHOTO: Page 213, 215–218, 221**

The name for this route comes from the Hopi people's subterranean religious chambers that were built into the pueblos. Kivas are present in the Anasazi's Cliff Palace at Mesa Verde. I use the term to give respect to the line; it felt like a religious experience skiing over so much exposure in such a beautiful place. I feel this line is one of the most aesthetic in the entire range. The 1,100' route descends from a saddle just below the true eastern summit of Hopi. You can get a summit ski of the line by skiing the upper East Face of Hopi and then traversing to the line. The line is a mellow narrow ledge at first that morphs into a steep ledge traversing 200' cliffs; in places it's 50+ degrees and off fall-line over massive air. The ledge ends at an

To "Hopi Peak" —

Kiva Ramp

Exit 1

Exit 2

Lone Eagle Peak

"Hopi Peak"

Looking back at Exit 1 from the top of Exit 2.

exit option that skis clean, or you can mount the last rib and ski a longer chute down to the Hopi Glacier moraine. In many ways it's similar to Broadway Ledge and Sky Pilot on James Peak. Climb it before you ski it to make sure you know what the snow is doing. I skied it with a whippet and an ice axe.

Combine with other routes in the area to maximize the return on the effort involved in getting back into this zone.

Making turns down Exit 2.

"Hopi Peak"

44b – "Hopi Peak"	Hopi Glacier	
DIFFICULTY: Expert	DISTANCE: 14 Miles Roundtrip	VERTICAL: 5,700'
SUNHIT: Sunrise + 2 Hours	ASPECT: North	SEASON: Spring
TRAILHEAD: Monarch Lake	MAP PAGE: 274, 276	PHOTO PAGE: 213, 215, 218–219, 221

This route is less intense than Kiva Ramp, but it doesn't go from the true summit of "Hopi;" it goes from the lower, western summit. Hopi Glacier isn't marked on the official USGS map, unlike the Peck and Fair Glaciers. The entrance is the crux as there are usually cornices here. Even when the cornices have fallen, you're looking at near 60 degree entrances. There are two entrances at the ridge; the one closer to the summit is usually easier. The lines dropping in from the hump to the west of the main couloir are cliffed out.

The chute to get back to Crater Lake.

Hopi Glacier

Kiva Ramp

Take the Cascade Creek trail first to Mirror Lake, then to Crater Lake. Ascend the snowfield on the south side of the lake up to the moraine below Hopi Glacier. Ascend the couloir to the ridge and ski your ascent route. Average angle is in the high 40s. Wait for sun hit or the super steeps will be terrifying. You may need a rope to deal with the transition around the ridge/cornice.

Combine with other lines in the area since you put so much effort into just getting back into the zone.

JOIN!

SUMMIT
CLIMBING GYM

CLIMB.
TRAIN.
GATHER.

The **ONLY** dedicated gym serving the Colorado High Country

Join our member-owned and operated climbing co-op located in Silverthorne, CO.

We are a not-for-profit gym offering the following

MEMBERSHIP BENEFITS

-Unlimited climbing!
-Quartely gym events
-Group climbing trips
-An awesome community

LEARN MORE & JOIN AT
www.summitclimbing.org

Lone Eagle Peak

There is so much great ski terrain above Crater Lake.

Lone Rabbit

Achonee

"Hopi"

45 LONE EAGLE PEAK – 11,890'

This is a spectacular mountain. It captivates the soul with its undeniable grandeur; you feel so insignificant at your campsite at Mirror Lake, neck craning skyward. The peak resembles an eagle emerging from an egg, looking skyward. According to USGS documents, the peak's name was intended to honor Charles Lindbergh's first solo flight across the Atlantic; "Lone Eagle" was his nickname. The knowledge of that nickname, however, became lost to the masses, and in 1978 the Colorado legislature put forth a joint resolution to change the name to Lindbergh Peak or Mount Lindbergh. The USGS kept the Lone Eagle Peak name when it revisited naming in 1981. This isn't an officially ranked peak as it is merely the first point on "Mahler Ridge" which extends to its higher neighbor "Iroquois."

45a – Lone Eagle Peak	Lone Rabbit Couloir	
DIFFICULTY: Expert	DISTANCE: 13 Miles Roundtrip	VERTICAL: 5,000'
SUNHIT: Sunrise + 4 Hours	ASPECT: Northwest	SEASON: Spring
TRAILHEAD: Monarch Lake	MAP: Page 274, 276	PHOTO: Page 221–222

This 800' couloir makes me feel like I'm skiing in Europe. Though not as long as many lines in Chamonix, the alpine rock and spires make me feel like I'm going for the Tour Ronde, a mini Gervasutti Couloir. The upper portion of the line reaches into the mid-50s in both upper top-outs; climber's left being the longer one. The rest of the couloir is in the high 40s. There aren't any crevasses like the lines in Europe, but later in the spring you can expect moating to create the holes that are Colorado's version of crevassing.

Lone Rabbit transition

Make your way to Crater Lake from Monarch Lake. You get a great view of the line from Crater Lake. It looks especially dramatic set against Lone Eagle Peak. Hike around the lake and ascend the snowfield, on the south side of Crater Lake, to the moraine below the line. Then head up the line. I heard a lot of rockfall while I was in this zone, so please wear your helmet. Climb it and ski it. There is a slight dogleg to the line, so make those turns or you'll go into the wall.

Fun and steep.

A look back at a classic.

It can be hard to tell if the upper line on "Cherokee" is in or not. But the middle choke melts out first.

"Cherokee"

46 "CHEROKEE" – 12,130'

This is another peak named in Gerry Roach's *Colorado's Indian Peaks: Classic Hikes and Climbs*. It keeps with his practice of naming significant points through the range after Native American tribes. The Cherokee people were originally from the southeastern United States. In the mid-1800s they were forcibly removed from that region to Oklahoma under the Indian Removal Act. According to the Cherokee.org website, the phrase "Trail of Tears" originated from a description of the removal of the Cherokee Nation in 1838. Today the Cherokee Nation is the largest federally recognized tribe in the United States. The peak is beautiful from the Cascade Creek Trail as you pass under its north slopes; look for moose in the meadows below the peak, south of the trail. It is the 602nd highest point in the state.

46a – "Cherokee"	North Gully	
DIFFICULTY: **Advanced**	DISTANCE: **10.7 Miles Roundtrip**	VERTICAL: **5,100'**
SUNHIT: **Sunrise + 1 Hour**	ASPECT: **North**	SEASON: **Spring**
TRAILHEAD: **Monarch Lake**	MAP: **Page 274, 276**	PHOTO: **Page 223–224**

If you're planning a trip to Mirror and Crater Lakes for ski backpacking, plan on doing this line first, on the way in; or last, on the way out. Accessing this route from Crater Lake, from the east, is reported to be in the 3rd class grade range but with all the ledges it looks to be time-consuming. Given the route's northerly aspect, an afternoon descent is reasonable if you have the weather window.

North Gully

Cherokee

"Cherokee" viewed
from Watanga Peak

Head up the Cascade Creek Trail from the Monarch Lake Trailhead 5.3 miles. If you get to the Pawnee Pass Trail Junction, you went too far. Head south to the base of the drainage gully and what may be a waterfall. There is usually a path through here even if some options are melted out. At the bench above the drainage gully, turn to climber's left and choose the option that goes through to the upper face, usually the climber's right option. Above this, head for the summit. The route is mostly in low-40 degree range with a few steeper sections up high and in the middle.

Getting around Blue Lake's cliffs can be tricky. Be sure to plan your exit on the uphill.

Blue Lake

47   MOUNT TOLL – 12,979'

This popular peak rising above Blue Lake is named in honor of Roger W. Toll, the superintendent of Rocky Mountain National Park from 1921-1929. He later became superintendent of Yellowstone. He was also the author of *The Mountain Peaks of Colorado* (1923) and *Mountaineering in the Rocky Mountain National Park* (1919). According to the American Alpine Journal, he was a charter member of the Colorado Mountain Club, where he originated the club's system of trip reports and designed the club's peak register cylinders, which are now widely used in the Rocky Mountain region. Mount Toll is a beautiful, striking peak with its steep North Face and North Ridge. Since it is visible from the plains, I like to use it to orient myself. The peak is also a popular spring skiing destination from the easy access provided by one of the busiest wilderness trailheads in the country, Brainard Lake. Toll measures in as the 651st highest point in the state rankings.

47a – Mount Toll	Southeast Slopes	
DIFFICULTY: **Advanced**	DISTANCE: **7.6 Miles Roundtrip**	VERTICAL: **2,900'**
SUNHIT: **Sunrise**	ASPECT: **Southeast**	SEASON: **Spring**
TRAILHEAD: **Brainard Lake**	MAP: **Page 277**	PHOTO: **Page 225–226**

This is a Front Range classic and a great introductory line. It is very popular, so most likely you will see other groups on this line. Brainard Lake is one of the busiest wilderness trailheads in the United States. One way to avoid the crowds is to bike into the Mitchell Lake Trailhead from the winter closure.

Make your way to Mitchell Lake Trailhead via skins, bike, or on foot. Hike or skin the trail to Mitchell Lake and pass it, heading west up-valley to Blue Lake. The line rises to the southwest over Blue Lake; head around the lake, taking the south shore. There is a cliff to navigate that

A look at the upper mountain.
photo: Dave Reed

Paiute Peak

rises directly out of the lake; take the couloir that cuts through the climber's left side of the cliff. Once on top of the cliff, make your way up the line. The angle is in the mid-30s on average. There is a short section of low-40 degrees near the top of the lower section. Above that, the aspect moves more southeasterly. The upper snowfield is in the mid-30s. The line from the lake to the summit is 1,600' of vertical.

As mentioned earlier in this section, you can expect to see other groups. Please be respectful of other users in the line, both ascending and descending. Try to set boot-packs off to the side to minimize exposure to other people's mistakes. As this is an easier line, other groups may not have the experience to do it the right way. Speak up if you see poor mountain craft. Let the other parties know that their actions may impact the lives of others.

If you're going to pond skim across Blue Lake, remember that if you go under the ice, that's probably the end.

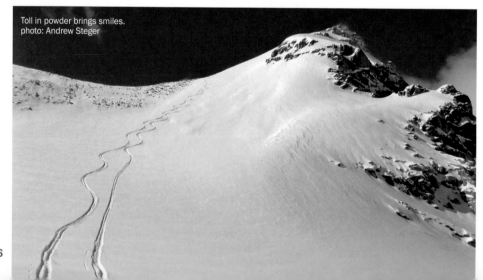

Toll in powder brings smiles.
photo: Andrew Steger

48 MOUNT AUDUBON – 13,233'

The 458th highest peak in the state was named to honor John James Audubon, the famous ornithologist, naturalist, and painter. His work *The Birds of America* is considered by many to be one of the finest illustrated books ever completed. A copy that recently sold at auction brought more than $11.5 million, the second most ever for a single book. Obviously naming a peak in as beautiful a place as the Indian Peaks for someone so in tune with nature was the right choice. Mount Audubon is visible from many miles away on the plains and along the Peak to Peak Highway; its position east of the divide lends itself well to this. Access is easy for this popular peak as it's the closest 13er to the one of the busiest wilderness trails in the country.

48a – Mount Audubon	Crooked Couloir	
DIFFICULTY: Advanced	DISTANCE: 7.6 Miles Roundtrip	VERTICAL: 3,100'
SUNHIT: Sunrise + 2 Hours	ASPECT: South	SEASON: Spring
TRAILHEAD: Brainard Lake	MAP: Page 277	PHOTO: Page 227–228

photo: Erik Stevens

Above the crook the angle is in the high 30's.
athlete: Allison Seymour

At the crook you get to the crux
and mid-40 degree turns.
photo: Jon Bloomfield

The Blue Lake's Basin is such a great zone for skiers, and this line is one of the reasons why. The 1,700' line from the ridge to the lake is steep and holds snow surprisingly late in the spring for a south-facing route. Access is easy as all the Brainard Lake routes are. Since this route is steeper than the Southeast Face of Toll, you are less likely to see other groups on this line; down by Blue Lake is a completely different story.

Make your way to Blue Lake via the Mitchell Lake Trailhead and trail. Contour around the lake on the north side, to the base of and up the couloir. "Couloir" is French for hallway, and this route's lower section is only a one-sided hallway. Follow the couloir up to the crook or dogleg and the steepest section of the line; it goes about 50 degrees at the steepest point. The rest of the couloir is in the low to mid 40s. Above the crook the angle eases to the high 30s. At the ridge, hike east to reach the summit of Audubon; this section melts out first and by spring usually isn't skiable. Ski the line via your ascent route.

This route combines well with the Coney Couloirs, Paiute's Southeast Face, and Toll's Southeast Face.

Audubon/Paiute
Saddle Couloirs
↓

Coney Couloirs
Summit option

From Coney Lake you get a good
look at the Coney Couloirs

48b – Mount Audubon	Coney Couloirs	
DIFFICULTY: Advanced	DISTANCE: 8.3–9.1 Miles Roundtrip	VERTICAL: 3,900'–5,200'
SUNHIT: Sunrise + 2 Hours	ASPECT: North–Northeast	SEASON: Spring
TRAILHEAD: Upper Coney Flats or Brainard Lake	MAP: Page 277	PHOTO: Page 229–230

This line should be a classic and it would be if it wasn't so far. Access from the Upper Coney Flats Trailhead makes this line reasonable but most likely you will be coming from the Lower Coney Flats Trailhead; this is 16.1 miles and 4,900' of vertical. From Brainard Lake you only have 9.1 miles roundtrip, but the gain is huge at 5,200' as you need to climb back out of Coney Basin. You get more vertical by going this route because you access the Coney Couloirs by ascending and returning via the Crooked Couloir. Between Coney Lake and Upper Coney Lake you have your choice of seven separate lines that descend from the Northeast Ridge of Audubon all the way west to the main Coney Couloir just east of the top of the Crooked Couloir. The main Coney Couloir is a 2,100' line to Upper Coney Lake.

Pick your poison and swallow the pill. If you're going from Coney Flats, take the Coney Lake Trail to Coney Lake. If there's a lot of snow in the valley—enough to cover the horrendous willows—ascend to Upper Coney Lake and then the Coney Couloir to the ridge and back east to the summit. If the willows aren't covered, ascend the gully to the south of Coney Lake to the Northeast Ridge of Audubon then on to the summit and the Coney Couloir just west of the summit. Or you could ascend and ski any of the couloirs between Coney Lake and Upper Coney Lake.

If going at it from Brainard Lake, ascend to Blue Lake and then the Crooked Couloir. Top out on Audubon by hiking east along the ridge to the summit; you will pass by the Coney Couloir just east of where the Crooked Couloir reaches the ridge. Ski the Coney Couloir and enjoy steep snow. The crux is a narrow section in the mid-50s. There are other steep sections to skier's left. The rest of the couloir averages in the mid-40s. The lower section just above Upper Coney Lake sees less loading and melts out first. Due to its north-facing nature, the return to the ridge shouldn't be sloppy, but your ski of Crooked Couloir to get back to Brainard Lake might be. Factor this in to your planning.

The Coney Couloirs offer surprisingly steep turns.
Get it early in the spring as it melts out fast.
athlete: Jon Bloomfield

49 PAIUTE PEAK – 13,088'

Ellsworth Bethel was the person behind the naming scheme for the Indian Peaks, having been inspired by the naming of the Arapaho Peaks. The USGS used seven of the names he put forth, according to the USGS decision cards. He originally chose Ute Peak as the name for Paiute, but with many other places in Colorado that bore the name Ute, he needed to come up with a different name for this one. Other peaks named by Bethel in the Indian Peaks were Apache Peak, Arikaree Peak, Kiowa Peak, Navajo Peak, Ogalalla Peak, and Pawnee Peak. The Paiute people come from California, Idaho, Nevada, Oregon, Arizona, and Utah. Paiute is an impressive peak especially when viewed from the west or from the Coney Lakes; the summit is pretty impressive too as the peak is centrally located and the views from the top include most of the Indian Peaks. It is the 578th highest summit in the state.

49a – Paiute Peak	Southeast Face	
DIFFICULTY: **Intermediate–Advanced**	DISTANCE: **8 Miles Roundtrip**	VERTICAL: **3,100'**
SUNHIT: **Sunrise + 1 Hour**	ASPECT: **Southeast**	SEASON: **Spring**
TRAILHEAD: **Brainard Lake**	MAP: **Page 277**	PHOTO: **Page 231–233**

Paiute Peak's Southeast Face looms large over Blue Lake. The direct line is a beauty as it negotiates its way through a series of ledges that intersect the face. The angle on the face reaches the high-40s but given the no-fall nature of the line, it is more serious than its angle suggests. To viewer's left of the main face lies the mellow Curvaceous Couloir. This line is actually a gully as it doesn't have rock walls. I've been on the line but haven't skied it. The angle is in the mid-30s with short, steeper sections. I included it because it is a classic intermediate line on this beautiful peak.

A look down the
Southeast Face.

Each ledge poses a threat
if you fall, so don't fall.

From Brainard Lake, make your way to Mitchell Lake and on to Blue Lake. Skin or hike around the north side of Blue Lake under Crooked Couloir and up a series of ledges to the unnamed lake below the Southeast Face. Ascend the line, taking note of the moats that develop on the face. It would be really bad to fall into a moat on this line. The central ledge had a 15' deep moat the last time I was on the face. At the top, you will get to the south summit. The north summit is the actual highpoint and requires some fun, moderately exposed scrambling.

Combine this line with Toll, Curvaceous or Crooked Couloirs.

49b – Paiute Peak	Paiute/Audubon Saddle Couloirs	
DIFFICULTY: Advanced	DISTANCE: 8 Miles Roundtrip	VERTICAL: 3,100'
SUNHIT: Sunrise + 1 Hour	ASPECT: Southeast	SEASON: Spring
TRAILHEAD: Brainard Lake	MAP: Page 277	PHOTO: Page 231, 233–234

This route isn't really an objective but a tool to facilitate traverses. Though the saddle is the low point between Paiute and Audubon, it is much closer to Paiute and so it is included here. The couloir on the south side is about 500' of steep, rock-walled goodness with another 300' of apron; maximum angle is right at 50 degrees. The north side of the saddle is 1,400 of vertical to the base of Paiute's Northeast Face, at the head of the Coney drainage; maximum angle here is about 45 degrees

Ski these lines if you need to access the Coney drainage for Coney Couloir, Paiute's Northeast Face, or are linking valleys while doing a traverse.

Summit

Curvaceous

Southeast
Face

Paiute/Audubon
Saddle Couloirs

photo: Dave Reed

The Paiute/Audubon Saddle Couloir
is a great way to get to Coney Lakes
from the Blue Lakes Basin.

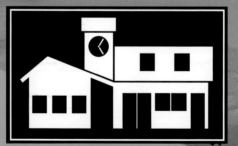

As seen from the South Slopes of Hiamovi, access is very easy.

West Slopes

50 MOUNT IRVING HALE – 11,754'

According to the USGS decision card, this peak was named in 1931 by the Colorado Geographic Board for General Irving Hale. A Denver East High School graduate, he served in the Spanish-American and Philippine-American Wars. Camp Hale, the site of the 10th Mountain Division training camp during World War II, is also named for the general. He was one of the founders of the Veterans of Foreign Wars (VFW). He died on July 26, 1930, and is buried in Denver's Fairmount Cemetery. The gendarme on the east face of the mountain strongly resembles a soldier standing at attention.

50a – Mount Irving Hale	West Slopes	
DIFFICULTY: Intermediate	DISTANCE: 6.3 Miles Roundtrip	VERTICAL: 3,600'
SUNHIT: Sunrise + 3 Hours	ASPECT: West	SEASON: Winter or Spring
TRAILHEAD: Roaring Fork	MAP: Page 276	PHOTO: Page 235–236

Summit

The West Slopes are nice and mellow.

From Watanga you can see the other
options between Hiamovi and Irving Hale.

This mellow tour to the western Indian Peaks offers awesome views. The route finding through the trees is difficult and you will benefit from a GPS unit. All the trees and the lower angles keep the avalanche danger on this line minimal. If you go for the summit, be sure to use care near the edge. If there is a cornice overhanging the East Face and you were to trapdoor through it, you would take a 600' fall before hitting the ground.

From the trailhead, hike up the steep Roaring Fork Trail. This is very low and south facing, so you'll find minimal snow here. Once at the falls and in a shadier zone, the snow cover will be better. Travel is much easier on the west side of the Roaring Fork. Follow the creek to about the 1.6 mile mark and cross the creek, heading east, up a treed gully that joins up with the Grouse Creek drainage. Maintain your easterly heading through fairly open trees at treeline and then up to the summit of Irving Hale. Retrace your steps for the descent. There are some steeper options to skier's left of the gully below Grouse Creek, leading back into the Roaring Fork drainage.

Combine this route with Watanga and Hiamovi as well as the teaser line on Twin Peaks.

51 WATANGA MOUNTAIN – 12,375'

According to *Native American Placenames of the United States* by William Bright, the mountain was named for an Arapaho leader. The name is said to mean "black coyote." There is also mention of a Watanga in Oklahoma that was the site of Cheyenne sun dances. This Watanga was located a few miles from the Washita River, according to an account in *The Cheyenne, Volumes 1-2* by George Amos Dorsey. The peak is ranked 1,093rd highest in the state.

51a – Watanga Mountain	Watanga Lake Gully	
DIFFICULTY: Advanced	DISTANCE: 9.2 Miles Roundtrip	VERTICAL: 4,600'
SUNHIT: Sunrise + 3 Hours	ASPECT: Southwest	SEASON: Winter Spring
TRAILHEAD: Roaring Fork	MAP: Page 276	PHOTO: Page 237

Summit

From Watanga Lake you can see multiple options coming almost directly off the summit of Watanga Peak.

Like Irving Hale and Hiamovi, this is a great zone to access in the winter and combines very well with the aforementioned peaks. The western Indian Peaks are beautiful with a glaciated history that delivers beautiful scarps and glacial knobs. It's best to stick to the trail when in this zone as the terraced nature of the terrain can see users getting cliffed out.

Head up the Roaring Fork Trail about 2.3 miles to Watanga Creek. Use the creek for navigation as the sign will probably be covered. The creek will take you to Watanga Lake. The last pitch to the lake is steep enough to slide. You can head to the east side of the lake and up the South Slopes of Watanga, keeping the avy danger minimal by being on a shallow angle.

From the summit, drop in on a west-southwesterly heading to get to the Watanga Lake Gully and the other options above the lake. The steep pitch is only 300' of high 30 degree slopes, but that's enough to get you in trouble so be sure of your stability; if it's not stable, ski the South Slopes.

Watanga Lake would be a good base for skiing all the peaks in the zone, including the teaser section Twin Peaks.

Watanga Peak's Southwest Slopes
offer wilderness winter turns.

51b – Watanga Mountain	Southwest Slopes	
DIFFICULTY: Intermediate	DISTANCE: 9.3 Miles Roundtrip	VERTICAL: 4,600'
SUNHIT: Sunrise + 2 Hours	ASPECT: South–Southwest	SEASON: Winter–Spring
TRAILHEAD: Roaring Fork	MAP: Page 276	PHOTO: Page 238

This is the easy line on Watanga, if a 4,600' vertical day can be called easy. At least the skiing is easy and the views are amazing. I had the good fortune to ski this route as a sunset ski. This is the ascent route for Watanga's Lake Gully as well as its safe route if the conditions merit. This is a great winter ski camping route to combine with Hiamovi and Irving Hale.

Head up the Roaring Fork Trail about 2.3 miles to Watanga Creek. Use the creek for navigation as the sign will probably be covered. The creek will take you to Watanga Lake. The last pitch to the lake is steep enough to slide. You can head to the east side of the lake and up the Southwest Slopes of Watanga, keeping the avy danger minimal by being on a shallow angle. Go up the Southwest Slopes to the summit.

For the descent, either return the way you came or ski into the Roaring Fork drainage directly. Be careful around the East Face, where you'll need to skirt the south end. Be aware of cliffs and keep your speed in check.

This solo, sunset ski of Watanga was one of the truly special moments from this past spring and finishing the guidebook.

Looking back at Hiamovi from the ridge
between Hiamovi and Irving Hale

52 HIAMOVI MOUNTAIN – 12,395'

According to *Indian Placenames in America, Volume 1* by Sandy Nestor, the peak "was thought to have been named for a Cheyenne chief who contributed songs and legends to *The Indian Book* by Natalie Curtis in 1908, his name was interpreted as 'god,' 'spirit' or 'high chief.'" Ranking for the peak is 1,074th highest in the state.

52a – Hiamovi Mountain	West Slopes	
DIFFICULTY: **Advanced**	DISTANCE: **9.7 Miles Roundtrip**	VERTICAL: **4,700'**
SUNHIT: **Sunrise + 3 Hours**	ASPECT: **West–Southwest**	SEASON: **Winter–Spring**
TRAILHEAD: **Roaring Fork**	MAP: **Page 276**	PHOTO: **Page 239–240**

Twin Peaks

Watanga

Approaching the steeper
turns on the West Slopes.

Lots of great options coming off the ridge between Hiamovi and Irving Hale.

Here's another relaxed route for this zone that makes it ideal for a winter descent. I've made it an advanced line due to the distance and the skills needed for navigation, but the skiing is intermediate. You will have a better time on this line if you have a GPS unit as the trees can be thick.

Follow the Roaring Fork Trail to the saddle of Irving Hale and Hiamovi, about 6 miles in. Go north from here and take the South Ridge of Hiamovi to the summit. Use care along the ridge's edge as Hiamovi's East Face has some massive, overhanging cornices. Do not trust the edge; it's farther back than you think. To your left going up the ridge are the West Slopes. They are steep enough to slide but you will get be in a great position to assess stability on your ascent.

Either ski back down the ridge and return the way you came; or via the West Slopes and then down along the Roaring Fork Creek proper to meet back up with the Roaring Fork Trail.

53 SAWTOOTH MOUNTAIN – 12,304'

This is one of four Sawtooth Mountains in the state, the others are in Routt, Mineral and Saguache Counties. This is the second highest of the four and the 1,140th highest peak in the state. This is another striking peak with a dramatic south face, almost a mirror version of Mt. Toll. The peak is visible for miles on the plains due to its unique saw-toothed jagged appearance. Access to this summit isn't easy without a solid 4x4 vehicle to get up Coney Flats Road. Embrace the approach.

53a – Sawtooth Mountain	Southeast Bowl	
DIFFICULTY: Advanced	DISTANCE: 6.3 Miles Roundtrip	VERTICAL: 2,900'
SUNHIT: Sunrise + 1 Hour	ASPECT: East–Southeast	SEASON: Spring
TRAILHEAD: Coney Flats or Middle St. Vrain	MAP: Page 277	PHOTO PAGE: 241–242

Approaching the choke.

Many people ski the Northeast Face of Sawtooth, but this is a different option that is worth your attention. On the Northeast Face you can't really see the defining face of this beautiful peak: the dramatic 600' South Face. The Southeast Bowl line is a little less direct from the top than the Northeast Face, but you get the South Face as your skier's left horizon. I think this should be the new standard for skiing Sawtooth.

This route is also a little more adventurous. From the upper Coney Flats Trailhead take the Coney Lakes Trail to Coney Lake. From Coney Lake, head up the drainage to the north of the lake. This will put you below the Southeast Bowl and South Face. Climb the bowl to the summit ridge and on to the summit. Return the way you came. If there is snow, descend the valley to the Buchanan Pass Trail, and then east to Coney Flats. If there isn't snow, return to Coney Lake the way you approached. Alternatively, you could approach this peak via the Buchanan Pass Trail and drop into the line from the top. Then at the bottom, regain the Buchanan Pass Trail to get back to the Middle St. Vrain Trailhead.

It stays steep below the choke.

Ogalalla
Express

Dalkes
Couloir

54 OGALALLA PEAK – 13,138'

This is another peak named by Ellsworth Bethel, the botanist. He was the driving force behind the naming of the Indian Peaks and this is one of seven summits named by him. The northernmost Indian Peak, this summit is also the southernmost 13er in Rocky Mountain National Park. The peak is dramatic at the head of the Middle St. Vrain drainage. It is the 540th highest summit in the state.

54a – Ogalalla Peak	Dalkes Couloir	
DIFFICULTY: Advanced	DISTANCE: **10.5–17.8 Miles Roundtrip**	VERTICAL: **4,000'–5,700'**
SUNHIT: Sunrise	ASPECT: Southeast	SEASON: Spring
TRAILHEAD: Middle St. Vrain/Camp Dick	MAP: Page 276–277	PHOTO: Page 243–244

This 1,300' line, dropping in directly from the summit of Ogalalla, is a beauty. The average angle is in the mid-40s, with a few sections that touch the low-50s. It's narrow at the bottom with decent walls to make it feel confining. In the middle it widens substantially and is a bit less steep; near the top it tightens again and gets very exposed at the summit. There often is a deep runnel; this is caused by rockfall and snow sluffing. It's a long way to get to this line. Even from the Upper Middle St. Vrain Road Trailhead, you're looking at 10.5 miles roundtrip. You need a solid vehicle and driving skills to make it to this point. If you go from Camp Dick, add 7.3 miles roundtrip and 1,700' of vertical. This is best as an overnight trip. The best place to check out conditions on this line is from the Upper Coney Flats Trailhead.

From the upper trailhead, take the Buchanan Pass Trail to the St. Vrain Glacier Trail. When you finally get to treeline at about the 4 mile mark, you get a beautiful view of Elk Tooth

and finally Ogalalla. At about the 5 mile mark, you will find yourself at the base of Ogalalla's Southeast Face and the entrance to the Dalkes Couloir. The lower and middle sections have the most pronounced runnelling. Ascend the line and use care as you approach the ridge as a fall on the top section could put you off the North Face of Ogalalla. The final section to the summit is around 50 degrees. Return the way you came.

The first opening in the trees.

55 MEADOW MOUNTAIN – 11,632'

This mountain was named in 1911, at the suggestion of ecologist William S. Cooper. According to Wikipedia, the Ecological Society of America recognizes Cooper's work in the discipline by bestowing its annual William Skinner Cooper Award on scientists who produce outstanding publications on geobotany, physiographic ecology, plant succession, or the distribution of plants along environmental gradients.

55a – Meadow Mountain	East Slopes	
DIFFICULTY: Intermediate	DISTANCE: 5 Miles Roundtrip	VERTICAL: 2,900'
SUNHIT: Sunrise	ASPECT: East–Southeast	SEASON: Winter
TRAILHEAD: Meadow Mountain	MAP: Page 277	PHOTO: Page 245–246

Just so you know you're on the right track.

Anthony Orig getting multiple laps in some winter pow.
photo: Becca Orig

This route reminds me a lot of Butler Gulch. You have a fairly flat approach for about 1.75 miles along a trail that is essentially a road. Above that, you have lightly-treed slopes with a few spots that could cause you some avalanche trouble but are generally safe. This is a great place to look at the wind's effects on the snowpack, as this mountain on the southeastern edge of Rocky Mountain National Park sees a lot of wind. The summit is in RMNP but the East Slopes are not.

From the trailhead, take the St. Vrain Mountain Trail up the valley. At about 1.75 miles, you will come to an opening in the trees. Take the line of least resistance up toward the saddle of St. Vrain Mountain and Meadow Mountain, angling more toward Meadow Mountain to save some distance. Top out and enjoy an outstanding view of Wild Basin to the west, and Meeker and Longs to the northwest.

Ski your ascent route. It makes sense to get multiple laps on this route. Skin, ski, and repeat until there's no more powder and you're a quivering mess. Take it easy on the exit trail as it is tight and sees a fair amount of use.

Looking south from the summit of Meadow into the basin.

TRAVERSES

At the beginning of the book, I talk about embracing the approach as a means for success in the Front Range, and Indian Peaks more specifically. Well, this section flies in the face of that concept, utilizing point-to-point traverses or getting multiple lines in on your visits to or through the zones covered. Maximizing the approach is what I was trying to accomplish by traversing the whole range; that concept failed twice due to weather. By cutting down on the size of the traverse, you can increase your chances of completing it. The goal of these traverses isn't to merely stay on the ridge to your eventual drop-in above your exit gully; these traverses are all about skiing routes, as many as you can. With weather always a concern, it's important to have alternate routes built into your plan to help minimize the danger of lightning.

Eisenhower Tunnel to Butler Gulch		
DIFFICULTY: Expert	DISTANCE: 9.7 Miles Point to Point	VERTICAL: 6,600' Up/ 7,200' Down
SUNHIT: Sunrise	ASPECT: All aspects	SEASON: Spring
TRAILHEAD: Eisenhower Tunnel West Portal North to Jones Pass		

This was one of my favorite days of last season—five great lines on five 13ers. "Golden Bear," Hagar, "Citadel," Pettingell, and "Hassel" were all great skis. I also had some excitement getting back to the ridge and probably cut it too close. The thunder was going off a few ridges to my west as I was running up the west side of "Hassel" to get back to the east side of the divide. With more stable weather, I would have liked to ski the Woods Creek Pinner (covered in the Teaser Section) as well.

Begin by ascending the West Gully of "Golden Bear." Ski the Northeast Bowl

to the base of Hagar's Southwest Ridge. Ascend Hagar and ski its Southeast Face or the Boomerang Couloir. Take a left to the base of Snoopy's South Collar and ascend it. Decide whether or not you want to ascend to the summit of Snoopy. It will add time; do you have the weather?

At the Saddle of the Collar, drop into the North Collar Couloir and ski to the flank of UN13418. Head up the south slope to the summit of Pettingell Peak. The North Face of Pettingell is the jewel of this traverse. The 1,700' face is more of a steep couloir ski with the steepest turns of the traverse at about 53 degrees. Make sure the weather is stable enough to give you enough time to get back to the east side of the divide. After Pettingell you will need to ascend to near the summit of "Hassel" or you could ski Woods Creek Pinner. You could then add Hassel for six lines. If you need to get into Butler Gulch quickly, you can ski down the North Ridge of "Hassel" to a direct entrance into Butler Gulch from the divide. From there, ski Butler Gulch to the Jones Pass Trailhead.

Berthoud Pass Super Tour		
DIFFICULTY: Advanced	**DISTANCE: 6.9 Miles Point to Point**	**VERTICAL: 3,600' Up/ 4,700' Down**
SUNHIT: Sunrise	**ASPECT: East– Northeast–North**	**SEASON: Winter or Spring**
TRAILHEAD: Berthoud Pass Summit to Zero Creek		

This is an all-time classic and it's still just as awesome. Berthoud Pass has a history going back to 1937; it was the site of the first lift-served skiing in Colorado and it was all about the backcountry before that. The lifts are gone now and the zone has been returned to the backcountry skiers and boarders. In 1940, Winter Park opened and it wouldn't surprise me if that year a much longer version of the super tour was completed; longer because Winter Park has been steadily expanding toward the pass and

wasn't nearly as close back in the day. Go get this one done and try to ski as many lines as you can along the way. This isn't a traverse along a ridge but instead involves skiing as many quality lines as you can through each drainage: Current, Second, First, and Zero. There are lots of options for routes to ski along the way; even the last line has options.

From the summit of Berthoud Pass, skin west up to the summit of Mt. Russell and ski the North Gully. You could ski anything into Current Creek, such as the 90s, Weebles, or SkullBite. Russell offers the most vertical and if you cut left you can throw in some more quality vertical with X, Y, or Z Chutes. From there, catch the Aqueduct or ski down to the bottom of Tea Cup Bowl. Ascend to Corner Pocket and ski it or get more vertical and ski Frankenstein Chute. Ascend the spine that divides Second and First Creek to the top of Chimney Chute. This is a great steep line.

After you ski the Chimney, skin up to the ridge separating the First Creek drainage from the Zero Creek drainage. If the weather is turning on you, just drop in on Zero Creek at the top of it. But the goal is to ski to Winter Park, so it's best to just continue on to the top of the Panoramic Express at the top of Parsenn Bowl. This is a backcountry book, so ski Zero Creek back to US 40 for the completion—not that having a beer at Mary Jane would be a bad thing, though. If you ski into the area, make sure it's during operating hours, as you may get in trouble if you're on the ski runs after close.

Berthoud Pass to Moffat Tunnel		
DIFFICULTY: Advanced – Expert	DISTANCE: 12–20 Miles Point to Point	VERTICAL – 12,300' Up/ 14,400' Down
SUNHIT: Sunrise	ASPECT: North–Northeast– East–Southeast	SEASON: Spring
TRAILHEAD: BP Summit to Moffat Tunnel		

Colorado Mines Peak

This traverse was the product of my second attempt of a complete traverse of the range. The goal was to go from Berthoud Pass to Wild Basin, while skiing as many lines as I could along the way. I was shut down by weather. I spent too much time near treeline due to lightning threat. But this section was so much fun that I decided to include it in the book.

There are a ton of options on this traverse. With five named 13ers and 10 named peaks, you can mix and match as you like. For my traverse, I skied the East Cirque of Colorado

Mount Flora

Mines, Flora's South Chute and Northeast Bowl, Wittter's Welcome Couloir, "East Eva" North Chute, James Peak's Bailout and North Face, and Haystack's North Face. As I mentioned, lightning kept me low, near the trees for much of it. This route is good because you have that option with a developed trail network leading to the east slopes of James.

You could add Breckinridge Peak, Eva, Parry, or Bancroft to the mix if the weather cooperates. There is a really cool cabin at

Seeking shelter at the James Peak Lake cabin.

James Peak Lake that offers a nice place to stay. It feels refreshing to have a roof over your head. I spent two nights out on my traverse. The first night out was under Witter's Welcome Couloir. I stayed there so I could get an early start for my ski of Witter. Lightning kept me off James Peak's summit but adding Starlight Couloir would be ideal for the traverse. The Iceberg and Crater Couloirs would fit nicely into the tail end of the traverse. Do your weather research and find a window to get it done.

Brainard Lake to Wild Basin		
DIFFICULTY: Expert	DISTANCE: 20.5 Miles Point to Point	VERTICAL: 11,400' Up/ 13,300' Down
SUNHIT: Sunrise	ASPECT: South–Southeast– East–Northeast–North	SEASON: Spring
TRAILHEAD: Brainard Lake to Wild Basin		

My first attempt at a traverse of the Front Range went from Wild Basin and got as far as Brainard Lake; again it was the weather that ended my bid at getting it done. This was a cool trip but would be better from south to north. Skiing south-facing snow in the afternoons was a little scary as it was often crusty and unpredictable. By going south to north you could ski north-facing snow in the afternoons and not have to deal with refrozen lines. Speaking of lines, there are a lot of lines to choose from. Should the weather rear its ugly head, you have the Buchanan Pass Trail and the Middle St. Vrain valley to stay low in while still making progress northward.

From Brainard Lake, make your way to Blue Lake. Your first choice of the traverse is which line to ski to get into the Coney drainage. Coney Couloir is an obvious choice; this will also

View from the summit of Ogalalla.

give you your first summit. Another great option is the Paiute/Audubon Saddle Gully, as this will place you higher in the Coney Drainage and can allow you to get Paiute's Southeast Face. You could spend a couple days in the Coney drainage skiing the Teaser lines on Paiute and "Algonquin." From Upper Coney Lake or Coney Lake proper, make your way up Sawtooth and ski the Southeast Bowl route, re-ascend, and make your way along the divide to "Red Deer." Ski the Northeast Slopes of "Red Deer" and then descend to Middle St. Vrain valley. Take the St. Vrain Glacier Trail to the base of Ogalalla. In the morning, ascend and ski Dalkes Couloir. There are a lot of options back in this zone with the Vrain Glaciers and Elk Tooth providing great lines. Re-ascend Ogalalla and traverse the ridge to Ouzel Peak. The North Slopes of Ouzel make for a fun descent to Blue Bird Lake. Gain the East Ridge of Mahana and ski the Southeast Couloir back to the trail and on down to the Wild Basin Trailhead.

Ogalalla Peak

Navajo – Apache Trifecta		
DIFFICULTY: Advanced	DISTANCE: 12 Miles Roundtrip	VERTICAL: 6,000'
SUNHIT: Sunrise	ASPECT: East–Northeast	SEASON: Spring
TRAILHEAD: Brainard Lake		

This isn't really a traverse, it's more of a combination, taking advantage of the approach to get in multiple lines and maximize the return on your work to get all the way back into the zone. You could easily add a few more lines to this route. Shoshoni has some great couloirs that empty onto Isabelle Glacier. The infamous Airplane Gully usually doesn't have enough snow for skiing, but if it's in you could add it to the itinerary. One could even turn this plan into a loop by connecting with Mt. Toll and exiting via the Blue Lake drainage and the Mitchell Lake Trailhead.

From Brainard Lake, make your way to Long Lake and on to Lake Isabelle. Follow the valley up to the Isabelle Glacier and the base of your first line, Queen's Way. Ascend and summit Apache. Ski the line, staying to skier's right at the bottom to glide over to the base of the Navajo Snowfield. Ascend to the top of the snow and descend. Stay to skier's left at the bottom and glide to the base of the Apache Couloir. Ascend the couloir to the top of the snow and descend your ascent route. Return via your approach. Three classics in a day—it doesn't get much better than that.

WARNING
READ THIS BEFORE USING THIS GUIDEBOOK

SKIING AND SNOWBOARDING ARE DANGEROUS SPORTS THAT CAN RESULT IN SERIOUS INJURY OR EVEN DEATH. BACKCOUNTRY SKIING IS EVEN MORE DANGEROUS THAN RESORT SKIING.

USE THIS BOOK ONLY AT YOUR OWN RISK.

This guidebook is intended as a reference tool for advanced and expert skiers and snowboarders. The terrain and routes it describes can be or are extremely dangerous and require a high degree of ability, fitness and experience to negotiate safely. This book is not intended for inexperienced/novice skiers and snowboarders. It is not intended as an instructional manual. If you are unsure of your ability to handle any situations that you may encounter, employ the services of a professional guide. Avalanche education is essential. There is a listing in the appendix on page 311 of Avalanche Education schools throughout Colorado

The information in this book is unverified, and the author and publisher cannot guarantee its accuracy. Assessments of the difficulty and risks associated with the terrain are based on opinions and are totally subjective. Numerous hazards exist that are not described and which are not marked on the mountains. Skiing or snowboarding any of the terrain in this book, regardless of its description or rating, may cause injury or death. The easiest runs in this book would be black diamond terrain at virtually every ski resort in the US. In the backcountry, you will encounter danger, hazards, and conditions that you won't find at any ski resort in the US. Ski areas have avalanche control teams. The backcountry does not. In addition to expert skiing ability, you must also possess at least a basic level of mountaineering and route finding skills. The ability to use a map and compass are essential. It is imperative that you own, carry, and know how to use an avalanche beacon, shovel, and probe when skiing the routes and terrain described in this book. More importantly is an understanding of avalanche assessment and safety protocols. Know what to look for, know the signs, and know when to turn around. If you don't know these then use a professional guide service. You must accept this risk.

The author and publisher make no representations or warranties, expressed or implied, of any kind regarding the contents of this book, and expressly disclaim any representation or warranty regarding the accuracy or reliability of the information contained herein. Use this book and the information contained herein at your own risk.

TEASERS

The concept of this section is to inspire you to go and get it done. I couldn't accomplish these; the reasons are explained. Use this beta to succeed where I failed. I tried to provide good photos so you know what you're getting into. The rest is up to you. Get on the internet and do some research. Check the maps and look for a weather window. I know I'm going to try to revisit these lines and some of the other lines I didn't include. There are so many options. New ones develop some years and others develop other years. Hopefully some of these will make it into the second edition of this book. But then I'll just add the 10 other lines I saw at the top of the last summit I visited.

Berthoud Pass to Wild Basin

I tried twice to get this done; once from the north and once from the south. The weather got me both times. It felt like I was running for cover from lightning most of the time. The winds howled and I had to take the lower option off the ridge both times. Weather can pin you down and throw off the logistics you've worked out with your partners.

Along with solid logistics, you'll also need stable weather. The thunderstorms seem to crop up in the afternoon or any part of the day if the monsoonal flow has started. If the flow is from the southwest, reschedule. If you need to ski lines to get a book done, don't carry too much weight to feel good about skiing them. I was going for a lot of lines and I got a lot done when the weather was coop-  erative, but then the lightning came and I just had to get low. There are plenty of options to detour at or below treeline.

This traverse involves skiing as many lines as you can. My original plan was about 90 miles and 50,000' of vertical. Going south is the wrong idea. This results in skiing refrozen, crusty snow with a heavy pack, in the evening when you're tired. Going from south to north allows you to potentially jump on winter snow in the afternoon and evening.

Really, what it came down to was that I was missing too may lines to get this book finished. I was going under them. I was doing neither well: the book routes nor the traverse. I will be back, though. Caching will be involved, I think. That way if you need to, you can hang tight for a couple days and wait it out. Some sort of communication is also needed so you can reschedule with partners if you are running late. A satellite phone would be useful.

The segments that I did get done all make for excellent adventures on their own. They are described in the Traverses section. Since I did it, I can write about it.

Woods Creek Pinner

I had intended to ski this line as part of my Eisenhower Tunnel West to Butler Traverse. The weather had other ideas and instead of running up to get this line, I ran up "Hassel Peak" West Face while the thunder rang out a couple ridges away. It was intense; 1,700' of vert, nonstop full-out. All I wanted to do was get back to the other side of the divide and get low. I pulled off the fastest changeover of my life in way under a minute.

This short shot combines ideally with Pettingell Peak's North Face. Skiing it sort of gets you back to Herman; you still need to do a fairly low-elevation traverse, though it is still above treeline. I mention Herman, but the line is in Woods Creek. This is an issue, as the access is closed by Urad Mine. The easement is summer only and for the Hassel Lake Trailhead. By combining with Pettingell and accessing from Herman, you get two for the price of one. Next time I hit Pettingell for sure.

Parnassus Southwest Couloir

Every time you drive by Parnassus, this line is in your face. I was planning on skiing this one but the weather this spring was a little crazy. By the time I went for it, the line was out. It's too bad I didn't get it as it was in. This doesn't happen every year. The winds can get kind of wild on this cross-loaded gully. There is also some serious off-fall-line action here; the benefit of this kind of terrain is that you end up skiing it in sections and automatically do sluff management. I'm looking forward to getting turns on this one as I really like to drive the highway and see all the memories.

Englemann Disney Chute

Back in 1954, this chute earned its name. Disney set up its cameras and CDOT set off the charges. The slide was massive and went all the way to the road. The cameraman who was set up on the road and a technician were unable to move out of the way in time and were buried under 30' of debris. They died. The footage is now only available for avalanche education.

This is a serious line with serious consequences. On my three attempts I failed due to human issues, wind loading, and too much new load with high temps and minimal freezing. With 100 degree temperatures in Denver this past June, by the time I went back for it there was no more snow.

One big issue that makes the line really tough is that you must ascend it. Since it is at low elevation, this can get dicey. We had a lot of snow in May and there was minimal time for stabilization between storms. Then the heat wave wrecked it.

Engelmann North Ramp

This mountain just loves to deliver and deny skiers. There is so much terrain to choose from on this massive mountain. I got some lines completed but not others. This line is almost never in. The upper interesting ramp needs a big spring to get filled in sufficiently. Lower down the line there is usually enough snow but you have to wait for the hard slabs to resolve their issues. The lower zone resembles Loveland Pass' Sheep Creek in many ways, including aspect and angle as well as cross-load. The wind usually scours the top of the mountain. I am looking for a fat snow year and some wet, late season upslope storms to fill this one in.

UN12704 East Bowl

Every year I look at this line and salivate. It doesn't help that it is early season as I write this and I've been watching a bunch of new ski porn. I'm stoked to be back at Jones Pass for the beginning of a new season. I'm amped and wanting to ski something fun; perhaps I'm pushing the limit of what I want from watching all those big lines get shredded by the pros. From the pass it all looks good. It's so far, though; perhaps in the spring when the snowpack is better. I've just never gotten back there. This one is more a reminder for me to go get it done.

UN12696 Northeast Couloir

One of the really fun parts of doing the skiing for the book was trying to go places for which I had no information. While I was skiing one of those lines, I found another line and another and it never seems to end. This is one of the lines from that day. The weather wasn't quite good enough to get two that day. The couloir I did get was worth it and now I have an excuse to go back for this one.

photo: Doug Evans

Witter South Couloirs

Witter is front and center in the psyche of those who drive from Denver and the Front Range up I-70; most of them don't know it, though. One of the peaks in the Genesee Bridge view is Witter. You can see the Northeast Face clearly, as well as the profile of the steep South Face. This aspect of Witter only fills in once a decade, and its southerly aspect means that the snow is fleeting at best. This is a pretty rowdy set of lines. I checked out the possibilities when I skied Witter for the book, but they were no longer in. The gendarmes that line the couloirs remind me of Tenmile Canyon's upper lines.

James Peak Super Star

This is the test piece on James Peak's East Face. Dopes with ropes: this is the kind of roped line I like. Use it for access to surmount an obstacle, then ski it. I like skiing, not messing around with gear and setting up anchors in the middle of things. I love steep skiing and this is the real deal. I plan to put this route in the next edition. On my last visit to the face, I was chased by cornice fall. The giant cornice on Super Star weighs heavy on my mind as I contemplate this descent.

"Heartbeat Peak" Y Gully

This line was spotted while approaching the West Couloir of James Peak. You're in the trees for a while and then you turn the corner and there it is. How did this not get in the book? Well, I planned to be in the zone for spring to go after the West Couloir. Once that route was ready, this line wasn't anymore. I'm looking forward to spending time in it this coming winter. Beyond just the Y Gully, there are multiple options in the tighter trees on either side. There are also other chutes farther up valley, between the Y Gully and James' West Couloir.

"Old Baldy" South Bowl

Embrace the approach to get this one done. If you wait until the Fourth of July Trailhead is open, you will not ski this line, or at least not much of it. You need to get up before the road opens and the line melts. Hessie to Fourth of July is a long way to go, especially for a line that isn't very spectacular. But it is an official 13er, so someday I'll go back for this one—maybe if I get some rando racing gear and spandex.

North Arapaho North Face

The approach is the big issue with this route as well. Just getting to this line while the North Face is still holding is an achievement. For some reason, the north aspect of North Arapaho doesn't hold snow very well. This is strange because the west-facing North Star holds snow reliably, almost every year. Once you get there you have to get out of there. The North Face itself is pretty inspiring. Hopefully one day I can add this route.

Achonee Arrow

Achonee Arrow is the one that got away. I didn't do my research on this line and assumed it would be obvious. I didn't realize my mistake until I was on Paiute looking at the correct way to approach the line. The line goes through but you can't see it from Crater Lake. The entrance looks very steep and what I thought were multiple rock steps to negotiate aren't even part of the descent. I wish I'd done better planning for this one. This is just another excuse to get back up there for more fun. I think I'll try to go in a little earlier in the spring to get some of the other lines I saw in the zone as well.

UN11893 "Pillow Peak"

I'm not going to say where this one is. I can promise you though that you will see a trip report from me up here this coming winter, provided we have a decent snowpack. This zone reminds me of the North Face of Crested Butte Ski Area. There are so many ledges, drops, and pillows in this zone. Access is pretty far in the winter but I think this is going to be a ski backpack getaway. We'll need to bring some solar power to operate the cameras.

Apache South Couloir

Like the North Face of North Arapaho, this is a long way to go for a line. Perhaps this route could be combined with North Arapaho as a multi-night expedition to one of the deepest parts of the Indian Peaks. The line is intriguing. It drops right from the summit of Apache and looks like it gets pretty narrow and steep. This zone of the Indian Peaks Wilderness is amazing, so jagged and wild. It actually looks like there are two lines on the south aspect.

Shoshoni South Couloirs

If you wait until the road to Brainard is open, you probably won't get to ski these lines. A start from the winter trailhead with a bike ride is always fun—well, at least the downhill is fun. The last few times I've gone in by bike I went to the Blue Lake drainage. I always seem to wait until later in the spring to visit the Isabelle Glacier. By that time, these south-facing lines are only remnants. It looks like there are a few choices, moderately steep and gnarly. If you get there early enough in the spring, I bet you could even link the lines to the summit.

Toll North Face

This line is gnarly and could be one of the most serious in the Front Range. It's very aesthetically pleasing, with a beautiful fall-line over some serious exposure. It almost looks like it should be in the Alps. It does get skied, though not very often. I was hoping to add this one to the traverse, but got sidetracked by other routes. With the heat wave, the line was gone by the time I got back to this zone. Perhaps the next time I'm in the area working on more projects from this section, I will give it some thought. I like the fact that even though the line is over a giant cliff, you can still ski it clean. Some may want to ski this on belay, but it goes clean so you don't have to use the rope.

Paiute Ghost Dancer

This is another technical line that I didn't get done, despite going in twice to try it. The first was on the first traverse from Wild Basin. I slept near the bottom of it and was shut down by weather and lack of visibility. I did end up skiing the Paiute Audubon Saddle Couloir that day instead. There are a couple of beautiful lines on this face. Both are steep. The summit line will need at least one rappel. The bottom ledge could be traversed or rappelled; both would break the flow. The line to looker's left is the cleaner option. Paiute's summit is a wild place and I'm looking forward to visiting it many more times in the coming years.

Paiute West Couloir

Solo in the backcountry is the best place to discover yourself and new lines to ski. While I was on the summit of Irving Hale I noticed this awesome line. Descending from the south summit of Paiute, this is a nice long couloir. I thought it might be there after all the snow we got this past spring, but the heat wave did away with it by the time I got to the summit of Paiute. This would be a good combination line but the timing would be tough since you would end up skiing the west aspect then the east aspect; that's backwards to the timing of the warmup. Maybe a better call would be to camp after skiing it, savoring the descent from its base. Then you could climb back out and ski a proper corn run back to Brainard or Coney.

"Blackfoot" North Couloir

This peak is really hard to access. I checked out the lines from the summit of Paiute and they looked fun, though short. By the time I got to them it would have been mostly walking both ways. If you really want to do this route and the lines down the ridge in the zone, it might require a ski backpacking trip. Set up a base camp and just go to town on the lines in the zone. You'll have so much more energy to enjoy the skiing if you don't try to do it in a day.

Algonquin East Couloir

"Algonquin" is another summit named by Gerry Roach. This route makes me want to spend more time in the Coney Lakes zone. Combining this route with the northeast lines of Paiute would be ideal. This one would be pretty painful, though; skinning the Coney Flats road with overnight gear, ropes, and enough food to spend some time in the zone adds up, weight-wise. You could also go at this one from Brainard after a ski of Paiute, but it would be tough to ski Paiute with so much gear. Guess I need to tell myself to "suck it up, buttercup."

Twin Peaks East Chute

Here's a line that got away. I went up to this beautiful zone and got Watanga, Hiamovi, and Irving Hale. It was a great trip with fun skiing. I went right under this peak and it looked like there was no way through the summit cliffs. I went on to Watanga for an amazing sunset ski. The next morning I ascended Hiamovi and saw that the line was indeed clean. Oh well, you win some, you lose some. At least this gives me an excuse to go back for it. Now that I have the beta it's just a matter of putting in the effort to get it done.

Hiamovi East Face

On the same trip that I missed Twin Peaks, I also missed this line. I didn't know I missed it until a few weeks later when I looked at this face from afar. I'm glad I didn't venture there solo—and with a broken finger—the time I was on Hiamovi. There is a giant cornice guarding the entrance. Perhaps a rappel is in order; below the cornice it looks clean. This route opens up a lot of other options as well. The western Indian Peaks feel like a wild, unexplored frontier. Let's hope that the current pattern of strong upslope storms in the spring continues.

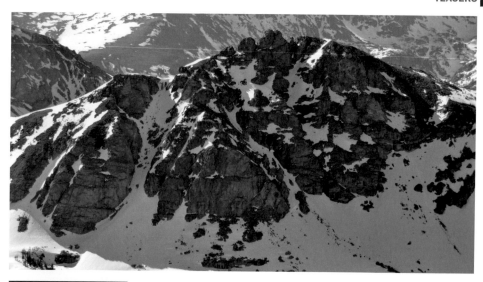

Marten West Couloir

There are so many great lines in the western Indian Peaks. This was one that I want to come back for in a slightly bigger snow year. Base camping would be tough in this area because most of the lines are spread out, with a few per drainage; then it's time to move to the next zone's set of routes. But this may be the way to go. I could see being entertained in this zone for about four or five days. That would be a lot of teaser skiing.

Elk Tooth North Face

During my first attempt of the giant traverse across the central Front Range, I spied this line while making my way up Ogalalla. It was getting late and I ended up skiing a great line on Ogalalla and making for lower ground to get out of the wind. In the morning the winds were howling up high. This is one of those lines that would have been good to ski at the end of the day, to avoid the crustiness. By the time I had recovered from the traverse, the line was gone. I love this rarely visited zone of Rocky Mountain National Park. Any excuse to get up there is a good excuse in my book.

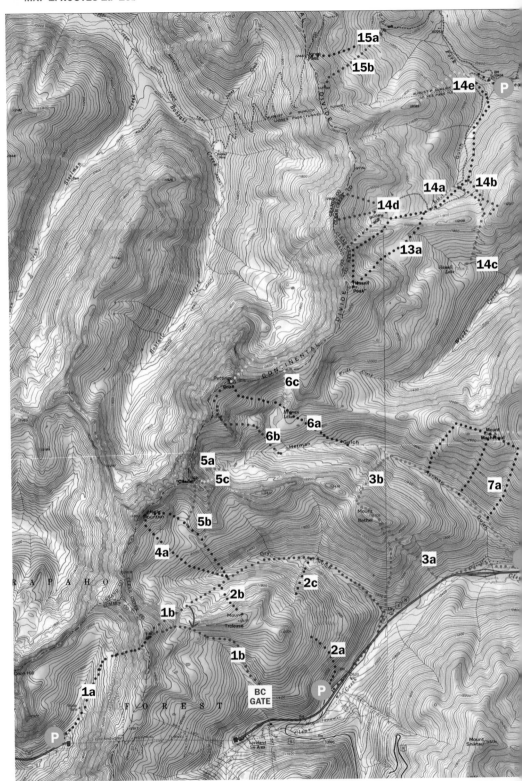

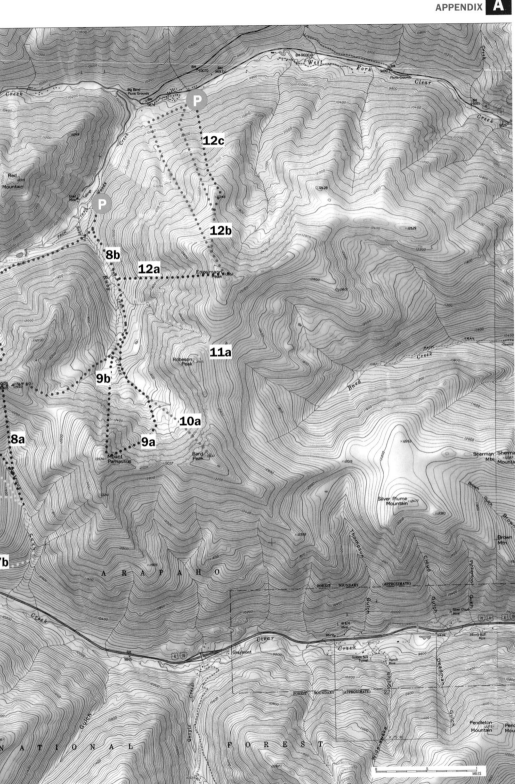

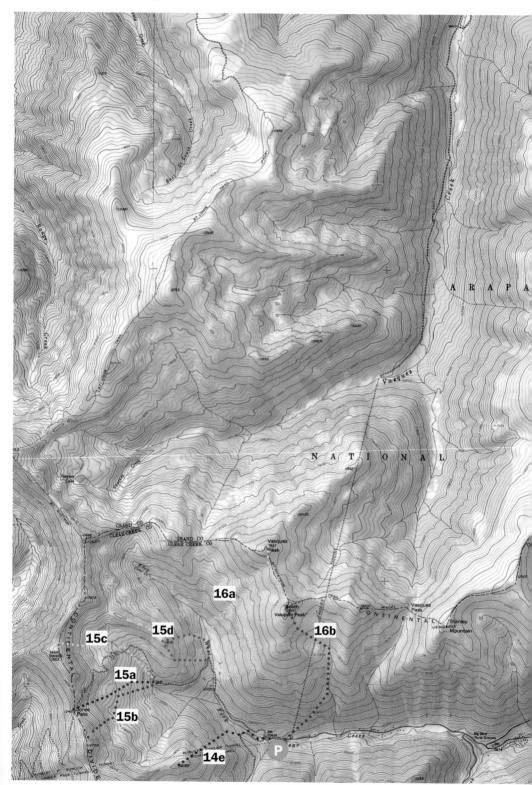

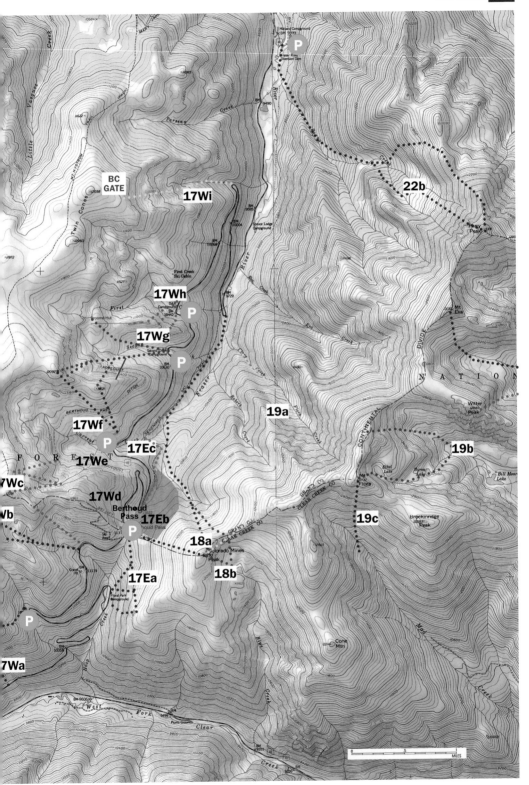

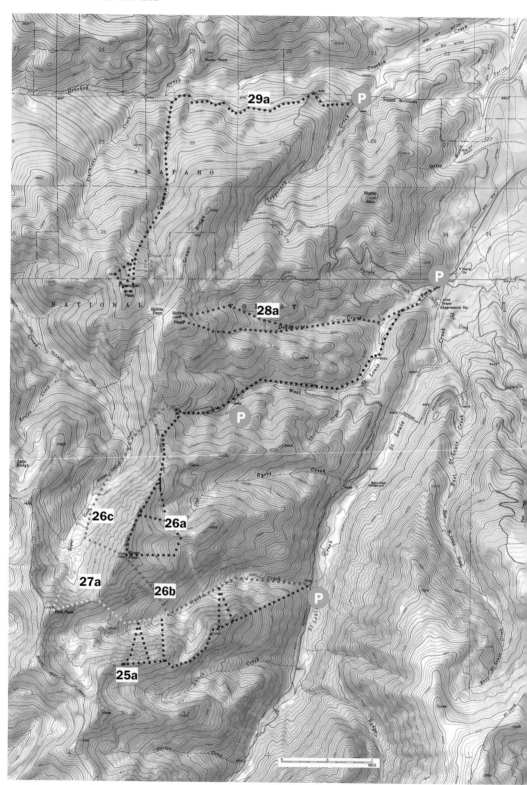

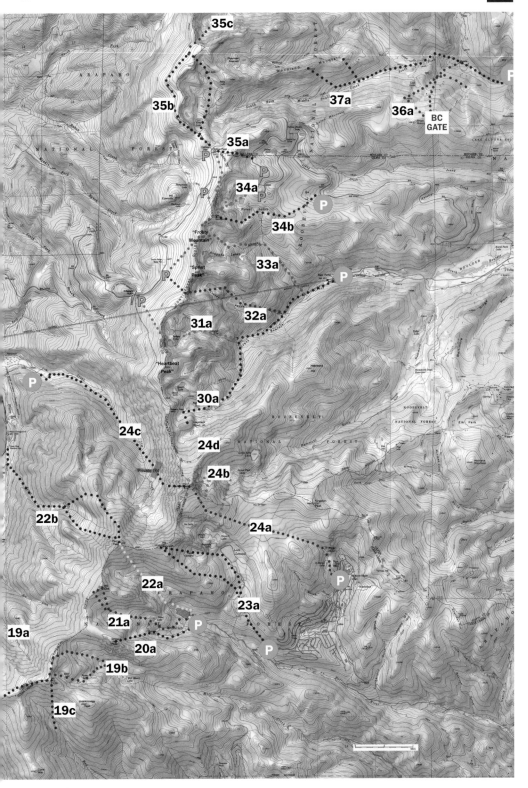

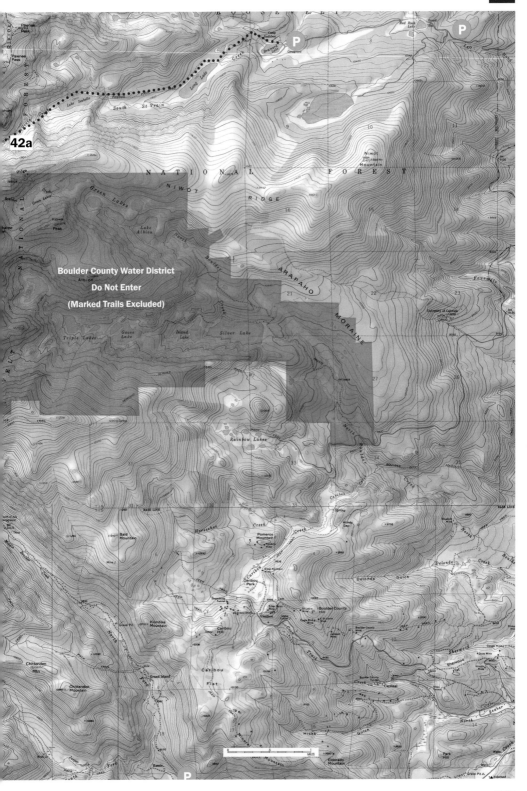

42a

Boulder County Water District

Do Not Enter

(Marked Trails Excluded)

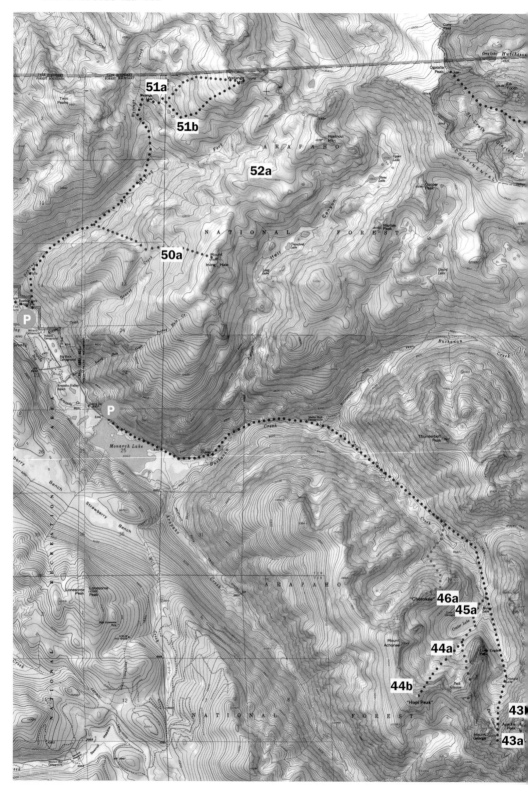

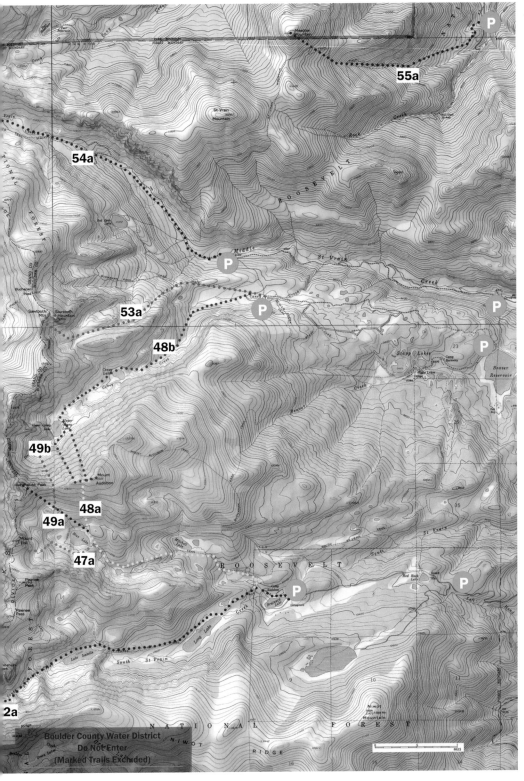

GLOSSARY OF TERMS

Adze: This is the shovel-like end of the ice axe. It can be used for chopping out steps on steep terrain. It also helps the axe from plunging too deep into the snow.

AT: Alpine touring is the name of the game for this book. AT bindings allow you to free your heel for the ascent. Most of these bindings feature ascension risers that ease uphill progress on steeper terrain. AT boots feature Vibram soles to make hiking safer. They also have a walk mode that allows you to flex your ankle, giving a more natural stride.

Beacon: This is another word for transceiver. This device sends out a signal while skiing. If the user is buried, their partners switch the device to receive. The unit will then pick up the buried signal. It's up to the user, and their partners, to learn how to locate that signal as quickly as possible.

Belay: A belay is a type of protection used in climbing. The rope is connected to the climber by a knot. The climber's partner uses a device to play out or take in rope. This connection can protect a fall. Training should be received before using this technique.

Chute: This is another word for couloir. This terrain feature is created by avalanches or other moving phenomena. Some chutes have rock walls others are more gully-like with lower sides. Care should be used when in chutes as there may be avalanche danger present.

Col: This is another word for saddle. This is the low point between two high points, usually on a ridge.

Cornice: This snowy terrain feature is created by wind transport. At an abrupt aspect change where there is significant windward action, snow will be compacted on the leeward side of the terrain feature. These can be stable or highly fragile. Care should be used around these features.

Couloir: This is another word for chute though this pertains only to chutes with rock walls. This terrain feature is created by avalanches or other moving phenomena. Care should be used when in couloirs as there may be avalanche and rockfall danger present.

Crampons: This contraption is worn on the soles of your ski boots. It is equipped with sharp metal spikes that allow for better traction on steep snow and ice.

Crown: This is the upper zone of a slab avalanche. Specifically this is the plane of failure for the slab. It is what remains of the slab.

Facet: This is a crystalline formation of snow. These crystals can wreak havoc on a snowpack. Their angular nature doesn't allow them to form strong bonds with their neighbors.

Gully: This is another word for chute. This terrain feature is created by avalanches or other moving phenomena. Some chutes have rock walls others are shallower with lower sides. Care should be used when in gullies, as there may be avalanche danger present.

Hangfire: This avalanche feature is the remnant slab that remains behind after a slab avalanche. There can be chunks of slab that do not run with the main slab. They can be located at the crown or along the avalanche's flanks. Care should be used if there is hangfire present, as the hangfire may release during rescue operations.

Leeward: This is the aspect that does not face the wind. If the wind blows from the west then the leeward aspect is east.

Pick: This is the pointy end of the ice axe. It can be used for gaining purchase in hard snow. The point can be driven into ice. In hard snow this is the end that one will use for self-arrest. It usually has serrated teeth. These teeth limit tool slippage in mixed terrain, like rocky sections you may need to negotiate during your ascent.

Probe: This folding pole assembles for use in avalanche rescues. The pole is pushed into the snow to search for the buried victim. It can also be used to find snow of suitable depth for a snow cave. If you are digging very deep snow pits they can be used as a depth gauge as they are usually marked with measurements

Randonee: French for hiking. The Europeans use this term as we use the word touring. This would include skinning as well.

Rappel: Rappelling is a descent using a rope affixed to an anchor. The user slides down the rope using a device and their lower hand to control speed.

Saddle: This is another word for col. This is the low point between two high points usually at ridgeline, but not necessarily.

Scree: Very fine loose rock. More accurately this is loose pebbles or gravel. Scree can be very pleasant to descend on but this can cause erosion scars on the mountain.

Shear Plane: As the snowpack builds through successive storms throughout the year, layers are formed with each new storm. The plane where each new layer forms has a bonding quality. One can test this quality by the ease of which the layers slide along this shear plane.

Skin: This is a piece of directional, synthetic fur that is applied to the bottom of skis or a split-snowboard. The fur allows forward progress and limits slide back, allowing for easier uphill travel.

Slab: Each new layer of snow that falls has the potential of becoming a slab. This homogeneous layer sits on other layers of snow below it. These layers may also be slabs. Between these slabs there is a bond. If the bond isn't strong enough the slab with fail and become a slab avalanche.

Sluff: This is a type of avalanche. This is the surface snow that moves with you as you ski or as temperatures rise throughout the day. Sluff should be planned for on steep slopes.

Talus: Loose rock that is rather large, from baseball to VW Beetle sized. This rock can break an ankle very quickly. Use care when traveling through talus.

Transceiver: This is another word for beacon. This device sends out a signal while skiing. If the user is buried, their partners switch the device to receive. The unit will then pick up the buried signal. It's up to the user, and their partners, to learn how to locate that signal as quickly as possible.

Whippet: This great tool is a pick from an ice axe that has been joined to a ski pole handle. This can be very useful in providing a means for self-arrest while skiing in steep terrain.

Windward: This is the aspect that faces the wind. If the wind blows from the west then the windward aspect is west.

SUNRISE SUNSET CHART

In the spring, timing is essential for success and safety. Use this chart to estimate when the sun will hit your intended line and the lines you will travel near. Assessing radiation affect is an important skill not only for avalanche hazard assessment, but also to find ideal riding conditions.

Day	Jan Rise Set HrMn HrMn	Feb Rise Set HrMn HrMn	Mar Rise Set HrMn HrMn	April Rise Set HrMn HrMn	May Rise Set HrMn HrMn	June Rise Set HrMn HrMn	July Rise Set HrMn HrMn	Aug Rise Set HrMn HrMn	Sept Rise Set HrMn HrMn	Oct Rise Set HrMn HrMn	Nov Rise Set HrMn HrMn	Dec Rise Set HrMn HrMn
1	0725 1651	0712 1724	0637 1756	0549 1828	0506 1858	0439 1925	0441 1935	0504 1917	0532 1835	0600 1747	0632 1703	0705 1641
2	0725 1652	0711 1725	0636 1757	0547 1829	0504 1859	0439 1926	0441 1935	0505 1916	0533 1834	0601 1745	0633 1702	0706 1641
3	0725 1653	0710 1727	0634 1758	0546 1830	0503 1900	0438 1927	0442 1935	0505 1915	0534 1832	0602 1744	0634 1701	0707 1641
4	0725 1654	0709 1728	0633 1800	0544 1831	0502 1901	0438 1927	0442 1935	0506 1914	0535 1831	0603 1742	0636 1700	0708 1640
5	0725 1655	0708 1729	0631 1801	0543 1832	0501 1902	0438 1928	0443 1935	0507 1912	0536 1829	0604 1741	0637 1658	0709 1640
6	0725 1656	0707 1730	0630 1802	0541 1833	0500 1903	0437 1929	0443 1934	0508 1911	0537 1828	0605 1739	0638 1657	0710 1640
7	0725 1656	0706 1731	0628 1803	0539 1834	0459 1904	0437 1929	0444 1934	0509 1910	0538 1826	0606 1738	0639 1656	0711 1640
8	0725 1657	0705 1733	0627 1804	0538 1835	0457 1905	0437 1930	0445 1934	0510 1909	0539 1824	0607 1736	0640 1655	0712 1640
9	0724 1658	0704 1734	0625 1805	0536 1836	0456 1906	0437 1930	0445 1933	0511 1908	0540 1823	0608 1734	0641 1654	0713 1640
10	0724 1659	0702 1735	0624 1806	0535 1837	0455 1906	0437 1931	0446 1933	0512 1907	0541 1821	0609 1733	0642 1654	0713 1640
11	0724 1700	0701 1736	0622 1807	0533 1838	0454 1907	0437 1931	0447 1933	0513 1905	0542 1819	0610 1731	0643 1653	0714 1641
12	0724 1701	0700 1737	0621 1808	0532 1839	0453 1908	0437 1932	0447 1932	0514 1904	0542 1818	0611 1730	0645 1652	0715 1641
13	0724 1703	0659 1738	0619 1809	0530 1840	0452 1909	0437 1932	0448 1932	0515 1903	0543 1816	0612 1728	0646 1651	0716 1641
14	0723 1704	0658 1740	0618 1810	0529 1841	0451 1910	0436 1933	0449 1931	0516 1901	0544 1815	0613 1727	0647 1650	0716 1641
15	0723 1705	0657 1741	0616 1811	0527 1842	0451 1911	0437 1933	0449 1931	0517 1900	0545 1813	0614 1725	0648 1649	0717 1641
16	0722 1706	0655 1742	0614 1812	0526 1843	0450 1912	0437 1933	0450 1930	0518 1859	0546 1811	0615 1724	0649 1648	0718 1642
17	0722 1707	0654 1743	0613 1813	0524 1844	0449 1913	0437 1934	0451 1929	0518 1857	0547 1810	0616 1723	0650 1648	0718 1642
18	0722 1708	0653 1744	0611 1814	0523 1845	0448 1914	0437 1934	0452 1929	0519 1856	0548 1808	0617 1721	0651 1647	0719 1642
19	0721 1709	0651 1745	0610 1815	0522 1846	0447 1915	0437 1934	0453 1928	0520 1855	0549 1806	0618 1720	0652 1646	0720 1643
20	0721 1710	0650 1746	0608 1816	0520 1847	0446 1916	0437 1935	0453 1927	0521 1853	0550 1805	0619 1718	0654 1646	0720 1643
21	0720 1711	0649 1747	0606 1817	0519 1848	0446 1917	0437 1935	0454 1927	0522 1852	0551 1803	0620 1717	0655 1645	0721 1644
22	0719 1712	0647 1749	0605 1818	0517 1849	0445 1917	0437 1935	0455 1926	0523 1850	0552 1802	0621 1716	0656 1645	0721 1644
23	0719 1714	0646 1750	0603 1819	0516 1850	0444 1918	0438 1935	0456 1925	0524 1849	0553 1800	0622 1714	0657 1644	0722 1645
24	0718 1715	0645 1751	0602 1820	0515 1851	0443 1919	0438 1935	0457 1924	0525 1848	0554 1758	0623 1713	0658 1644	0722 1645
25	0717 1716	0643 1752	0600 1821	0513 1852	0443 1920	0438 1935	0457 1923	0526 1846	0554 1757	0624 1712	0659 1643	0723 1646
26	0717 1717	0642 1753	0558 1822	0512 1853	0442 1921	0439 1935	0458 1923	0527 1845	0555 1755	0626 1710	0700 1643	0723 1647
27	0716 1718	0640 1754	0557 1823	0511 1854	0442 1922	0439 1935	0459 1922	0528 1843	0556 1753	0627 1709	0701 1642	0723 1647
28	0715 1719	0639 1755	0555 1824	0509 1855	0441 1922	0439 1935	0500 1921	0529 1842	0557 1752	0628 1708	0702 1642	0724 1648
29	0714 1721		0554 1825	0508 1856	0441 1923	0440 1935	0501 1920	0530 1840	0558 1750	0629 1706	0703 1642	0724 1649
30	0714 1722		0552 1826	0507 1857	0440 1924	0440 1935	0502 1919	0531 1839	0559 1749	0630 1705	0704 1641	0724 1649
31	0713 1723		0550 1827		0440 1925		0503 1918	0531 1837		0631 1704		0724 1650

GEAR LIST

You should have enough gear to be able to survive an unplanned night out. Help can be a long wait away, so being prepared is essential to your survival should things go wrong. Some gear may not be right for some trips, but this is a list of the gear I generally have with me. During winter you might not need crampons or a sun hat and most routes have no call for a rope and harness. Additional required gear will be noted in the route description.

Avalanche Beacon
Probe (Not connected ski poles)
Shovel
Snow Study Kit
Snow Saw
Cornice Cutter
Skis or Splitboard
AT Boots
AT Bindings
Climbing Skins
Ski Crampons
Crampons
Ice Axe with Leash
Helmet
Goggles
Sunglasses
Headlamp
Ski Poles, 1 w/ Whippet (optional)
Backpack/Airbag Pack
Water
Food
Hard Shell Jacket with Hood
Soft Shell Jacket
Extra Sweater
Base Layers
Ski Pants
2 Pairs Gloves
2 Pairs Socks
Sun Hat
Wool Hat
Balaclava
Compass
Topo Map for Planned Route
Cell Phone
Camera
JetBoil Stove
Lunch
Extra Batteries

Emergency Bivy
Sunscreen
Lip Balm
Ski Wax
Glop Stopper Skin Wax
9mm Climbing Rope 30m or 55m
Climbing Harness
Selection of Protection
Belay Device
First Aid Kit
 Bandages
 Ace Bandage
 Gauze
 Athletic Tape
 Ibuprofen
 Sam Splint
 CPR Mask
 Wound Closures
 Iodine
 Alcohol Pads
 Latex Gloves
 Suture Kit
 Scissors
 Tweezers
 Percocet
Repair Kit
 Zip Ties
 Bailing Wire
 Various Spare Buckles
 Nylon Strips
 P-Tex
 Multi Tool with Pliers
 Lighter
 4 Rubber Ski Straps
 Sewing Kit
 Duct Tape
 Extra Batteries
 Nylon Cord

FURTHER READING

This isn't exactly a bibliography. Some of the sources below were used in the writing of this book and they were credited as used. I avoided the use of lots of footnotes to make the info easier to process. This list basically provides a resource for further study of the area. My favorite avalanche books should certainly be read multiple times. I've also included some of my favorite online resources.

Graydon, Don (Editor), *Mountaineering Freedom of the Hills 8th ed.*, Seattle: The Mountaineers, 2010

Tremper, Bruce, *Staying Alive in Avalanche Terrain*, Seattle: The Mountaineers, 2008

LaChapelle, Edward R., *Secrets of Snow: Visual Clues to Avalanche and Ski Conditions*, Seattle: University of Washington Press, 2001

Roach, Gerry & Jennifer, *Indian Peaks: Classic Hikes and Climbs*, Golden: Fulcrum Publishing, 1998

Fredston, Jill & Fesler, Doug, *Snow Sense: A Guide to Evaluating Snow Avalanche Hazard*, Anchorage: Alaska Mountain Safety Center, 1999

Fredston, Jill, *Snowstruck In the Grip of Avalanches*, Orlando: Harcourt, 2005

McClung, David & Schaerer, Peter, *The Avalanche Handbook*, Seattle: The Mountaineers, 1993

Bronski, Peter, *Powder Ghost Towns: Epic Backcountry Runs in Colorado's Lost Ski Resorts*, Berkeley: Wilderness Press, 2010

Fay, Abbott, *A History of Skiing in Colorado*, Lake City: Western Reflections Publishing Co., 2008

Roach, Gerry & Jennifer, *Colorado's Thirteeners 13,800 to 13,999 Feet From Hikes to Climbs*, Golden: Fulcrum Publishing, 2001

Dawson II, Louis W., *Dawson's Guide to Colorado's Fourteeners Volume 1 The Northern Peaks*, Colorado Springs: Blue Clover Press, 1999

Reed, Jack & Ellis, Gene, *Rocks Above the Clouds*, Golden: The Colorado Mountain Club Press, 2009

Wells, Charles A., *Guide to Colorado Backroads & 4-Wheel Drive Trails,* Monument: FunTreks Inc., 2005

Dyer, John L., *The Snow-Shoe Itinerant*, Lake City: Western Reflections Publishing Co., 2008

Taylor, Andrew M., *Guide to the Geology of Colorado*, Cataract Lode Mining Co, 1999

Hall, Frank, *History of Colorado*, Lake City: Western Reflections Publishing Co., 2008

Lipp, Jordan, *Backcountry Skiing Berthoud Pass*, Example Product Manufacturer, 2005

Faughey, Eileen & Haddad, Ron, *Front Range Descents: Spring and Summer Skiing and Snowboarding In Colorado's Front Range*, Sigma Books, 2003

AVALANCHE EDUCATION

As I've stressed multiple times throughout this book, avalanche education is a very important part of safe ski mountaineering. Below are the AIARE approved avalanche schools in Colorado. The organization provides avalanche education to more backcountry travelers than any other single avalanche education organization in the U.S.

Alpine World Ascents, Inc.
2705 Overlook Dr.
Broomfield, CO 80020
(303) 350-0366
alpineworldascents.com

Apex Mountain School
PO Box 8621
Avon, CO 81620
(888) 686-7685
apexmountainschool.com

Aspen Alpine Guide
PO Box 659
Aspen, CO 81612
(970) 925-6618
aspenalpine.com

Aspen Expeditions
0133 Prospector Road
Ste 4115
Aspen, CO 81611
(970) 925-7625
aspenexpeditions.com

Buena Vista Mountain Adventures
P.O. Box 5212
Buena Vista , CO 81211
(719) 966-9939
bvmountainadventures.com

Colorado Adventure Guides
50 Magnum Bonum Dr
Breckenridge, CO 80424
(303) 908-0595
coloradoadventureguides.com

Colorado Mountain Club
710 10th Street, #200
Golden, CO 80401
(303) 279-3080
cmc.org

Colorado Mountain College—Leadville
901 South Hwy. 24
Leadville, CO 80461
(719) 486-2015 Ext.4272
coloradomtn.edu

Colorado Mountain College—Steamboat
1275 Crawford Ave.
Steamboat Springs, CO 80487
(970) 870-4527
coloradomtn.edu

Colorado Mountain College - Vail-Eagle - Edwards
150 Miller Ranch Rd.
Edwards, CO 81632
(970) 569-2913
coloradomtn.edu

Colorado Mountain School
2829 Mapleton Ave.
Boulder, CO 80301
(800) 836-4008 Ext.3
totalclimbing.com

Colorado Snowboard Guides
PO Box 4110
Dillon, CO 80435
(719) 244.7779
coloradosnowboardguides.com

Colorado Wilderness Rides and Guides
4865 Darwin Court
Boulder, CO 80301
(720) 242-9828
ColoradoWildernessRides
AndGuides.com

Crested Butte Mountain Guides
PO Box 1718
Crested Butte, CO 81224
(970) 349-5430
crestedbutteguides.com

Eldora Avalanche School
2861 Eldora Ski Rd.
Nederland, CO 80466
(303) 440-8700 Ext.248
eldora.com

High Mountain Institute
531 CR 5A
Leadville, CO 80461
(719) 486-8200 Ext.107
hminet.org

Irwin Guides
330 Belleview Ave.
Crested Butte, CO 81224
(970) 349-5430
irwincolorado.com

Kling Mountain Guides
1205 Camino Del Rio
Durango, CO 81301
(970) 259-1708
klingmountainguides.com

Majestic Heli Ski
172 Red Bluff Vista
Glenwood Springs, CO 81601
(970) 366-6600
majesticheliski.com

Peak Mountain Guides, LLC
PO Box 992
Ridgway, CO 81432
(970) 318-1011
peakmountainguides.com

Pikes Peak Alpine School
10 S. Limit St.
Colorado Springs, CO 80905
(719) 630-3934
pikespeakalpineschool.com

Red Rocks Community College
13300 W 6th Avenue
Lakewood, CO 80228
(303) 914-6238
rrcc.edu/outdoor

Renaissance Adventure Guides, LLC
730 E. Center Ave.
Denver, CO 80209
(303) 988-2943
raguides.com

Rocky Mountain Guides
11 Grey Fox Ln.
Dillon, CO 80435
(970) 409-9555
rockymountainguides.com

San Juan Mountain Guides, LLC
PO Box 1214
Ouray, CO 81427
(970) 325-4925
mtnguide.net

San Juan Outdoor School Telluride Avalanche School
PO Box 3679
302 Adams Ranch Rd#8
Telluride, CO 81435
(970) 728-4101
tellurideadventures.com

Silverton Avalanche School
1228 Snowden
Silverton, CO 81433
(970) 903-7039
avyschool.org

Southwest Adventure Guides
PO Box 3242
Durango, CO 81302
(800) 642-5389
swaguides.com

Steamboat Powdercats
1724 Mt. Werner Cr.
Steamboat Springs, CO 80477
(970) 879-5188
steamboatpowdercats.com

INTERNET RESOURCES

GiterdunPublishing.com: www.giterdunpublishing.com
MakingTurns.com: www.makingturns.com

avalanche

Colorado Avalanche Information Center: avalanche.state.co.us/index.php
Colorado Snowtel: http://www.wcc.nrcs.usda.gov/snow/index.html
Avalanche.org: www.avalanche.org
American Institute for Avalanche Research and Education(AIARE): www.avtraining.org

beta

Mountain Project/Climbing: www.mountainproject.com
14ers.com: www.14ers.com
Backcountry Coalition: www.backcountrycoalition.com
Wildsnow: www.wildsnow.com
CamptoCamp: www.camptocamp.org

blogs

MakingTurns.com: www.makingturns.com
14erskiers: www.14erskiers.com
Wildsnow: www.wildsnow.com

community

Colorado Fourteeners Initiative: www.14ers.org
Teton Gravity Research: www.www.tetongravity.com

government

Colorado Department of Transportation: www.cotrip.org
US Forest Service: www.fs.fed.us
Rocky Mountain National Park: www.nps.gov/romo

maps

CalTopo: www.caltopo.com
Hillmap: www.hillmap.com
Google Earth: www.google.com/earth
CamptoCamp: www.camptocamp.org

weather

Colorado Snowtel: http://www.wcc.nrcs.usda.gov/snow/index.html
OpenSnow Weather Ski Forecasts: www.opensnow.com
National Weather Service: forecast.weather.gov
MeteoStar: wxweb.meteostar.com/models/
Intellicast:www.intellicast.com/

SHOPS DEDICATED TO THE SKI MOUNTAINEER

It's important to have shops that support your sport. Having the ability to pick up an item that you need locally not only makes getting back into the mountains quicker it helps the environment by not having to burn a bunch of gas going to the city for what you need. You never know—you might find your best new partner while frequenting one of these great stores.

Alpine Quest Sports
34510 US Hwy 6, Edwards
(970) 926-3867

Bent Gate Mountaineering
1313 Washington Ave., Golden
(303) 278 7658

Boone Mountain Sports
2962 Evergreen Pkwy., Evergreen
(303) 670-0039

Bristlecone Mountain Sports
781 E. Valley Rd., Basalt
(970) 927-1492

Clear Creek Outdoors
1524 Miner St., Idaho Springs
(303) 567-1500

Colorado Mountain School
2829 Mapleton Ave., Boulder
(303) 865-3521

Cripple Creek Backcountry
582 Colorado 133, Carbondale
(970) 355-4279

Estes Park Mountain Shop
2050 Big Thompson Ave.,
Estes Park
(970) 586-6548

High Alpine Sports
899 Steinfelt Pkwy., Fairplay
(719) 836-0201

Icebox Mountain Sports
505 Zerex St., Fraser
(970) 722-7780

Jax Home Office
PO Box 469, Bellvue
(800) 336-8314

Leadville Outdoors
225 Harrison Ave., Leadville
(719) 486-7392

Mountain Chalet
226 North Tejon St.,
Colorado Springs
(719) 633-0732

Mountain Outfitters
112 S Ridge St., Breckenridge
(970) 453-2201

Neptune Mountaineering, Inc.
633 S. Broadway #A, Boulder
(303) 499-8866

Ouray Mountain Sports
732 Main St., Ouray
(970) 325-4284

Outpost Sunsport
931 E Harmony Rd. #1,
Fort Collins
(970) 225-1455

Ptarmigan Sports
137 Main St. C-104, Edwards
(970) 926-8144

Red Fox NA
424 Main St, Lyons
(303) 823-6867

REI
1376 E Woodmen Rd.,
Colorado Springs
(719) 260-1455

1789 28th St., Boulder
(303) 583-9970

1416 Platte St., Denver
(303) 756-3100

5375 S Wadsworth Blvd.,
Lakewood
(303) 932-0600

9637 E County Line Rd.,
Englewood
(303) 858-1726

4025 S College Ave., Fort Collins
(970) 223-0123

14696 Delaware St., Westminster
(720) 872-1938

5375 S Wadsworth Blvd., Littleton
(303) 932-0600

Rocky Mountain Underground
500 South Park Ave.,
Breckenridge
(970) 453-6405

Salida Mountain Sports
110 North F St., Salida
(719) 539-4400

Summit Canyon Mountaineering
732 Grand Avenue,
Glenwood Springs
(970) 945-6994

Tin Shed Sports
112 East 2nd Street
Nederland
(303) 258-3509

The Trailhead
707 Hwy 24 North, Buena Vista
(719) 395-8001

Ute Mountaineer
210 S. Galena St., Aspen
(970) 925-2849

Wilderness Exchange
2401 15th Street #100, Denver
(303) 964-0708

Wilderness Sports
701 E. Anemone Trail, Dillon
(970) 468-5687

INDEX

"Algonquin" East Couloir..................265
"Golden Bear".....................................41-43
"Blackfoot" North Couloir.................265
"Cherokee"...223-224
"Frosty Mountain"...........................179-180
"Hassell Peak".....................................91-92
"Heartbeat Peak" Y Gully.................260
"Hopi Peak".......................................215-219
"Old Baldy" South Bowl....................260
"Sprint Peak"...................................177-178
"The Citadel"......................................57-62
110s, Berthoud Pass...........................119
31 Iceberg Couloirs...........................175-176
418 Chutes, Pettingell Pk. 64-65
80s/90s/100s, Berthoud Pass 117-118
Achonee Arrow 261
Apache Couloir, Apache Pk..............209-210
Apache Peak..209-214
Apache South Couloir 262
Appendix...268-285
Audubon, Mt.......................................227-230
Avalanche Education 283
Avalanches 4-7
Bancroft, Mt. 147-148
Bard Peak...81-82
Bear Claw, Parry Pk. 144-147
Berthoud Falls Trailhead....................21
Berthoud Pass 110-124
Berthoud Pass Current Creek Trailhead..............24
Berthoud Pass First Creek Trailhead.............25
Berthoud Pass Pump House Trailhead................23
Berthoud Pass Second Creek Trailhead.............25
Berthoud Pass South Corner Trailhead.............22
Berthoud Pass Stanley Slidepath
      Access Trailhead...........................23
Berthoud Pass Summit Trailhead........................24
Berthoud Pass Super Tour 248-250
Berthoud Pass to Moffat Tunnel 250-251
Berthoud Pass to Wild Basin...............255
Berthoud Pass Zero Creek Trailhead 26
Bethel, Mt...51-54
Bills Peak 167-168
Bobtail BM, Jones Pass 104
Bottle Peak...169-170
Brainard Lake to Wild Basin 251-252
Brainard Lake Trailhead.....................37
Brainard Lake Winter Trailhead 36
Breakfast Chute, Engelmann Pk. 89-90
Broome Hut, Berthoud Pass................120
Butler Gulch..93-100
Byers Peak 161-166
Cabin Creek Couloirs, Mt. Jasper.............197-198
Camp Dick/Middle St. Vrain Road Trailhead.....39

Camping and Permits.........................2-4
Caribou Lake Bowl, Mt. Neva 201-202
Caroline Bowl, Mt. Bancroft..............147-148
Challenger Glacier, Rollins Pass........188
Chimney Chute, Berthoud Pass.............. 120, 122
Colorado Mines Peak 129-132
Communication 13
Coney Couloirs, Mt. Audubon............229-230
Coney Flats Road Trailhead................38
Corner Pocket, Berthoud Pass............120
Cornices..10
Crater Couloirs, "Sprint Pk.".............177-178
Crooked Couloir, Mt. Audubon............227-228
Crystal Bowl, Ptarmigan Pk. 171-172
Current Creek, Berthoud Pass............119
Dalkes Couloir, Ogalalla Pk..............243-244
Deadhorse Bowl, Bottle Pk. 169-170
Deadhorse Creek Trailhead.................29
Devil's Thumb Pass Trailhead.............34
Divide Chutes, Butler Gulch...............97
Drainpipe, Mt. Parnassus 78-80
Dry Gulch Trailhead............................20
East Bowl and Slopes, Mt Machebeuf...........69-71
East Bowl, Byers Pk. 161-162
East Cirque, Colorado Mines Pk. 131-132
East Cirque, James Pk. 151-154
East Face, Radiobeacon BM 183-184
East Ridge Flank, Mt. Jasper...............196
East Side "Frosty Mountain".............179-180
East Slopes, Meadow............................245-246
Eisenhower Tunnel to Butler Gulch...........247-248
Eisenhower Tunnel West Portal North
      Trailhead....................................19
Eldora Backcountry 189-190
Eldora Backcountry Gate Trailhead.............33
Elk Tooth North Face..........................267
Engelmann North Ramp.......................257
Engelmann Peak....................................85-90
Engelmann Disney Chute.....................257
Etiquette and Philosophy 14
Eva, Mt...141-142
Fair Glacier, Apache Pk.....................212-214
Fairway, Berthoud Pass 126
Fall River Reservoir Trailhead............27
Fingers, Berthoud Pass.......................127
First Creek, Berthoud Pass 122-123
Flora Creek Bowl, Mt. Flora 133-135
Flora, Mt..133-138
Floral Park Zone, Berthoud Pass 126-127
Floral Park, Berthoud Pass................126
Fourth of July Road Trailhead............34
Frankenstein, Berthoud Pass.............120
Further Reading 282

INDEX

Gaffney's, Berthoud Pass......................................115
Gear List 281
Glossary 278
Great Divide, Berthoud Pass 115
Hagar Mountain 55-56
Halfpipe Gully, Butler Gulch 93-94
Haystack Mountain.......................................173-174
Headwall, Berthoud Pass 122
Hells Half Acre Zone, Berthoud Pass.........127-128
Hell's Half Acre, Berthoud Pass..........................127
Herman Gulch Trailhead 20
Hessie Winter Closure Trailhead 33
Hiamovi East Face..266
Hiamovi Mountain 239-240
Hopi Glacier, "Hopi Pk."...............................218-219
Hourglass Gully, Butler Gulch........................ 94-95
Internet Resources 284
Interstate Gully, Mt. Bethel 51-53
Introduction 1-17
Iron Creek Couloirs, UN12393.................... 159-160
Iron Creek/Byers Peak Road Trailhead................29
Irving Hale, Mt. 235-236
James Peak 149-158
James Peak Super Star...259
Jasper, Mt. 193-198
Jenny Lake Bowl, Rollins Pass 185-186
Jim Creek Trail Trailhead 27
Jones Brothers Chutes, Butler Gulch............ 98-100
Jones Pass..101-106
Jones Pass Trailhead..22
Kiva Ramp, "Hopi Pk."..................................215-217
Knob, Berthoud Pass 124
Knuckles, Berthoud Pass.....................................127
Lake Bowl, "Hassell Pk." 91-92
Lift Line, Berthoud Pass.....................................115
Lightning and Weather.................................... 7-8
Lightning Gully, Engelmann Pk..................... 87-89
Lone Eagle Peak...221-222
Lone Rabbit Couloir, Lone Eagle Pk. 221-222
Long Lake Trailhead 37
Lost Lake Bowl, Eldora Backcountry 189-190
Loveland Ski Area Chair 8 Gate...........................19
Machebeuf, Mt..67-71
Mainline to The Roll, Berthoud Pass........115-116
Maps...268-277
Marijuana 13
Marten West Couloir 267
Meadow Mountain.......................................245-246
Meadow Mountain Trailhead...............................40
Mines 1 and 2, Colorado Mines Pk. 129-131
Mitchell Lake Trailhead.......................................37
Moats..11
Moffat Tunnel East Portal Trailhead 30

Monarch Lake Trailhead 35
Mount Audubon...227-230
Mount Bancroft 147-148
Mount Bethel 51-54
Mount Eva 141-142
Mount Flora 133-138
Mount Irving Hale 235-236
Mount Jasper..193-198
Mount Machebeuf.. 67-71
Mount Neva 199-202
Mount Parnassus... 77-80
Mount Toll..225-226
Mount Trelease 45-50
Mountain Craft.. 8-9
Mustang, Berthoud Pass.....................................115
Navajo Peak...207-208
Navajo Snowfield, Navajo Pk....................207-208
Navajo–Apache Trifecta 253
Neva, Mt. 199-202
Nitro Chute, Berthoud Pass...............................115
Nitro Cliff, Berthoud Pass..................................115
No Name - UN12424, Berthoud Pass 113
No Name Bench, Berthoud Pass.........................113
North Arapaho North Face 261
North Arapaho Peak....................................205-206
North Chute, Hell's, Berthoud Pass 127
North Chute, Russell, Berthoud Pass 115
North Collar Couloir, "The Citadel" 57-58
North Face, Bard Pk....................................... 81-82
North Face, Bills Pk.....................................167-168
North Face, Haystack Mtn. 173-174
North Face, Mt. Trelease 47-49
North Face, Pettingell Pk............................... 65-66
North Gullies & Trees, Mt. Trelease 49-50
North Gully, "Cherokee" 223-224
North Saddle Gully, Mt. Bethel 53-54
North Slopes, James Pk. 157-158
North Star Couloir, North Arapaho Pk. 205-206
Northeast Bowl, "Golden Bear" 42-43
Northeast Bowls, Mt. Flora.........................135-136
Northeast Cirque, Radiobeacon BM 181-183
Northeast Face, Mt. Jasper..........................194-195
Northeast Face, Mt. Neva............................199-200
Northeast Face, Mt. Parnassus 77-78
Northwest Gully, Robeson Pk....................... 83-84
Oatmeal Bowl, Berthoud Pass............................113
Ogalalla Peak 243-244
Paiute Ghost Dancer...264
Paiute Peak 231-234
Paiute West Couloir 264
Paiute/Audubon Saddle Couloir.................233-234
Parnassus Southwest Couloir 256
Parnassus, Mt...77-80

INDEX

Parry Creek Trail Trailhead 26
Parry Peak 143-147
Pass Bowl, Jones Pass 101-102
Pauly's Powderstash, Berthoud Pass 126
Perfect Trees, Berthoud Pass 119
Peter Rabbit Cabin, Berthoud Pass 119
Pettingell Peak 63-66
Pillows, Berthoud Pass 120
Plunge, Berthoud Pass 115
Postage Stamp, Berthoud Pass 119
Ptarmigan Peak 171-172
Queen's Way, Apache Pk. 211-212
Quicksilver Trail, Berthoud Pass 127
Radiobeacon BM 181-184
Retail Shops 285
Roaring Fork Trailhead 36
Robeson Peak 83
Rockfall 10-11
Rollins Pass 185-188
Rollins Pass Road East Side Trailhead 31
Rollins Pass West Side Trailhead 32
Ruby Gulch Trailhead 21
Rush Chute, Berthoud Pass 115
Russell Peak - UN12391, Berthoud Pass ... 114-115
Sawtooth Mountain 241-242
SE Slopes, James Pk. 149-150
Second Creek Ridge, Berthoud Pass 120
Second Creek, Berthoud Pass 120-121
Sentinel, Berthoud Pass 127
Seven Mile Trail, Berthoud Pass 128
Shoshoni South Couloirs 263
Skull Bite, Berthoud Pass 119
Skyscraper Glacier, Rollins Pass 186-187
Skywalker Couloir, South Arapaho Pk. 203-204
Snoopy 57-62
Snow Lion, Mt. Jasper 193-194
South Arapaho Peak 203-204
South Bowl and South Collar,
    "The Citadel" 58-60
South Bowl and Trees, Mt. Trelease 45-47
South Chute, Mt. Flora 137-138
South Face, Parry Pk. 143-144
South Peak (UN12900) SE Bowl,
    Vasquez Pk. 108-109
South Side – Hassell Lake, Butler Gulch 96
South Slopes, Pettingell Pk. 63-61
South Slopes, Woodland Mtn. 191-192
Southeast Bowl, Mt. Eva 141-142
Southeast Bowl, Sawtooth 241-242
Southeast Face, Hagar Mtn. 55-56
Southeast Face, Paiute Pk. 231-232
Southeast Gully, Byers Pk. 163-164
Southeast Slopes, Mt. Toll 225-226

Southwest Bowl and Gully, Vasquez Pk. 107-108
Southwest Slopes, Watanga Mtn. 238
St Mary's Glacier, James Pk. 149-150
St. Mary's Glacier Trailhead 28
Stanley Slide Path, Berthoud Pass 112-113
Steuart Road Trailhead 28
Sunrise/Sunset Chart 280
Tail and East Bowl, "The Citadel" 60-62
Tea Cup, Berthoud Pass 119
Teasers 255-267
Telegraph, Berthoud Pass 126
Ten Little Indians, Berthoud Pass 119
The Roll, Berthoud Pass 115
Toll North Face 263
Toll, Mt. 225-226
Trailheads 19-40
Traverses 247-253
Tree Wells 11
Trelease, Mt. 45-50
Triple Rock, Berthoud Pass 115
Twin Peaks East Chute 266
UN11893 "Pillow Peak" 262
UN12118 (First Corner), Jones Pass 105-106
UN12393 159-160
UN12696 Northeast Couloir 258
UN12700, Jones Pass 102-104
UN12704 East Bowl 258
Upper Tipperary Trailhead 30
Urad Bowl, Woods Mtn. 74-76
Using This Guidebook 15-17
Vasquez Peak 107-109
Watanga Lake Gully, Watanga Mtn. 237
Watanga Mountain 237-238
Waterfall Face, Berthoud Pass 115
Watrous Bowl, Woods Mtn. 73-74
Weebles, Berthoud Pass 119
Welcome Couloir, Witter Pk. 139-140
West Chute, "Golden Bear" 41
West Couloir, James Pk. 154-156
West Gully, Byers Pk. 164-166
West Gully, Engelmann Pk. 85-87
West Slopes, Hiamovi Mtn 239-240
West Slopes, Mt. Irving Hale 235-236
Wildlife 11-13
Witter Peak 139-140
Witter South Couloirs 259
Woodland Mountain 191-192
Woods Creek Pinner 256
Woods Mountain 73-76
X,Y Z Chutes, Berthoud Pass 115
Y - YNot - YYes Gullies, Mt Machebeuf 67-69
Y Couloirs, Mt. Jasper 197-198
Zero Creek, Berthoud Pass 124

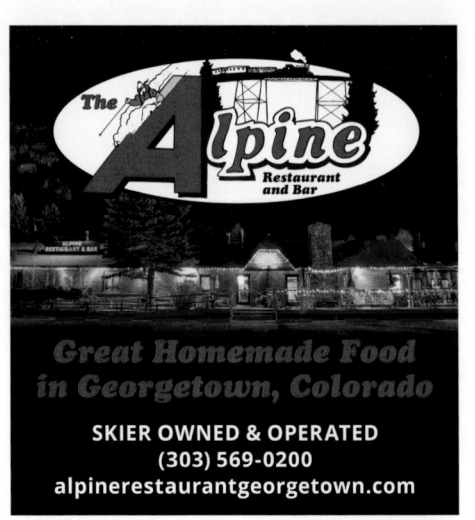